PRAISE FOR

The Death Class

"Readers will come away struck by Bowe's compassion—and by the unexpectedly life-affirming messages of courage that spring from her students' harrowing experiences."

—*Entertainment Weekly*

"[Hayasaki] skillfully weaves together difficult stories, finding unexpected connections. . . . The book's strength lies in the well-observed details of the lives portrayed, and in the recognition that the work Bowe and her students are doing is messy, necessary stuff. Hayasaki acknowledges this by bookending chapters with writing prompts from Bowe's syllabus—'Be a Ghost'—as if to encourage readers to consider the big questions on their own."

—*The New York Times Book Review*

"By chronicling the stories of Bowe and four of her students, Hayasaki imbues the austere topic of death with tangible narrative immediacy. It's a book of powerful scenes."

—*The Boston Globe*

"At its heart, this book spotlights a bumpy but certain road to resurrection and imparts its wisdom as it traverses a drama-filled landscape, one pocked with suicides and cold-blooded murder, abuse and addiction. . . . *The Death Class* manages to glide gracefully and delicately through the parts—say, the autopsy table—where you're sure you'll retch, if you can even keep your eyes on the page. And for sticking with it, you're rewarded with poetic passages and assorted revelations you'll likely not forget. . . . Hayasaki, through Bowe, drums in the essential lessons of how by finding purpose beyond ourselves, we infuse our lives with meaning and lessen our fear of death."

—*Chicago Tribune*

"Year after year, Norma Bowe faces a waiting list of students wanting to get into her death class at a college in New Jersey. Beyond the probing about last wills and good-bye letters and class trips to mortuaries and cemeteries is the underlying truth that a good, long stare at death can trigger a deeper appreciation of life. . . . Award-winning journalist Hayasaki spent four years following Bowe and her class and . . . offers a completely engaging look at death and the meaning of life."

—*Booklist* (starred review)

"Who would want to take a class on death? Everyone, it turns out. Norma Bowe, the most popular professor on campus and instructor of 'Death in Perspective' at Kean University is an unsung hero of our day. Erika Hayasaki takes us on an unforgettable journey with Bowe and the many people in her orbit touched by her wisdom and compassion. Erika's book is the last lesson you'd ever need on life."

—Ruth Davis Konigsberg, author of *The Truth About Grief: The Myth of Its Five Stages and the New Science of Loss*

"*The Death Class* is at once puncturing and redemptive, sharing humanity's most painful, violent face while at the same time revealing a fierce optimism and stunning generosity. It is more than a glimpse of a remarkable educational experiment. It shares the story of an extraordinary teacher whose very life is the class while weaving together the lives of students who struggle with complex, tormenting problems and find grace in each other. Its stories have lodged in me and will not soon let me go."

—Erica Brown, author of *Happier Endings: A Meditation on Life and Death*

"This is a beautiful book about courage—the courage to turn and face your own life and death, and the courage to make a difference in the lives of others. *The Death Class* points to a way of living fully, gratefully, and meaningfully every day."

—Elizabeth Lesser, author of *Broken Open* and cofounder of the Omega Institute

"At the end of every chapter, Hayasaki includes an assignment from Bowe's syllabus—e.g., write your own eulogy, pretend you are a ghost and record your observations, write a goodbye letter to someone or something lost. These assignments invite readers to consider the essential question of Bowe's course—and Hayasaki's book: How can we learn to celebrate life?"

—*Kirkus Reviews*

"[Norma Bowe] not only teaches her students about the physiology of death, its implications for all areas of life and thought; she rescues them from it. She answers calls in the middle of the night, and she answers the call to help humanity whence it comes, near or far. She is friend, counselor, aid worker, and revolutionary in the person of one woman, one 'who delighted in cemeteries, the overlooked classrooms beneath our feet.' Her subject, the end, is always just beginning."

—Melissa Holbrook Pierson, *The Barnes & Noble Review*

"Hayasaki has a reporter's way of winnowing out the facts, the interesting stuff, small details, and tiny secrets that make us want to know more. She immerses us so well into the story of the class, students, and the professor that it's almost easy to forget we're reading. We become part of what's happening, complete with triumphs, gasps, and life-affirming inspiration."

—Terri Schlichenmeyer, *The Bookworm*

"Erika Hayasaki has beautifully distilled her hands-on research, giving readers much useful information to digest while sharing important life lessons."

—BookReporter.com

"Hayasaki knows how to pick up one thread and tie it expertly to the next. She can describe the macro view of death, moving from denial to more openness, and also the micro view, taking us into the lives of at least five students in depth and of many others in broad strokes."

—*The Christian Century*

The Death Class

A True Story About Life

Erika Hayasaki

Simon & Schuster Paperbacks
New York   London   Toronto   Sydney   New Delhi

In memory of Carl Harris

Simon & Schuster Paperbacks
A Divison of Simon & Schuster, Inc.
1230 Avenue of the Americas
New York, NY 10020

First Simon & Schuster trade paperback edition January 2015

SIMON & SCHUSTER PAPERBACKS and colophon
are registered trademarks of Simon & Schuster, Inc.

For information about special discounts for bulk purchases,
please contact Simon & Schuster Special Sales at 1-866-506-1949
or business@simonandschuster.com.

The Simon & Schuster Speakers Bureau can bring authors
to your live event. For more information or to book an event
contact the Simon & Schuster Speakers Bureau at 1-866-248-3049
or visit our website at www.simonspeakers.com.

Designed by Esther Paradelo
Jacket design by Jackie Seow

Manufactured in the United States of America

3   5   7   9   10   8   6   4

The Library of Congress has cataloged the hardcover edition as follows:
Hayasaki, Erika.
The death class : a true story about life / Erika Hayasaki.
pages   cm
Includes bibliographical references and index.
1. Thanatology. 2. Thanatology—United States. I. Title.
HQ1073.H39   2014
306.9—dc23   2013002025

ISBN 978-1-4516-4285-8
ISBN 978-1-4516-4294-0 (pbk)
ISBN 978-1-4516-4295-7 (ebook)

Tell me, what is it you plan to do
with your one wild and precious life?

—Mary Oliver, "The Summer Day"

Contents

Contents

The Good-bye Letter

Just after 7 A.M. on a Wednesday in April 1995, a man left a place called Ponca City, climbed into a rented Ryder truck, and began to drive. He had a buzz cut and a face shaped like a butternut squash with a narrow beak of a nose. The words on his T-shirt read, SIC SEMPER TYRANNIS, alongside an image of Abraham Lincoln's face. The man did not stop driving for an hour and forty-five minutes, when he parked the truck next to a day care center crawling with babies, locked its doors, and walked away. Inside, a bomb fuse fizzed. At 9:02 A.M., the truck erupted.

I was sixteen years old, a high school student in Lynnwood, Washington, two thousand miles away, watching the carnage in Oklahoma City unfold over a television in a friend's home that day. A group of us had left campus early, and I remember sitting on a carpet as newscasters replayed the images of a fireman cradling a bloody baby and wires and pipes dangling from the wreckage of the Alfred P. Murrah Federal Building like veins. Nineteen children died in the attack, 168 people in all. But none of those lives concerned me. Not in that moment. Not on that day.

Shortly before Timothy McVeigh left for Oklahoma City, another man had been making his way toward the Whispering Pines apartment complex just a few minutes from where I lived. His name was James Yukon McCray. He had a broken heart and a gun. It was just after 4 A.M. in the Pacific Northwest when he arrived outside the complex dressed in dark clothes and a red-and-black stocking cap. There was a girl inside apartment 265, my schoolmate and friend Sangeeta Lal.

At sixteen, Sangeeta still had the face of a child, round and cheeky, with long, wavy black hair that she smoothed down with coconut oil. Later that morning she was supposed to be at school, where she usually showed up in lipstick the same shade as her nails and jeans four sizes too big for her five-foot frame, cuffed at the bottoms and held up with a long belt. It was a chilly morning, and she might have arrived to first period in her army green windbreaker over an Atlanta Falcons sweatshirt, and a pair of white sneakers.

Her family had relocated from the island of Fiji to our suburban town twenty-two minutes north of Seattle. The day before, in the parking lot after school, Sangeeta showed me the new white sedan she'd received for her birthday and told me we would go for a spin in it soon. She kissed its window and left cranberry-colored stains on the glass, then gave me a hug good-bye. Her single mother had purchased the car with money saved from her job at the Nintendo of America headquarters in Redmond, Washington, where she worked the early shift. On that morning, she had already left for work when the first phone call came in to 911.

At 4:18 A.M., a female voice connected on the line with an emergency operator, saying that she could hear someone knocking on her window. The caller's name was Sangeeta. She said the person was trying to break in. A neighbor woke up and heard something too, like glass breaking and boards creaking or steel nails being ripped from their foundation. The neighbor looked out her window and saw nothing.

But back at apartment 265, the intruder was already climbing inside. The line went dead. The operator called back, and an answering machine picked up. Police units headed to Whispering Pines to check on a burglary in progress.

WE KNEW HE sometimes beat her up, and we had tried to convince her to break it off. Once she hid from James inside the apartment where I lived with my mother and brother. James was five years older than Sangeeta and did not go to school with us, but he often picked her up from campus. He had a cruel streak, like the time he convinced one of Sangeeta's friends to let him perm her hair and slipped Nair hair removal cream into the so-called perm solution.

She had been trying to break it off with him for a while. The assistant principal knew that Sangeeta had filed a domestic violence report against him with the school police officer earlier that year. Several weeks earlier, she had broken up with him for good, but that had done nothing to convince him to leave her alone. Sangeeta talked to another police officer on campus about him the same day she showed me her car, and she stopped by to see her sixteen-year-old neighbor in apartment 267 around 4 P.M. to explain that James had threatened to hurt her and her mom. Sangeeta took down her neighbor's phone number in case she might need him.

SHE RAN OUTSIDE on that dark morning with James on her trail. Dogs barked as neighbors slept. Some residents heard shrieks and footsteps outside their windows, but did not get out of bed. Sangeeta made it to apartment 283, on the ground level. According to police reports, a thirty-nine-year-old man named Sherman was sleeping on the floor of the apartment near the sliding glass door when he heard someone banging on it. He got up and looked into the terrified eyes of a young girl. "Help me, help me!" she screamed. "Let me in!"

But before he could react, he watched a man about six inches taller than she was come from behind and drag her away from the porch and onto the lawn. Sherman saw him pull back the slide on his 9-millimeter automatic and aim it at her.

"Please don't!" Sangeeta screamed.

James looked through the glass doors at Sherman, who bolted out of the way, crouching behind a television. He heard one shot.

A neighbor in 284, next door, looked out of his window and saw a girl on the grass. It looked as if she was sitting down, as a man hovered over her. She'd been shot in the chest.

"Bitch!" he shouted. "Get up!"

"Please don't!" Sangeeta repeated. "Please don't!"

He fired a second shot.

Sangeeta collapsed, her face in the grass. James looked up and saw the neighbor in 284 peering through his window. Their eyes met, and James took off. He ran through an alley, straight back to Sangeeta's apartment, where he killed himself with a single bullet.

In three hours, the world would begin tuning in to Oklahoma. But at school, her friends would be steered to the career center, where grief counselors stood on guard. As a group, we were told of her death before the rest of the students. It didn't actually sink in until the campuswide announcement a few minutes later, as if the principal saying it over a loud speaker made it official. His voice came over the intercom: Sangeeta Lal, a Lynnwood High School sophomore, had been killed early that morning. In an instant, the room became a blur of wailing, disoriented teenagers.

We wandered around the school in a teary daze and continued our mourning off campus, as friends piled into my beat-up blue Honda Accord. We drove around until we ended up in a friend's living room, where we waited for news to come over the television. That was how it happened, right? People got shot and it ended up on television. Or in the newspaper. But we could find nothing on the newscast about Sangeeta that day. All the channels went back to firefighters and frantic parents in Oklahoma. When the newspaper mentioned the murder-suicide the next day, it printed her age wrong—she was in her late teens, or maybe twenty. It didn't mention her name at all. In the week that followed, her death was written up in the format the news business calls a "brief." There was not enough information, or it was simply not important enough, to merit an entire story.

Police found a gun, along with Sangeeta's school ID and driver's learner's permit in her bedroom, near James's body. At 12:55 P.M., a police officer and a chaplain had shown up at her mother's job at Nintendo to inform her that her daughter had been shot to death. They asked her to come to the medical examiner's office to view the body.

I saw her mother a couple of times in the following days. Inside the apartment where James had committed suicide, she lay on a couch moaning and looked into the face of my friend Rosemary, who resembled her daughter a little, and called her "My Sangeeta." I heard her bone-searing screams during the wake, as Sangeeta lay in a coffin, her body draped in a shimmering gown, a bindi dot on her forehead, the corners of her mouth turned upward. I heard her mother's delirium again at the funeral, especially before they took her Sangeeta to be cremated. She followed her daughter's casket out, as if she wanted to climb inside with her. I never forgot the image or the sound.

I was an editor at my high school newspaper, *The Royal Gazette,* at the time and wrote a front-page story about Sangeeta, trying to include all the details that local newspapers had not, and I wrote about her again weeks later for a regionwide teen newspaper operated under *The Seattle Times.*

Sangeeta was the first person I had known and cared about who died violently, and hers was the first death I ever covered as a reporter.

THEN IT WAS Monday, April 16, 2007. Newswires hummed. There had been a shooting at Virginia Tech University. Monitoring from my desk in New York City, where I had been stationed as a national correspondent for the *Los Angeles Times,* I read reports that said the estimated death toll had climbed to twenty, with the final count as yet unknown. I booked a flight to Virginia. There was a windstorm and the small plane rocked like a boat riding torrential waves, but we touched down safely and I rented a car and drove to the campus in Blacksburg, arriving as the sun was beginning to rise.

Not even twenty-four hours had passed since a twenty-three-year-old college senior named Seung-Hui Cho had gone on a shooting rampage, and some families still did not know if their loved ones were alive. That became clear during my first stop at The Inn at Virginia Tech, a hotel and conference center with a gray stone exterior, which had become a gathering center for family and friends. As I arrived, a red-eyed man was beginning to wade with desperation toward the hundreds of media trucks and satellite dishes blanketing the hotel parking lot. When I approached he told me that his daughter, Erin Peterson, an eighteen-year-old freshman in international studies, had not responded to his phone calls. She was a basketball player (his first daughter had died of cancer at 8). She would certainly have found a way to contact her family to let them know she was alive.

"She would have called," a woman behind him whimpered. "She would have called us by now."

The family told me they had visited hospitals in the area but could not find her. They had received word that she might be at one hospital and headed there, but the patient turned out to be someone else. Now Erin's father just wanted information, and he was willing to hurl himself before a gaggle of reporters just in case any one of us could help. He gave me his cell phone number and told me to contact him if I heard anything about his daughter.

There was a candlelight vigil on the Virginia Tech Drillfield that night as the sky turned from blood orange to plum blue and hundreds of people wrapped their bodies in blankets bearing the school's name and lit candles inside Dixie cups. The field shimmered with fire and murmured with prayers: "Just bring this campus comfort."

I glanced over at Norris Hall, a stone structure. Inside, thirty-one of the thirty-three students and faculty present had died the previous morning. The highest death toll had occurred in room 211, an intermediate French class, where Cho had killed twelve others and wounded six, before taking his own life. Erin Peterson, I soon learned, had been killed in 211 also. That was the room I decided to write about, focusing on the people who had lived and died in it.

It took a week to track down the few survivors who made it out, and from each interview the same character emerged as the heart of the class, its professor Jocelyne Couture-Nowak, also known as "Madame Couture." She had been killed trying to protect her students. Madame Couture adored the French language and reveled in teaching it, punctuating her comments on students' papers with exclamation points and breaking into French songs during class, flailing her arms like a conductor as students followed her lead, botching lyrics and singing out of tune. Sometimes she got so excited about a lesson that she had to interrupt her sentences to take a deep breath.

Her funeral was held at the Peggy Lee Hahn Garden Pavilion eight days after the shooting. I walked across campus to the funeral with some of the students she'd taught who had survived. Madame Couture's wooden coffin was draped in the Acadian flag. Her husband, Jerzy Nowak, was head of the horticulture department, and his wife loved flowers and plants as much as he did. Her funeral took place on his birthday.

"Jocelyne, my darling, if Heaven exists, this is your Heaven," he said in front of the crowd of seven hundred. "You are surrounded by family and friends you cherish, by students you respect and passionately help to succeed."

One student who spoke at the funeral was supposed to have been in room 211 on the day of the shooting but had awakened late and not gone to class. He had lost his best friend in the rampage and offered these words about his professor on his classmates' behalf: "Madame, have you touched all of us in a profound way that we will never forget, and will we always love you?"

He paused and continued. "Mais oui, Madame. Mais oui."

Those were the final words I wrote. The article was published, and I flew back to New York a few days later, spent and sad.

In the dozen years since Sangeeta's death, I had attended scores of funerals, written hundreds of obituaries, knocked on the doors of victims and survivors of tragedies, and interviewed family members and friends of the dead. I had become a journalist to try to explain and interpret the world and its stories. But death's mercilessness and meaning, I could not figure out, no matter how many stories I wrote.

Winter had not yet eased its clench on New York City in the days after my return from Virginia. One morning, a Web link popped up on my screen in a condensed search engine feed on New Jersey, which immediately caught my interest. A student from a campus not far from New York had written about a popular teacher. The headline read, "Gaining a Little Life Perspective: Capture each moment of your life in Death in Perspective, an amazing class offered at Kean."

A professor of death. Maybe I could write an article about her class? Who knew, maybe I would even learn something in the process.

HER NAME WAS Dr. Norma Bowe, a registered nurse who also held a master's degree in health administration, a PhD in community health policy, and a tenured professorship at Kean University in Union, New

Jersey, a thirty-minute drive without traffic or two quick train rides away from New York City. A proud mother who had raised two daughters, she had spent two decades working in emergency rooms, intensive care, and psychiatric wards before coming to Kean University, where she taught classes on mental health, nursing, and public health. But Norma was most widely known around campus as the professor who had created the most popular class at Kean University. Rivaled only by Human Sexuality, Death in Perspective had a three-year waiting list.

The professor and I hatched a plan. She agreed to allow me to shadow her class as a journalist documenting the experience for as long as it took. But I would also have to participate in her class as a student.

And so the official odyssey began on the first day of the Spring 2009 semester, although I had been following her around for about six months already. The moment I stepped into her office, Norma made it clear that she was no stranger to her own death dramas. She often found herself cast in the center of them.

She launched into a recap of the winter break, speaking almost without pause: "A student of mine called me on New Year's Day, hysterically crying. I was home by myself. . . . Her father, because of the financial crisis, had decided to blow up the house with his wife and son in it. He figured, in his crazy thinking, it would be better for the mother and son to go to Heaven."

When the girl arrived home, the house was filled with gas. Norma knew the man needed a psychiatric evaluation. Norma picked the student up and drove her father to the hospital.

Meanwhile, another student's mother had tried to commit suicide right after New Year's Day, and a young man she knew had succeeded in killing himself. Norma had been called upon for crisis relief in each case.

Norma pulled out a pile of photocopied syllabi. A bumper sticker stuck to her filing cabinet read: WATCH OUT I'M FRESH OUT OF ANTI-DEPRESSANTS. Taped to the office door was an article: "One Year After Virginia Tech." Videos and books spilled onto the floor, with titles such as *Killer Disease on Campus: Meningitis; The Autobiography of Dying; Life, Death and Somewhere in Between; Forced Exit: The Slippery Slope from Assisted Suicide to Legalized Murder; Remembrances and Celebrations: A Book of Eulogies, Elegies, Letters and Epitaphs; The Realities of Aging; There's No Place Like Hope: A Guide to Beating Cancer in Mid-sized Bites; Young Shooter; Jesus Camp; Jumping off Bridges.* . . . On her desk lay a photocopied suicide note that a student had given her—written not by him but by his mother. It had dried blood staining its edge, and the scribbled words on it read, "I know you guys diserved [*sic*] better I'm sorry I was what u got."

Nearby was a printout of an email titled "Hi I'm in Iraq again." It had been written to Norma by a former Death in Perspective student who was now assigned to a hospital at Balad Air Base. The staff sergeant described treating a two-year-old boy with burns over 70 percent of his body and a thirty-eight-year-old Iraqi gunshot victim. "I swear she was shot more times than Tupac, Biggie Smalls and 50 Cent," he wrote, requesting that she share his letters with her classes. Norma tucked the letter into her pile of syllabi, gathered up her keys and books, and click-clacked down the hall toward the classroom in her black high-heeled Mary Janes.

FOR MUCH OF the early twentieth century, talking openly and honestly about death was considered poor taste—especially inside classrooms. But by the 1960s, some scholars had come to believe that death education was as important as sex education, if not more important—since not everyone had sex.

Pioneers such as the psychiatrist Elisabeth Kübler-Ross had begun dragging "death out of the darkness," as a 1969 *Time* magazine article put it, and the first college class on death was taught at the University of Minnesota in 1963. Others followed, and the burgeoning field soon came to be referred to as thanatology.

By 1971, more than six hundred death courses were being offered across the United States, and five years later that number had nearly doubled. Now thousands of such classes can be found across disciplines from psychology to philosophy to medical science to sociology. Scholarly research journals focusing on death and dying have emerged, as well as textbooks and death education conferences. Some colleges offer degree and certificate programs with death, dying, and bereavement concentrations, and increasingly, as at Kean University, undergraduates can take such classes as general electives.

Teachers take their own approach to death classes; some stick to pedagogy, lecturing about academic research and theory, while others put their own spins on it, with students lighting candles and sitting in silence before beginning class.

But Norma had hardly heard of any of those other death classes when she designed her curriculum more than a decade ago.

WHEN THE DOOR to room 426, Hennings Hall, swung open that January afternoon, two dozen students greeted the professor. The early ones sat at desks lined up in rows, their faces illuminated by white lights, the kind you might find in a hospital ward. A sunbeam of dust particles fluttered through half-raised window blinds.

"Hi, everybody," Norma said, dimming the lights. "The first thing we're going to do is set up in a circle."

The students began scooting chairs and desks. I took a seat near the door.

"This is a health class," she continued, "but it's not like any kind of health class that you've ever had before. It's probably not like any class you've had before in any subject."

She distributed the copies of the syllabus and began to go through each section. She would use a variety of books, she explained, including *Tuesdays with Morrie,* by Mitch Albom, stories about visits to a former teacher on his deathbed, and *The Diving Bell and the Butterfly,* by Jean-Dominique Bauby, a memoir he wrote after a stroke that left him with locked-in syndrome, a condition in which his mind and consciousness worked, even though he could not move or talk. He wrote the book by blinking his left eye, Norma told the class, as an assistant read him letters of the alphabet.

She held up the *Death, Society, and Human Experience* textbook, which each student was required to purchase, but if she spent each class lecturing from it, she said, "You all would be very bored and drooling out of your mouths." She mimicked a person keeled over atop her book, as a few students chuckled. The class would be more heavily focused on discussions, with some lectures and exams based on readings. "So be on top of your reading." But the core of the class, she explained, would be the personal assignments and field trips.

"Most of you are here for a reason," she said. "Maybe someone's story in this room, or someone's experience, might press on some scar tissue for you. So that's okay. We're sitting in a circle right now because we're really beginning a bereavement group."

The students tried not to look at one another. Norma gave out the first assignment. They opened their notebooks and waited for her cue to take notes: "Write a good-bye letter to someone or something that you've lost," she said. "I'd like you to say whatever you need to say to that person, and then I'd like you to sign and date the letter. Whatever popped into your head first when I said those words, that's where you should go."

"Any questions?" she concluded. The students shook their heads and began zipping coats and bags. "All right, have a good week."

A FEW DAYS later, on assignment for the newspaper, I met one of the survivors of the US Airways flight that had landed in the Hudson River at a Dunkin' Donuts near his home in Long Island. At twenty-three, Bill Zuhoski was not much older than most of Norma's students.

He told me how he had been sitting in the very back of the plane when it started to plummet. The second of five siblings, he had quickly begun to agonize that his family would learn of his death on television. The man sitting to his right did not say a word, but the man to his left squeezed his arm and prayed, all the while asking "Are we over the water? Are we near the airport?" Bill peered out the window, giving updates.

The back of the aircraft slammed into the water first, bashing Bill's forehead against the seat in front of him and busting up his face. People raved afterward that it was such a smooth landing, but it certainly did not feel like that in the back. His glasses flew off. Without them he could hardly see his hand in front of him. Frigid water poured into the plane, rapidly rising to his waist. No, he thought, it would not be the crash that killed him; he was going to drown. He stripped down to his underwear, bolting over the top of the seats like a lizard. He slithered so fast that soon there was no water, just the fabric tops of seats. He missed the first emergency exit, which he might have been able to spot had he been wearing his glasses, but found his way to an exit at the front of the plane and onto a slide that led to a floating dinghy.

People saw his shirtless, shivering body in the raft on television screens and in photos around the world. "Hey," some said to him afterward, "you're the naked guy!" It seemed that no one else on board had stripped down in a panic as he had, but in the moment all he could think about was becoming as weightless as possible so he could swim, fast. Survive.

In the weeks that followed, people from across the country sent him letters tucked in Bibles and told him, "Congratulations on being alive." Dozens of reporters like myself kept asking the same questions: What was it like to cheat death? How has this changed your life?

He had a hard time answering. "I don't really know. I will tell you when it sets in."

Others wondered whether he'd found God. But Bill never really felt he'd lost God. There had been no immediate revelation, no overnight awakening, no obvious rebirth. It almost seemed to frustrate him that he couldn't come up with something more profound to say about his world-captivating brush with death, besides "I don't sweat the small stuff anymore, like traffic." He offered a half smile, as if he knew how insufficient that sounded.

I bade farewell to Bill and took a seat in a cold, empty station on Long Island. The next train was an hour away. I opened a blank page on my computer screen and sat there for a moment, remembering what Norma had told the class: "Whatever popped into your head first when I said those words."

Then I began to type: "Dear Sangeeta . . ."

PART

I

Death's Secrets

DEATH IN PERSPECTIVE

The following course excerpts are from the syllabus, class outline, guidelines, and assignments created and designed by Dr. Norma Bowe, PhD, RN, MS, CHES.

FROM CLASS OUTLINE

- Introduction, Attitude Survey, Definitions
- What Is Death? Biomedical Interpretations

TAKE-HOME WRITING ASSIGNMENT:
The Good-bye Letter

Write a good-bye letter to someone you have lost.

Erika Hayasaki

Dr. Bowe

Death in Perspective

Good-bye Letter

I wrote an article about you for the school newspaper, The Royal Gazette. *On the day it came out, a teacher came storming into the journalism classroom and unleashed on me: How could I have published such gory details about a classmate's murder? How dare I upset the school even more?*

It was then I realized how taboo the subject of death was and how scared people were to face it.

ONE

The Professor

When it came to death, Norma Bowe had the fearlessness of a swift-water rescue team; when everyone else wanted to get away from the force of the current, she went charging straight into it instead. Not many threats in this world seemed to rattle her: not guns, murderers, or the criminally insane, and certainly not death. With cheeks that swelled when she smiled as if she'd stuck a Tootsie Pop beneath each one and a high-pitched reverberating laugh, she made you feel as though, if you could only hold on to her hands long enough, you might just be the one person lucky enough to escape.

There was an air of invincibility surrounding her, a feeling so magnetic that long after class had been dismissed students found themselves wanting to hang out with "Dr. Bowe," which was what they called her, despite her insistence that they call her Norma. They lingered in her office for hours, even when she wasn't there. When she actually did get sick or injured, some of them reacted with stunned disbelief, as if they didn't think a woman like that could be mortal. But she knew there was an art to surviving. That is what she wanted her students to learn.

Norma had a fondness for cemeteries and could spend hours perusing inscriptions on tombstones or kicking back on a freshly mowed patch of grass next to the grave of a stranger. If she had enough free time, which was rare, she might even bring along one of her favorite Jodi Picoult novels to read. When traveling to a new city, Norma did not think it at all odd to pay a visit to the local graveyard, snapping photos as if it were a regular tourist destination. She believed cemeteries held the stories that history books could not always document; they were the overlooked, underused classrooms beneath our feet, so it made sense to her to teach a lesson inside one every once in a while.

The Rosedale & Rosehill Cemetery in Linden, New Jersey, where her students convened one summer night, was bordered by an auto-stripping business, a school-bus yard, a truck repair shop, a warehouse, and a headstone company, Payless Monuments. As dusk fell, students parked their cars in a line as if part of a funeral procession along a quiet road that meandered through the cemetery. The memorial grounds would have been mostly empty without her class, except for the squirrels, crickets, and crows. Norma planned to give a lecture here on the biology of dying, and she had warned the students beforehand that it would be important to take notes; questions about it could end up on the final exam.

"Hi, everyone," she said, waving with a wide smile as she pulled up late to the cemetery in her silver Mazda minivan full of students. Norma and her students jokingly referred to it as the "party bus," because the van spent its days shuttling students on field trips to prisons, funeral homes, hospice care centers, mental hospitals, and morgues. Its bumper sticker read AMERICA NEEDS A WOMAN PRESIDENT, and its floors and seats were littered with pink highlighters, an unopened Doritos bag, a dozen stuffed purple bunnies, a Celtic Thunder CD, the sound track of *Hairspray*, and clusters of straws sealed in paper wrapping.

She emerged like a fairy godmother before her students, hopping out of the van and hurrying into the graveyard with all eyes on her, walking with a side-to-side wag, a slight stoop of the shoulders, her feet nudged outward like a pair of wings.

"Nothing like a good cemetery, right?" she asked, rounding everyone up.

She had long brassy hair that she usually wore down, like today, or in a high ponytail when it frizzed in humidity. Her eyes changed colors in the light, like speckled brown jade, and her skin was flushed in the face, more suntanned on the arms and chest with a spattering of freckles. Her underactive thyroid made it easy for her to gain weight and hard to lose it, and she barely ate with her nonstop schedule, subsisting on unsweetened iced Dunkin Donuts' lattes. She was pear-shaped and pretty, with a sturdy frame that locked her soft edges into place. During non–work days, she dressed folksy: long, flowing skirts, walker's sandals, turquoise and silver jewelry, and trinkets the color of bones. At work, she sometimes dressed as if she might be called to attend a funeral at any moment, which happened occasionally: black skirts, black dresses, black stockings, black heels. For color, she'd add a bright scarf.

Today she wore black billowy pants and a black cardigan over a pink blouse, with scarlet lipstick and a green gemstone bracelet. Her heavy key chain jangled as she walked, containing more keys than any one person could possibly need, along with membership cards for places such as Petco Pals, Borders, Brooks Memorial Library in Brattleboro, Vermont, and Curves health club for women.

"Guess what?" she said in her singsong voice, which always seemed as though it were stuck in falsetto. "There's a crematory across the street." That was where they burned bodies, she explained to the students, suggesting that maybe they could stop by and check it out later.

The professor led everyone on a tour of the grounds, straightening roses on graves and standing tipped-over fences and flags upright. Dandelions and white clover pushed through the ground as Norma took moments of silence to pay tribute to the bodies beneath.

The cemetery was divided into neighborhoods, mirroring a typical big city: Chinese, Spanish, Ukrainian, Polish, Russian, Greek.

If the Chinese section had been a real neighborhood, it probably would have boasted the highest property values. Its tall arched pillars bore the name Greater Chinatown Community Assn. Rows of polished pink or shiny gray headstone blocks, some as big as refrigerators, stretched into the horizon. Engraved into the facades were intricate bamboo designs and horizontal Chinese characters, but English lettering could also be found on some, names such as Low, Lam, Lau, Chung, Wong, Kong. Small red rocks balanced atop some headstones, as if placed there as offerings.

Norma parked herself here, sitting cross-legged in front of a thirty-six-ton granite sculpture of a 1982 diesel Mercedes-Benz 2400 with a license plate reading RAY TSE. Rising from a low stone slab behind a Roman-style pillared mausoleum, the memorial had been built to look like an entombed car, right down to the headlights, windshield wipers, door handles, and Mercedes logos on the trunk, nose, and rims—except for a missing hood ornament, left off because it would have been too easy to break off and pocket.

Students rubbed their fingers along the smooth granite. As the story went, fifteen-year-old Raymond Tse, Jr., had wanted his own Mercedes, but he had died in a car accident in 1981 before ever having a chance to earn his driver's license. His millionaire older brother, the landlord and businessman Raymond David Tse, paid for the tribute, estimated at $250,000.

"When I think about what the body does when we die, it's not like there's a point where everything shuts down," Norma noted. "It doesn't happen all at once."

She made clear that she was speaking of natural deaths from disease and physical ailments, not sudden deaths from murders or car accidents. In violent deaths, bodies don't have time to make those little adjustments for our comfort. "It's wild how the body works," she went on. "Our bodies take care of us our entire lifetime, take care of us when we're sick, when we're ill. At the very end it does that too."

"The first thing that happens is, the circulatory system begins to shift the blood supply to all of the major organs," Norma said. "We're very hardwired to survive, so the brain gets the message; rather than the heart pumping blood all the way to the tips of the toes and back up again, it really just starts to pool to the major organs, heart, lungs, brain, digestive system, kidneys, liver. So a lot of times people will begin to complain of feeling cold. They will ask for a blanket, even if it's a hundred degrees in August."

That meant death is near, she explained, three weeks away, maybe two. The body temperature can drop a degree or more. Hands and feet take on the frigid feel of refrigerated poultry. Arms and legs begin to look pasty, draped over bones like pie dough, sometimes gray or violet, blotchy, like a web of bruises. Nail beds turn blue; the lines around the mouth, blue too. Blood vessels protrude near the surface of the skin, like varicose veins. The blood lacks oxygen and is no longer cherry red, as healthy blood should be. Instead, it turns a deep, black merlot, so dark it appears blue beneath the skin. This, Norma explained, is called "cyanosis."

Another sign of impending death: fading eyesight. A dying person might want brighter lighting, the curtains open. While sight is among the first senses to go, she said, hearing is last. You must not assume that a dying person doesn't know what is going on around him or her, she explained, but carry on as if he or she can hear everything. You can read the newspaper to him or her, leaning close to his or her ears as you speak.

A week or so before death, the blood shifts again, this time away from the digestive system and to the kidneys, heart, lungs, and liver. "That makes it so people stop feeling hungry," she said. "They don't want to eat any more." Favorite meals do not spark the same glimmer of delight. They won't complain of hunger or thirst, even in the absence of intravenous feeding tubes. The body won't miss the satisfaction of an overstuffed belly, won't crave what it no longer needs. If you hold a stethoscope to the abdomen, Norma said, listen for bowel sounds: the contracting movement of muscles pushing food down the digestive tract—or *peristalsis*—has slowed, maybe even stopped. "So what do we do?" she said. We who love them want to feed them anyway. "We tell them, 'You'll like it, it's good,'" she said. They might become bloated, nauseous, constipated, or begin vomiting. "We force-feed people," she said. "It makes *us* feel better, folks, it doesn't make *them* feel better."

When the liver has begun to shut down, usually a few days before death, a person might become more agitated, shifting around in bed, and the whites of the eyes turn yellow. "It might look like they're in agony," Norma explained. Toxic waste has been building up in their bodies because the liver has stopped filtering it as it used to.

The breathing becomes rapid and shallow, up to fifty breaths per minute, mostly through an open, drooling mouth. The respiratory rate slows, the heart beats staccato. Death may be just hours away now. At times it might seem as if there is little attempt to breathe at all, a pause of ten seconds, as when a sleeping person snores deeply, then does not inhale for a few seconds, before letting out a long, rapid *whoosh* of air. "Those periods of apnea will get longer and longer," Norma said. This phase might be accompanied by short heaving gasps or barking: the "agonal phase."

Saliva, unable to be swallowed, builds up deep in the back of the throat, too deep for nurses to suction it out, causing a congested, purring sound—the "death rattle."

This is known as Cheyne-Stokes respiration, named after John Cheyne and William Stokes, two physicians who first described and documented the breathing pattern in the nineteenth century. "Air comes into the mouth, and it just goes about as far as the trachea, that's it," Norma said. "Breathing is more rapid. Cheyne-Stokes breathing, when it starts, you have just a few hours, maybe twenty-four hours."

"It is like asthma?" a student asked.

"No," she replied. "With asthma, bronchioles are constricted, you can hear wheezing and people struggling to breathe." Cheyne-Stokes breathing, she said, "is very peaceful. It's just a little bit of air being exchanged."

Euphoria sets in. The body takes care of the dying mind. The mind takes care of the dying body. "You know that great feeling, when you first meet somebody you're really attracted to, when you fall in love? We've all had that feeling," Norma said. It's caused by seratonin, dopamine, and norepinephrine. "Those chemicals will continue to increase, and they are at peak in the moment when you die."

The neurotransmitters that carry nerve impulses between cells, causing feelings of joy or euphoria, counter pain, even as the blood pressure continues to plummet, the skin turns a dull grayish hue, and the capillaries in the nose thicken. "Imagine, your dying brain gets flooded with this stuff," Norma went on.

Little by little, the pulse rate and blood pressure go up and within an hour start to drastically drop. "Your heart rate will continue to drop until your heart stops."

"Your breathing will stop first," Norma said. "The heartbeat will stop last."

The time of death will be recorded once the heart has stilled, she said. If you examine the pupils, they will look dilated and dull, vacant.

"The appearance of a newly lifeless face cannot be mistaken for unconsciousness," wrote Sherwin B. Nuland in *How We Die: Reflections on Life's Final Chapter*. "Within a minute after the heart stops beating the face begins to take on the unmistakable gray-white pallor of death; in an uncanny way, the features very soon appear corpselike, even to those who have never before seen a dead body. A man's corpse looks as though his essence has left him and it has."

The body temperature cools by one degree per hour. Livor mortis, a red marbling of the skin, sets in. Within twenty-four hours, rigor mortis, a stiffening of tissues, ensues, beginning with the face and moving down through the corpse. Then, as though thawing, the body again goes limp. Norma had seen all of this happen hundreds of times while working as a nurse, in places such as the neurology intensive care unit. But, she added, "there's a lot we can't explain. We just don't know everything that happens when people die."

To EMPHASIZE THAT point, she followed her biology of dying lecture with a story from when she had been a young nurse on hospital rounds. As she explained to her students, patients often awoke from very bad illnesses or cardiac arrests, talking about how they had been floating over their bodies. "Mm-hmmm," Norma would reply, sometimes thinking, Yeah, yeah, I know, you were on the ceiling.

Such stories were recounted so frequently that they hardly jolted medical personnel. Norma at the time had mostly chalked it up to some kind of drug reaction or brain malfunction, something like that.

"No, really," said a woman who'd recently come out of a coma. "I can prove it."

The woman had been in a car accident and been pronounced dead on arrival when she was brought into the emergency room. Medical students and interns had begun working on her and managed to get her heartbeat going, but then she had coded again. They'd kept on trying, jump-starting her heart again, this time stabilizing it. She'd remained in a coma for months, unresponsive.

Then one day she awoke, talking about the brilliant light and how she remembered floating over her body. Norma thought she could have been dreaming about all kinds of things in those months when she was unconscious.

But the woman told them she had obsessive-compulsive disorder and had a habit of memorizing numbers. While she was floating above her body, she had read the serial number on top of the respirator machine. And she remembered it. Norma looked at the machine. It was big and clunky, and this one stood about seven feet high. There was no way to see on top of the machine without a stepladder.

"Okay, what's the number?" Another nurse took out a piece of paper to jot it down. The woman rattled off twelve digits.

A few days later, the nurses called maintenance to take the ventilator machine out of the room. The woman had recovered so well, she no longer needed it. When the worker arrived, the nurses asked if he wouldn't mind climbing to the top to see if there was a serial number up there. He gave them a puzzled look and grabbed his ladder. When he made it up there, he told them that indeed there was a serial number.

The nurses looked at each other. Could he read it to them? Norma watched him brush off a layer of dust to get a better look. He read the number. It was twelve digits long: the exact number that the woman had recited.

The professor would later come to find out that her patient's story was not unique. One of Norma's colleagues at the University of Virginia Medical Center at the time, Dr. Raymond Moody, had published a book in 1975 called *Life After Life,* for which he had conducted the first large-scale study of people who had been declared clinically dead and been revived, interviewing 150 people from across the country. Some had been gone for as long as twenty minutes with no brain waves or pulse.

In her lectures, Norma sometimes shared pieces of his research with her own students. Since Moody had begun looking into the near-death experiences, researchers from around the world had collected data on thousands and thousands of people who had gone through them—children, the blind, and people of all belief systems and cultures—publishing the findings in medical and research journals and books. Still, no one has been able to definitively account for the common experience all of Moody's interviewees described.

The inevitable question always followed: Is there life after death?

Everyone had to answer that question based on his or her own beliefs, the professor said. For some of her students, that absence of scientific evidence of an afterlife did little to change their feelings about their faith. For others, it put that much more pressure on this life.

In the cemetery that evening, the sky had turned the color of slate. Some of the students were sitting on a curb listening to the lecture with outstretched legs, their feet clad in flip-flops and sneakers. Others leaned against cars. One young man wore his fraternity letters. A couple of young ladies were dressed in business attire: white collared shirts, slacks, and high heels. No one could have known it that day, but a year from now one of those students—the short-haired woman in glasses, holding her spiral notebook, with a beige cardigan over her Kean University T-shirt— would be dead herself, a victim of a house fire that started after she had fallen asleep without putting out her cigarette.

Norma dismissed her students. They climbed into cars and SUVs, filing out minutes before total darkness fell.

MOST PEOPLE SAY they do not fear death or barely think about it at all, according to Gallup polls. But Ernest Becker, a cultural anthropologist who won a Pulitzer Prize for his book *The Denial of Death*, argued that we're kidding ourselves; fear of death makes us want to engage in activities that render us unique, allowing us to reach a level of putative immortality. Death anxiety, Becker believes, is the powerful undercurrent stirring human behavior.

"What does it mean to be a self-conscious animal?" he wrote. "The idea is ludicrous, if it is not monstrous. It means to know that one is food for worms. This is the terror: to have emerged from nothing, to have a name, consciousness of self, deep inner feelings, an excruciating inner yearning for life and self-expression and with all this yet to die. It seems like a hoax, which is why one type of cultural man rebels openly against the idea of God. What kind of deity would create such a complex and fancy worm food?"

But if death is terrifying to most people, Norma knew that her job was to impart the more useful lesson about it: how to live a good life while always under the sharp tip of mortality. The narratives behind the bodies on the autopsy field trips to coroners' offices on which she took her students told those truths. Like the seventy-three-year-old splayed on a metal table one morning, his face peeled from his skull, his forehead folded in a flap over his chin. The medical examiner's report noted that he had hung himself in his garage. His wife had recently died, and it seemed that he could not bear to live on without her.

Displays of life's daily horrors, usually hidden from the public's view, ended up naked and spliced open by blue-gloved technicians, right before her students' eyes. There was the married thirty-year-old father of three, his mouth open, his arms rigid and cocked. He had been shot in the head. Someone had found him at 9:41 the night before; his belongings had ended up spread across a white sheet on the medical examiner's floor: a tangerine-and-red flame-colored T-shirt and sneakers that matched, a blood-soaked white undershirt, four packs of Newport cigarettes, a few dozen MetroCards for the New York City subway, $211 in cash.

And there was the boy who must have been about twelve. He had apparently hung himself in a basement with a dog leash. Norma just could not let that one go. After watching his autopsy on one field trip, she hunted down the information as to where the child's funeral was being held and decided to attend.

There was no denying it: life's edges brimmed with misery and cruelty. No wonder people often concluded that the dead were better off. In our youth, we looked forward to our futures, like "children in a theatre before the curtain is raised, sitting there in high spirits and eagerly waiting for the play to begin," the nineteenth-century German philosopher Arthur Schopenhauer once wrote. "It is a blessing that we do not know what is really going to happen. Could we foresee it, there are times when children might seem like innocent prisoners, condemned, not to death, but to life, and as yet all unconscious of what their sentence means."

By the time many of Norma's students came to her, they were already exhausted and confused about life and looking to find out how not to carry it out like a sentence.

In 1985, two researchers from the University of Louisiana at Lafayette embarked on what would become a twenty-year study to solve this question: what kind of students take death education courses in college, and why?

Sarah Brabant and Deann Kalich surveyed more than nine hundred students enrolled in Brabant's Sociology of Death and Dying course and found that nearly 24 percent wanted to deal with their own grief issues; but, most startlingly, close to half of the students surveyed had "seriously contemplated committing suicide at some time in their lives." Even more distressing, 10 percent of the students said they had actually tried to kill themselves at one point.

Norma saw all of this in sentences sprinkled through her students' essays. Like this one from a student who had been homeless: "I used to pray every day until one day I lost hope and it felt like it was pointless." Or this one: "After I was raped I wanted to curl up in a ball and die."

The professor referred students to the college counseling center on a regular basis. They called her in the middle of the night, in the early morning, during class, during lunch; they sent urgent text messages, knocked on her office door in tears, broke down sobbing with her in hallways. She kept a school mental health counselor's phone number in her cell phone. But some students simply threw it away when Norma jotted it down for them. They didn't want to talk to a stranger. They only wanted to talk to her.

So Norma's message was that happiness takes hard work. It should be approached like a series of homework assignments. She kept a small book in her office, *A Short Guide to a Happy Life* by Anna Quindlen, which she often quoted to students from memory. This was one of her favorite lines: "Life is made up of moments, small pieces of glittering mica in a long stretch of gray cement." Quindlen went on, "We have to teach ourselves how to make room for them, to love them, and to live, really live."

Living a long life didn't come with any promises that it would be a happy one either. Norma learned this lesson on her own when she was a twenty-something nurse in Virginia. On home visiting duty, she met a 110-year-old woman living alone in a trailer in the woods. Mary Manly was her name. Her only son had died in his eighties, and all she had left was a little black mutt with a gray chin that seemed as old as his owner, hobbling around on his little legs. Mary had a wound on her leg, and Norma stopped by to tend to it every few days.

One day, she treated the wound with a wet-to-dry sterile dressing, chatting with Mary. As she was leaving the trailer, Norma looked back over her shoulder. Through a window, she watched Mary grab a bag of cornmeal, rip off the dressing, and stuff the ground dried maize into her wound.

Norma went back later and confronted her. "Look, Mary, I saw the cornmeal. What was that about?"

Mary looked at her. "I don't like the feel of the wetness!" she snapped. "I want it to be dry."

"Okay, but you can tell me that," she said. "Cornmeal is going to make it stay like a wound. It's not going to heal."

Mary turned quiet, looking embarrassed.

In that moment, Norma realized that Mary did not want the wound to heal. She had no family left, no friends, and no other visitors to speak of. She must have looked forward to the dressings. It was the only time she had face-to-face conversation in days.

Norma called up the local church to tell them about the 110-year-old woman in a trailer, suggesting that maybe they could bring her a pie once in a while. She also continued to visit Mary regularly, even if not summoned.

Still today, on a wall in her office, she kept a black-and-white framed photo of her younger self, kneeling next to Mary. From her patient, Norma had learned that the deepest wounds can never be healed with ointment and gauze. It was a lesson more valuable than anything found in a textbook or dissertation.

She always held on to that tenderness she had for the elderly like Mary, those forgotten and overlooked. It was the same kind she felt for forlorn strangers, her students, and her own children. They needed her. And she didn't mind being needed.

So when it came to defining her Death in Perspective class, the professor developed the habit of handing out a poem by Khalil Gibran called "On Death" at the end of every semester. Part of it went like this:

Then Almitra spoke, saying, "We would ask now of Death."
And he said: You would know the secret of death.
But how shall you find it unless you seek it in the heart of life?

TAKE-HOME WRITING ASSIGNMENT: The Fire Story

Write about the time you walked through fire—your life's hardest moment—and how you came out of that experience alive. Who was there for you? How did you get through it? How did it change you?

TWO

Life Stories of Norma Lynn

Her home was a haven of fresh-baked cookies, porcelain dolls, and Christmas carols—nothing close to the images of high cerebral pretense or mystical musings that a professor of death might conjure up. Musical compositions of Richard Wagner did not fill her living space, and neither did the essays of Michel de Montaigne. There were no black votive candles, no altars swirling with Nag Champa incense, no household decor inspired by a Día de los Muertos celebration.

Norma lived with her family in a seafoam-colored two-story colonial house with an eggplant purple door on a quiet block across from a school in a Highland Park neighborhood, within walking distance of an earth-friendly mattress shop, a bubble tea café, three synagogues, and a vitamin, herbs, and organic foods store. The area's newspaper racks offered *The Star-Ledger* and the *Highland Park Mirror,* which featured articles on the local arts festival and an upcoming Zumba Latin dance aerobics demonstration. The professor and her partner of more than two decades, Norman, a child psychologist and also the father of their teenage daughter, had lived in that house for fifteen years. Norma and Norman. Norma's older daughter from her first and only marriage (she didn't feel the need to walk down the aisle a second time) was a college student studying law at Rutgers University and had lived there too before she went off to school.

One morning, Norma decided to explain the meaning behind various objects in her home, such as the quilt on the sofa—it was made of swaths of childhood dresses, bedroom curtains, and favorite shirts that had belonged to her older daughter, Melissa. "I said to her whenever she was sad or upset, she could wrap her childhood around her in the quilt." The professor continued the tour, pointing out a menorah that had belonged to her grandmother and a statue of a black Jesus given to her by Norman at Christmas.

Norman had been raised Jewish. Norma's mother and grandmother were also Jewish, and her father was Catholic. She'd grown up going to both synagogue and Catholic Mass and attending a private Catholic school, where the nuns terrified her—tying students' left hands behind their backs to force them to use the right one, yanking boys by the neck with their ties, slapping students with sticks. The family welcomed both religions into the household these days but didn't stick firmly to the rules of either, although they did celebrate all the holidays with fervor.

Norma had met Norman when they were both working at a mental health center, and on one of their dates he'd introduced her to an ashram, where everyone wore white and looked like zombies. It was a little too weird for her. Then he introduced her to the Omega Institute in Rhinebeck, New York, a retreat of workshops, family activities, and organic food in the woods, which she enjoyed. In the years since, they have visited Omega annually with their daughter, Becca, and Melissa, from Norma's first marriage.

Norman came downstairs looking tired. A short, spectacled, bearded man thirteen years older than Norma, he'd graduated from high school at sixteen. He had been accepted into Cornell University but had gone to City College of New York instead, earning his PhD at Rutgers University by twenty-six. He was the kind of quietly brilliant man who always seemed to be contemplating the nature of the universe, such as microscopic cell division. Once, Norma remembered, he had been so lost in thought that he'd had no idea he'd put on two neckties.

"Do you have two minutes?" Norma asked him. "Just two minutes to move the clothes from the van?"

A few days ago, she'd taken their daughter and a student along to haul off a mountain of clothes from a widower's home. The grieving man had found her email address after reading about her students in the newspaper, and Norma had dropped by for about two hours, asking him to tell her the stories behind many of his wife's belongings before he let go of them forever. She'd thought that remembering would help him let go—grief therapy delivered right to his front door. But now the tweed jackets, polyester jumpsuits, worn vintage leather suitcases, and embroidered sweatshirts were cluttering up the party bus. "They're full of dog hair, and I can't breathe," she told Norman, "and there's a suitcase that smells a little funny too."

He nodded and went about unloading the items into a spare room, to be sifted through and donated another day, as Norma continued her tour. She explained the story behind a vase that a supervisor had given her, a thank-you for her help after his wife died of cancer. She explained the meaning behind a Mother's Day card given to her by a student who was a marine.

Norma seemed to have an anecdote for every ornament, every occasion, every important memory. She was a practiced storyteller. She knew when to pause for effect, when to wait for the laughter or the jaw drop. She'd figured out how to unspool her lessons inside of stories too. That was why attending one of Norma's classes often felt like having a front-row seat at a one-woman monologue, interspersed with improv moments drawn from audience participation; she could build an entire lesson out of one student's personal experience. You never knew what to expect from the show or its spectators. Some days it was laughter; other days, rage or tears.

So it made sense that when it came down to her own life and loved ones, she'd catalogued all of it into a series of entertaining stories too.

One day, Norma said she had a funny story about her Huffington Post–blogging neighbor Chris.

"Chris very often will walk the dog, right? And this dog . . . it has this huge head on a Labrador's body . . . a pit bull head. It just does nothing but drool. I call it Grizzle goo, it's like this slobber that just hangs . . . sometimes she'll walk across the street and stand in front of my house" while walking the dog.

Norma went on to explain that when her oldest daughter, Melissa, had been a senior in high school who also played varsity basketball and sang in the choir, she and a group of friends had ended up double-booked:

a Christmas concert and basketball championship back to back. The stern choir director wanted her students on time. "So I said I would offer up the party bus and I would drive the girls from the game straight to the school to the choir concert."

But the game went into overtime. When it finally ended, Norma threw the girls into her van and took off for the concert. "In the meantime, there's a bunch of them in the back of my car. They all start changing their clothes." The choir director required them to all wear white shirts, black skirts, and black shoes. Norma looked at her daughter and asked, "Where are your clothes?" To which her daughter replied, "They're at home." In that case, Norma told her, she might as well forget the concert. Her daughter started to cry. "So I'm flipping out and driving," Norma said. "All of a sudden, she looks at me and she goes, 'Mom, you have on a white shirt, a black skirt, and black shoes today.' I had just come home from work . . . I look down and sure enough, I did."

So Norma began to strip.

"At every stoplight, I'm taking my clothes off. She puts on my outfit, and I'm down to my bra and underwear. . . . But there was no way in hell I was going to put on her sweaty basketball uniform."

Norma pulled up to the school, shouting at them to get out of the car before someone spotted her. "And I'm half-naked. In the car. In December. So I'm, like, okay, I'll just drive down the block, go into the house and put on clothes, and go to the concert. So I pull in, and sure enough there's freakin' Chris with that dog. . . . I jump out of my car in my underwear, and I'm fumbling with my keys to get into the house."

By the next day, practically the whole block had heard the story of the naked professor running around outside her house in the snow, Norma said, chuckling at the image of herself.

Norma did not mind if people thought of her as ironic or eccentric. But fragile or wounded? That was a different story. She carried herself as if following the mantra of a therapist 24/7: *I'll listen to your issues, but you don't need to know mine.* Trying to understand her sometimes made you feel like the nosy kid with hands cupped around both eyes, peering through the curtains of a neighbor's window on a bright day. You had to tiptoe real close if you hoped to stand the slightest chance at seeing what was on the inside. When asked personal questions by her students, or by me, she sometimes responded with a joke: "If I told you, I'd have to kill you."

One day—more than a year into my following Norma around—her curtain parted a little. We were sitting on a bench in Raritan Bay looking toward Staten Island on a warm Saturday afternoon, after a balloon-releasing ceremony that Norma had just conducted at a cemetery with three former students who had been enrolled in her classes at different times: a mother and two daughters all grieving the death of the same man, the daughters' father.

The professor's story, as she told it to me that day at Raritan Bay, had started when she was still in her mother's tummy, a fist-sized fetus that nobody even realized was there, nobody except her seventeen-year-old mother, who seemed to wish she could strangle the weed growing inside right out of her belly with every girdle she layered over the next. The girdles suctioned her mom's midsection like a tourniquet, strings yanked tightly, creating an illusion of a stomach so flat that her grandmother couldn't even detect there was a baby under there.

"She never took a prenatal vitamin," Norma said, recounting what her grandmother, who was now dead, had told her years before. "She never had a doctor's appointment. It's, like, a miracle that I have all my fingers and toes."

Her mother, who had since died too, was named Linda, and the way Norma understood it, the woman back then had places to see, her own life to lead first, before having a child. She'd wanted to become a journalist when she left her hometown of Newport News, Virginia, and enrolled in the University of Miami. In her first semester, she'd met a young man named Norm, who was studying marketing.

Linda's Jewish parents had come from Austria and Russia, fleeing persecution. Norma's father was Catholic, from Baltimore, Maryland, but his family had later moved to New Jersey. His parents had come from Italy to Ellis Island, his father on the *Lusitania*, his mother on the *Saturnia*. He had topaz-blue eyes, a shock of blond hair, and a cocky machismo about him. He drove a 1956 Chevy convertible and had grown up poor and sheltered, fishing and hunting blackbirds to eat with polenta and cornmeal, working in a steel mill with his dad. Linda had developed a circle of wealthy girlfriends at school, but when it came to money her new romantic interest had barely any. It did not seem to matter, since Linda got pregnant soon after they met.

That summer, Norma's grandmother intercepted a letter from Linda's lover. It was about the unborn child. She confronted Linda and discovered the girdles. The deception was over. On August 22, the baby was born. They named her Norma Lynn (combining both parents' names). "My parents got married," Norma explained. "And that was, like, the worst thing ever."

Norma's parents moved to Florida. Her dad found a job at Cape Canaveral Air Force Station, earning about $75 a month as a service person. The newlyweds fought violently, and within a year and a half, they divorced, and her father, as Norma later learned, denied paternity.

Still a baby, Norma said, she was sent to live with her grandmother in Virginia, while her mother charged off elsewhere to try to put the pieces of her life back together. She spent her earliest years raised by her grandma and a maid; although Linda lived there too, she wasn't around much. "My grandmother and mother were at a movie theater. My mother had a stomachache in the movie theater and buckled over in pain," she said. "My grandmother rushes her to the hospital. I was at a neighbor's house. At the hospital, they take off her clothing to put on a patient gown and there she is again." Pregnant, "with five layers of girdles. And they cut off all the girdles, and she was delivering the baby, and that baby was stillborn."

Norma looked at me. "So how did I survive? And that baby didn't?" Her grandmother, who'd split from her grandfather long before much of it happened, told her that she'd buried the dead baby herself.

"You know," she went on, "years back there was a case in New Jersey, where a girl delivered a baby at the prom and put it in a waste-basket." The eighteen-year-old south New Jersey student gave birth in a bathroom stall in 1997, according to news reports, and choked the boy before putting him in a trash bag and throwing him away. The girl went back to the dance floor to rejoin her prom date when she was done, even eating a salad and dancing one last dance. After she was caught, her friends and family claimed they'd had no idea she was pregnant. "I was a psych nurse by then," Norma said. "I remember everyone saying 'How could people not know?'" She thought to herself: it was not as impossible as it might have seemed.

Her own father had not wanted her in the first place, she believed, and her mother had tried to hide her, perhaps even get rid of her, and then left her to be raised by her grandmother. She was just an unwanted kid; loved by her grandmother, definitely—the dear woman had no other choice. But unwanted all the same.

DECADES LATER, THE professor found herself standing at a whiteboard in front of her students, semester after semester, explaining how life and death are inextricably bound with birth.

Drawing a circle with eight points, she introduced her favorite psychological theorist by writing his name at the top: Erik Erikson. She had stumbled across his work when she was a college student. "He thought we grow, develop, and change throughout our entire life span," she told her students. "We never stay the same. Each experience molds us and changes us."

The German-born psychologist never knew his real father and was adopted at age six by his mother's husband, Theodor Homburger. At home in Germany, Erikson was treated differently from his three half sisters. At school, he was made fun of for being a tall, fair-skinned, blond, blue-eyed Jewish kid who looked Scandinavian, when his peers of the same religion were all shorter, with darker skin, hair, and eyes.

"Before long, then, I acquired the nickname 'goy' in my stepfather's temple; while to my schoolmates, I was a 'Jew,'" Erikson wrote in an essay in *Daedalus*. "Although I had tried desperately to be a good German chauvinist, I became a 'Dane' when Denmark remained neutral during the First World War."

Erikson's stepfather had insisted that he go to college to become a doctor, but he refused and instead set off to become an artist in Vienna, where he painted portraits of children. "I became intensely alienated from every thing my bourgeois family stood for," he wrote. "At that point I wanted to be different."

He began teaching art in an elementary school, where he met a psychoanalyst by the name of Anna Freud, a daughter of Sigmund Freud. Anna was impressed by Erikson's innate ability to relate to and understand children, and she invited him to learn psychoanalysis at her father's institute. Erikson took up the offer, while also earning a teaching degree, and Anna took him under her wing. In the years after he finished his training at the Vienna Psychoanalytic Society in 1933, Erikson went on to become a professor at Harvard. When he moved to the United States, he changed his last name from that of his adoptive father, Homburger, to Erikson. Some researchers have speculated that it was his own way of defining himself after a lifetime of suffering his own identity crisis and feeling as though he did not belong.

Erik Erikson gained international fame, as Norma explained, for his developmental theory that the human life cycle, from birth to death, is divided into eight stages.

Crisis encompasses each of Erikson's eight stages, and the evolution of a personality depends on how a human endures, flourishes, founders, or remains stagnant through each, Norma told her students. In each stage, an individual either gains a virtuous personality trait that will help him or her confront the subsequent crises throughout life, or they miss out on gaining that virtue, which makes it that much more difficult to cope with life's challenges as the next stages approach.

Critics of his theory claimed that it wasn't grounded in enough scholarly statistical research, that it was more applicable to males than females, and that it focused too heavily on childhood and not enough on adulthood. Others questioned whether his stages of psychosocial development were sequential: Does a person have to graduate successfully from one stage to make it into the next?

As Norma teaches, Erikson thought people were capable of changing up until that last stage of life. Norma believes that people can move between Erikson's stages out of order, sometimes reverting backward or sometimes getting stuck in one, perhaps for his or her entire life. But to learn to face death with integrity, according to Erikson, one first has to successfully develop all of those specific virtues from the prior seven stages of life. And it all begins with birth.

"What are some basic needs of a newborn?" Norma asked her students.

"Being fed," one answered.

"Yes, absolutely."

"Shelter."

"Being changed."

"Right. You don't want to be wet. A wet baby will cry and cry."

The infant develops a reliance on the adult who consistently comes to take away the child's pain from hunger or discomfort. Trust establishes hope. It becomes, as Erikson put it, "an actual sense of the reality of 'good' powers, outside and within oneself."

This trust in a mother or a caretaker becomes, as a child grows older, an underlying trust in life, a sense that life and the world are not so bad. So the first virtue an individual picks up is hope.

"Hope," Erikson wrote, "is both the earliest and the most indispensable virtue inherent in the state of being alive. . . . if life is to be sustained hope must remain, even where confidence is wounded, trust impaired."

But Erikson argued that adults who are deprived of these basic needs during infancy can find themselves destined for a life of despair. A distrustful child can grow into an adult with trouble finding a reason to live in a world that is full of disappointment and discontent. Erikson called this first stage of life "Trust vs. Mistrust."

"What else do newborns need?" Norma asked.

"Attention."

"Love."

"Yes, and how do we show that?"

"By holding?"

"Right," Norma said. "Newborns have to be held."

If a baby learns that he or she cannot trust his or her mother, father, foster parent, grandparent, nurse, or nanny, if the child feels abandoned or starved not only for nourishment but also attention—such as basic cuddling—it contributes to his or her basic sense of doubt in the world.

That is the first crisis of life.

"It's really very interesting, guys," Norma said. "If you're not held enough as a baby, your brain does not hard wire properly." If no one steps in to protect and cradle a child, "those babies can develop something called failure to thrive. They stop eating. They stop sleeping. They just die."

In the description of his theory, Erikson referred to the research of the psychoanalyst René Spitz, who released a silent black-and-white film, *Grief: A Peril in Infancy*, in 1947, in which he compared two groups of infants: the first raised in a home by nurses responsible for seven infants each and the other in a nursery at a women's prison in upstate New York, where mothers cared for their babies daily. The babies raised by nurses seemed withdrawn, spaced out, or in a state of terror. He filmed babies who did not make eye contact and did not seem remotely curious or responsive to play. Others had barely enough will to cry. Some had become emaciated and frail. They lagged behind those raised in the prison with their mothers; in Spitz's footage of the prison, those babies were seen crawling, climbing, and frolicking about.

Gaining virtues in every stage after childhood takes work. Norma knew that because she'd done the work herself. For those who have experienced mistrust, Norma told her students, "We will be battling against it for the rest of our entire time on the planet."

In the second of Erikson's stages, "Autonomy vs. Shame and Doubt," a child's physical growth takes off, going from a state of helplessness to suddenly being able to sit up, crawl, walk, and run. It is a time of exploration, she explained, when a child holds on and lets go, wanders off and returns, pushes away and wants to be held again. This is when a child learns a sense of independence and adequacy, a feeling of self-worth.

By the third stage of life, between ages three to five, "We have a very big cognitive growth spurt," Norma said. "Our vocabulary increases exponentially and kids begin to mimic what parents and caregivers are saying. If you come from a family that does a lot of cussing, chances are you will hear a three-year-old saying cuss words too or saying 'Mommy told Daddy to go to hell.'"

Erikson called the third stage "Initiative vs. Guilt." Children learn creative problem-solving skills, how to play, act out, and imagine all the behaviors that help them realize they have a sense of purpose. When parents excessively punish, beat, or verbally abuse a child for exploring the world and trying to figure it out, he or she can begin to feel shame or guilt for thinking or acting in such a way in the first place.

People who don't develop autonomy or initiative as children can become dependent on others later, as Norma interpreted Erikson's theory, or they can doubt themselves in every aspect of their lives. In this stage, shame emerges: *I am not good enough. Nothing I have to say is important. No one will ever love me.*

Between six and eleven years old, children reach Erikson's fourth stage of life, "Industry vs. Inferiority." This is when they begin to want to master the skills they have been learning, showing off their abilities in reading, gymnastics, writing, violin, painting, or Little League. Children develop a sense of competitiveness with their siblings and peers and want to prove to everyone, including themselves, that they are not worthless. So much of their success in doing so depends on the attentiveness and love of a caregiver.

If, throughout all of these ages, a child's impulsivity is stifled or his or her flitting mind punished, if he or she is abused or neglected, if he or she never feels real love and encouragement, Erikson said, the youngster might grow up with a wish to "force the world not to look at him, not to notice his exposure."

"He would like to destroy the eyes of the world," Erikson wrote. "Instead he must wish for his own invisibility."

As NORMA'S LIFE story went, when she was five, her mother decided to leave Virginia. She packed up her little girl's belongings, and told her to say good-bye to her grandmother. Linda carted Norma back with her to live in the Jackson Heights, Queens, neighborhood of New York.

Linda had found a job working for Pepsi-Cola in Midtown on Fifty-ninth Street and Park Avenue. Meanwhile, her father, at twenty-four, had been drafted and spent two years in the military before being transferred to the Fort Dix, New Jersey, military base, where he was close enough to reunite with Linda. He was ready to claim the little girl now too. There was no need for a paternity test to prove he was her father this time. He believed it now. He was ready to raise her and be a family.

Soon after, Norma's parents married each other—a second time. They were addicted like that: volatile and toxic when together, yet unable to loosen the choke hold they had over each other. They moved in with each other again too. They fought. They made up. They fought some more. Soon they had a son together, and there were no girdles this time around.

As Norma remembers it, Linda forbade her daughter to use the word "Mom" in public. Other times, her mother screamed at her, "You've ruined my life! I never wanted you. I would have been a journalist!" More than once, she remembered her mother telling her she wished she had never been born.

Some days, Norma said, she wished the same.

"I was sort of the buffer," she said. "If my mother took it out on me, she was less likely to get into it with my father. When my father got into it, then we had knives, then we had guns, then we had, like, next-level DEFCON 10."

WHEN NORMA WAS ten, she rode her bike through a patch of poison ivy. She was allergic, and it was the time of year when people burned piles of leaves in their yard. She must have been breathing in the fumes, because remnants of poison ivy got trapped in her respiratory tract. Her eyes swelled shut, her throat began to close. She ended up in the emergency room, where nurses tried to give her a steroid shot to reduce the symptoms. But they could not find a place on her body to inject the needle. Her body was completely covered in bruises.

Adults came into her room with questions: How did you get the bruises? Have your parents ever hit you? Terrified that they would take her away to an orphanage if they learned the truth and even more scared of her mother's reaction if she told, she came up with a story: "I fell off my bike . . . and then the bike fell on top of me . . . and I hit a bush." Oh my God, they're going to find out, she thought as the lies spilled out of her mouth.

When it was over, they did not take her away.

The truth was, sometimes her mother choked her until she nearly passed out. Sometimes she pulled her hair out of her scalp in chunks. Most days, she whacked her with wooden spoons. The family had an ornate living room that Norma could never remember them sitting in and an elaborate dining room with a big table they never seemed to use. Instead they ate at a smaller round table off the kitchen with four seats. Norma's seat was in front of her mother's cabinet. There was no way to move the chair to sit down without hitting the cabinet. Each time Norma bumped the cabinet she would get hit, mostly in the torso or below, but rarely in the face. Anything she did seemed to set her mother off, whether she was too quick to talk back or too slow to speak. Too fast to walk or too slow. She always heard she was too stupid for her own good, no matter how high her grades in school were.

It wasn't just her mother who hurt her. Once when Norma was seven, her parents went out at night and left her at home. She was sick and delirious, threw up in her bed, and was too weak to clean up her mess. When they came home, her mother flew into a rage and her father pushed her face into her own vomit. "Please don't, please don't!" she remembered crying, tears and vomit soaking her hair.

On some occasions, she thought her parents might kill each other. When she was old enough to drive, she took both of her parents to the hospital over and over again with bloody lips or dislocated hips or jaws. She felt most useful when she was taking care of them, saving each from the other. Norma Lynn. Keeper of their secrets. Scrubber of their messes. The rescuer. And when she came through for them in such a way, she could almost feel their gratefulness, their regard for her, even if they never said it.

Her brother was five years younger, and he had been born with pyloric stenosis, a narrowing of his stomach to his intestines, which caused severe vomiting throughout his first months of life. As a child, he erupted into tantrums so severe that he would stop breathing and turn purple. She grew up taking care of him too. Norma had no idea who among the family members would die first, whether from violence or illness.

Death, it seemed, taunted her like some kind of bedroom monster lurking in the closet. She learned how to be a very good girl, always tiptoeing around her parents' tempers, hiding in her bedroom reading Nancy Drew novels, throwing herself into science class at school.

Her sense of self-assurance came about as subtly as physical maturation. For months there were hints, but then all of a sudden there she was, practically full grown. Somewhere along the way she just stopped being afraid—afraid of her parents, afraid of her life, afraid of death. Maybe that sense of courage had existed inside her even before she was born, but all she knew now was that when violence broke out at home, she could dissociate from her body, go into a state of total calm. After all, it couldn't be that bad, she thought. Death. She had managed to outsmart it for this long.

She decided to try to go to medical school. Her father seemed to be making good money as a business administrator in public education in those days. He stashed wads of cash in their home, and sometimes Norma came across the bills, which were hidden near the guns. They had a drop-down ceiling, the kind that if you pushed the right spot, a block of tile would move, revealing the goods concealed inside. The basement filled up with stacks and stacks of books, reams of paper, pens, and pencils, framed pieces of art, and office furniture—stuff that looked as if it had come straight from a school reception office. Norma didn't really know why it was there. She knew better than to ask.

Her mother wore chocolate mink coats, smoked three packs of cigarettes a day, and spent nights out playing professional bridge and mahjong, and her daylight hours doting on her poodle, Pierre. Her father had a red convertible Fiat, and later an eggplant-purple Porsche, which he drove around town while holding a glass of red wine. He even had his own bodyguard, as well as a person who chauffeured him around when he didn't want to drive. Some nights, her dad dragged her along to Italian restaurants in places like Staten Island. She would sit in the corner of the restaurant and watch her father drink and yammer away with all of his friends and business partners, also Italian.

Once Norma stayed in a kitchen as some of her dad's friends went into another room, and she heard one man, his colleague of some sort, bawling and wailing. It sounded as though he was begging. Begging for what? she wondered. Why would a grown man cry like that? She had yet to figure it out for herself. All she remembered was that she never saw or heard from that man again. She never asked her father what had happened to him. Something told her she did not want to know.

AT THAT POINT in her story that day on the bench in Raritan Bay, Norma shook her head and grew quiet for a moment. "It's so hard to tell you this," she continued, taking a breath. As she grew older, she'd come to discover hidden truths about her family. Truths she wished she could undo.

"Um, my father," she began, "was involved in the Mafia."

Surely she was joking. Norma sometimes spent her free time attending drumming workshops, Native American sweat lodges, and sessions entitled "The Wisdom of Thirteen Indigenous Grandmothers." Nothing about her life said "Mafia." The punch line had to be coming. But she wasn't smiling. "He was a business administrator in the public school system, and therefore he could give the Mafia contracts—building contracts, maintenance contracts." What the Mafia couldn't hawk or had to store would end up in his family basement.

"Those people would sell anything," she said. "They would sell you if they could."

Her dad, now seventy-four, lived in Myrtle Beach, South Carolina, where he drove a cherry red Mustang with a convertible top. He'd left his days of jet-setting to Atlantic City and the Dominican Republic or attending parties with Playboy girls. But when I met him months later, he was still dropping names such as Paul Castellano and John Gotti, Sr.

AT FIFTEEN, NORMA had an exit plan. She hatched it one day not long after her mother raised a hand to her face for the last time. She would later remember standing up to her that day, grabbing her wrists, looking her straight in the eye, and saying "You are not hitting me today." To her surprise, her mother backed off.

In three more years she could legally leave without being shuffled into a foster home or a runaway shelter. She posted a countdown calendar in her room, crossing out the days until she could graduate high school and leave home for good.

She told her mother about her medical school plans. Her mother told her she'd be better off working in a bank. Fine, she decided, she would make it to med school on her own. Pay for it herself.

But Norma quickly realized that medical school would be nearly impossible to finance on her own, so she chose nursing school instead. She got accepted into the Muhlenberg School of Nursing, a program affiliated with Union County College, which she chose because she could receive an associate's degree and then transfer to earn a bachelor's degree. She went to work at the University of Virginia, near her grandmother. She would not regret leaving her parents, but she would miss her little brother. She trusted he'd be fine; he was the planned child. Norma left home, believing she'd be better off if she never returned.

Her on-the-job training as a psychiatric nurse at the University of Virginia Medical Center quickly proved to her that this was where she belonged—in a hospital dealing with the mentally and physically ill. Here she was in a psychiatric ward with people even more unhinged than the ones she'd grown up with—and she held the keys. She controlled injections and medications, and she could read people, especially when they were the least bit agitated.

"Oh, my God, crazy people? People screaming and yelling? Pounding on walls? Breaking furniture? This is great!" Norma said. "And I was really good at handling it."

She could sense a blowup before it started to build. When a patient began punching or bashing his head against a wall or ripping up the sheets in his room, other nurses ran away to find the body restraints. They wanted to strap the patient to a stretcher, shoot him full of Thorazine, an antipsychotic medication, and force him into isolation in a quiet room. But Norma told them, "No, let me talk to him." She would sit on the patient's bed and try to calm him. It didn't always work. Once a patient beat her up pretty badly, walloping on her as if she were a punching bag, but even that did not faze her. She slipped into the same disassociated state she had discovered in childhood.

One morning, she started making rounds on her shift, checking in on new patients who had been admitted overnight. She walked into a room and noticed a young man sitting on the bed. "Hi," she said with a smile. "I'm the charge nurse on the day shift."

He stared at her blankly. She noticed he was holding something on his lap. She walked closer and noticed it was a gun. She didn't raise her eyebrows or try to moonwalk out of the room.

"I'm really sorry, I know this is your property, but you're not allowed to have this in the psychiatric unit," she said without skipping a beat. "You'll have to give that to me, and I'll lock it up safely for you, and you can get it when you're discharged."

Here was this twenty-two-year-old nurse smiling with her hands outstretched, as if asking him to hand over his belt to ensure it wouldn't get lost. The man looked flummoxed. Norma had seen plenty of guns in her lifetime, and this one didn't intimidate her any more than the rest. "I'll take that for you," she said sweetly.

He handed it over.

"Thank you very much," she said, walking calmly over to the nurse's station with the pistol in her hands, as if balancing a tray of meds. She called security to come lock it up. A guard checked its chamber: the gun was loaded.

"Really?" Norma replied. Well, that was a close one.

LIKE HER FAVORITE theorist, when Norma got old enough, she changed her Italian last name. No longer wanting to be connected to her father through it, she decided to keep "Bowe," which belonged to her first husband, after the marriage ended in her twenties. She never changed it back after they divorced. Sometimes she wondered if she and her father really were biologically related. After all, she didn't think they looked much alike. He'd lost his power, and his powerful friends, long before. Still, he came around a couple times a year, mostly for holidays or graduations.

On the day Norma earned the right to add "Dr." to her title, she remembered that her father broke out of the graduation audience and headed for the steps of the stage as the PhD degrees were being bestowed.

Horrified, Norma looked on as Norman tried to stop Norm. (The fact that their names matched seemed fitting for her already unusual life.) But Norm (her father) shook off Norman (her partner) and barged onstage as the doctoral adviser pulled the hood over Norma's head.

Her father grabbed her arm in front of the crowd. Looking her in the eye, he managed to get one sentence out before being ushered offstage:

"From nuthin'," he told his daughter, "to somethin'."

CLASS FIELD TRIP: Medical Examiner's Office
TAKE-HOME WRITING ASSIGNMENT: The Rewind Button
If you had a rewind button for your life, what would you go back and change?
Caitlin
Dr. Bowe
Death in Perspective
If I Had a Rewind Button . . .

The thing is, I loved my mom so much and I still do. When I was little . . . I would follow her everywhere and want to be around her all the time. [But] when she was high . . . it was like a switch turned in me and I was evil. So many times she convinced me not to flush [her pills] down the toilet, and not tell daddy. She would swear on my life that she would never do it again. Well I'm 22 years old and it still happens. . . . I wish so bad that I had handled everything differently, or somehow forced her into rehab.

THREE

Rewind Button

Spring Semester, January 2008

For too long, Caitlin convinced herself that she could ward off death with homemade sacraments. Daily showers in her parents' house turned into heroic lifesaving missions. If the shampoo and soap bottles did not face in exactly the same direction, if the ends of the bathroom towels touched each other or were not perfectly aligned, Caitlin believed her father would die.

Day after day, the Kean University student methodically straightened the bathroom knickknacks, as if everyone else's life depended on it, all the while neglecting her own. No one told her this behavior might have been a symptom of a larger psychological challenge, until the fall of 2007, when she enrolled in a mental health class with Dr. Norma Bowe.

The professor immediately identified the behavior that Caitlin described in her papers and class discussions. She called it obsessive-compulsive disorder, a way of existing that made Caitlin reliant on rituals—habits that helped her feel as though she had some control in a world that was skidding all around her. But Caitlin didn't begin to clue the professor into where her need for control might have started until she enrolled in a second class with Norma, Death in Perspective.

The new semester began at the start of 2008 and would last five months. It was in this class that Caitlin revealed through her assignments how deep-seated her fears of death actually were. She explained to her professor in private how she couldn't bring herself to move out of her parents' house and leave them to themselves because she was terrified that something would happen to them. She woke up in the middle of the night sometimes, hurrying to the bedside of her sleeping parents, just to make sure they had not stopped breathing. She couldn't fathom the thought of losing either of them, but especially her dad. He was her fiercest protector. The one person in her life who made her feel important. Her shampoo bottles, she believed, would prevent catastrophe. And if not, the light switches would do the job; she flicked them on and off and repeated the words "God forbid" three times out loud.

She had not always wrestled with this need to monitor the fate of her family. When she was a little girl, she had found other ways to manage. Her mother could be screaming and thrashing around the house, all because her father had hidden her pills again, and Caitlin would kneel on the floor, lost in her crayons and coloring books, as if tuning out commercials on a television. She retreated into her own world of play.

In elementary school, Caitlin found a rusty copper key in her backyard. It was a skeleton key, believed to open multiple doors. She became a skeleton key collector. Her dad brought her new ones, and she cherished each of them, especially because they came from him. He told her she could accomplish anything she wanted in her life. "Don't ever give up," he said. "Don't be a quitter."

But as she got older, skeleton keys no longer held special powers that she imagined might offer a way out. Tuning out the arguments became impossible. She stopped believing that she could do anything. Only the rituals, such as organizing pennies in a precise order with all heads or tails matching, seemed to ease her anxieties.

Over the last ten years, the professor had developed a stockpile of writing-for-therapy exercises that she pulled out on a whim. She'd probably read more than two thousand good-bye letters. Midway through Caitlin's term in the death class, Norma asked students to answer the question "If you had a rewind button, what would you go back and change?"

Caitlin went home and wrote as honestly as she could, submitting the assignment in the next class. One afternoon soon after, Norma took her seat in the circle of desks in the classroom and announced to the students that one assignment had stuck out from the rest and she hoped that person would read it aloud. Caitlin looked around, wondering who among her three dozen peers the professor might be referring to.

"Caitlin," the professor said, looking in her direction.

Caitlin's jaw dropped. She couldn't be serious, she thought. Out of all these students, Norma had picked *her* to share? She felt put on the spot. But she was also surprised that her professor had paid enough attention to her story to even mention it. The other students had shared their good-bye letters in the second class. Some had lost family members and friends to accidents and diseases. Their struggles seemed far more tragic than hers. Who in this classroom, she wondered, would really care to hear about her?

At first Caitlin tried to ask the student next to her to read it for her, but Norma encouraged her to take ownership of the letter, read it herself. Reluctantly, she did.

"It was about two weeks after my fourth birthday when I found my mom unconscious in my backyard with one sock on," Caitlin began, her voice trembling as she felt all eyes on her. Tears blurred her vision as she blinked to make out the rest of the words on the paper. "She went into a coma. I don't remember how long because I was so young, but I do remember everyone telling me Mommy was sick. It wasn't until I was about eight years old that I understood she did it to herself. She is a drug addict and has been since before I was born. You might think I'd want to rewind and change the fact that I ever knew."

When Caitlin found her mom that day, she had no idea what was wrong with her. Caitlin tried to get her to wake up, but she wouldn't budge. Was she dead? She hardly even understood what dead meant at that age, but she knew it wasn't good. Caitlin yelled for her father, a firefighter, who was home that day. He came running, scooping her mom up like a sack of toys. But he didn't call an ambulance. Instead he decided to drive her to the hospital himself. Caitlin and her sisters crawled into the backseats of the minivan. Their dad deposited their mom's motionless body across their tiny laps. The girls held on to her arms and legs for the ride.

She had seen the scars on her mom's wrists since she was little. They ran across like raised veins. But she didn't learn until she got older that her mom had slit her wrists and set her bed on fire before Caitlin was born.

As Caitlin got older, she realized that the pills were the problem. Some of the labels had weird words, like Xanax, Vicodin, and Percocet. The pills were *bad*. The pills might *kill* her mother. "She loves the pills more than she loves you," her father would tell Caitlin, forcing her to look at her mother's swollen, drooling face.

Whenever her father found out her mother had been using while he was at the firehouse, he flew into a rage, even slapping her around. But her mom barely seemed to feel it. All drugged up, she did not even respond.

There were times Caitlin found her mother on the bathroom floor, unconscious with toothpaste smeared across her face and the sink. Imitating her father's reaction, Caitlin would yell and slap her and then tear the house apart searching for the sock full of pills. Sometimes her mother begged her not to flush the pills or tell her father. Feeling guilty, Caitlin obeyed.

One day, her mother noticed the rusty skeleton key that Caitlin kept on a chain around her neck and asked if she knew where it had come from. Caitlin always figured the key had magically appeared in her backyard, just for her to find, separate from the ones her father gave her. But her mom explained that someone had given it to her at the hospital when Caitlin was four. That meant her mom had received it shortly after Caitlin had found her facedown in the backyard. She must have lost the key in the yard.

Caitlin couldn't believe it. She threw the key away. She wanted nothing to do with anything tainted by such a horrible memory. That was when her hobby of collecting skeleton keys ended.

By the time she turned twelve, Caitlin had become withdrawn and despondent in school. She would not even reply when a teacher called on her, wouldn't open her mouth at all. She just sat there, paralyzed with fear.

Sometimes teachers would get upset with her lack of obedience and scold her in front of the class, which made her feel terrible. She wanted desperately to talk but just couldn't bring herself to do it. The thought of speaking mortified her, and she began to hate herself even more for it. When class was over, she would go looking for somewhere away from everyone else to cry.

To try to overcome this fear and shyness, she decided to try out for a school play. But she got so nervous before her audition that she ran to the bathroom and threw up all of the Doritos she had eaten beforehand. Throwing up horrified her. She had never thrown up before, at least not since she was a baby, and she couldn't remember that far back. She detested sickness in general and would lock herself in a closet with Lysol if ill people were around. She would wipe down the toilet seat in her own house each time she went to the bathroom, and even after it had been wiped down she still did not actually sit on the toilet seat. She rubbed her hands raw with soap and water. She needed neatness. If anything in her bedroom seemed an inch out of place, or if a pencil suddenly went missing, she would notice immediately and get upset. She couldn't stand the thought of anyone touching her stuff. After the vomiting incident, she got panic attacks in school, worrying that she might throw up again at any moment. Fear of vomiting consumed her now too.

By middle school, Caitlin was a C student, but she had become convinced that she could make life at home better if she excelled in sports. She knew the whole family enjoyed softball, and when Caitlin played in tournaments they all came to the games and acted so happy, like a normal family. Her mom was a huge Yankees fan. And her dad enjoyed playing catch. If Caitlin could become the best softball player, if she could play the game as much as possible, maybe then, she figured, everything would be okay. But it didn't work out that way.

Years passed, and Caitlin kept looking for new ways to cope, to make her imperfect life feel perfect. She had become obsessed with the idea of being skinny. She consumed 500 calories a day, subsisting on coffee, oatmeal, and fruit, and ran two to three miles or spent forty-five minutes at the gym daily. She was five feet, seven inches tall and had whittled down to 100 pounds in a matter of months. She stopped getting her menstrual cycle.

By college, Caitlin had willed herself to become a straight-A student, who panicked if she received anything less. She was now pretty *and* smart, or so everyone else thought. But passing herself in the mirror, she didn't always see the captivating young lady that others commented about on Facebook, using words such as "gorgeous" and "hot," one even saying she could be Britney Spears's twin. Caitlin was a long-legged blonde with a sharp chin and a waist narrow enough to hug with one arm. For makeup she used just smoky eyeliner, mascara, and a few strokes of lip gloss, yet it was still enough to make heads turn. But at school she preferred baseball caps and running sneakers. She sometimes stooped when she sat, like a weak stem holding up a heavy flower. When Caitlin looked at herself, she saw someone never quite beautiful or remarkable enough.

One day, while home from her college classes, Caitlin and her sister heard crashing sounds from downstairs, as if someone was chopping down a tree in the basement. Then they heard a blast. Caitlin knew her father owned a few guns. He kept them stashed in the basement in a cabinet, separate from the bullets. The sisters ran downstairs toward the noises. By the time they reached the basement, they realized their mother had locked herself inside with the guns. Their dad grabbed a sledgehammer from the backyard and tried breaking down the door. But before he could get through, Caitlin's mom pulled the trigger. The bullet lodged in a wall near the staircase her daughters had rushed down.

"You could have shot one of the kids!" Caitlin would remember her dad screaming.

"I'm constantly worrying, even when there is nothing to worry about," Caitlin told the class that day when Norma called on her to read her rewind button essay. "I stress myself out and overdo everything, like it's going to fill some void."

IN CLASS, CAITLIN found herself engrossed by the stories her professor shared about her years working as a psychiatric nurse. Norma would launch into a lesson on mental illness sometimes like this: "I had a patient say to me once, 'If only you would take me to the roof, I could prove to you that I could fly.' He was absolutely convinced. Sometimes people get these really grandiose ideas when they're manic."

Norma recounted her experience with another patient, also manic:

"This kid comes in, and he's just all over the place. We had to restrain him and take him to the psych unit, but he managed to jump up and run down the hall with the stretcher strapped to him. . . . The psychiatric unit was on one side and the geriatric unit was on the other, and these old people would walk by and he would be plastered to the wall because they just caught him buck-naked full frontal. This went on for about two weeks. One day, I went in and it was quiet, and this nurse says, 'You won't believe it. Go in and look.' And sure enough, I went into the room and he had his hands crossed over his chest with his eyes closed, and I said, 'What's wrong?' And he said, 'Can't you see I'm dead?' He had gone from really high to really low."

Norma also told her classes about an extremely bright Rutgers University student she had treated when she worked as a psychiatric nurse in an outpatient clinic. His family had come to the United States from India in the hope that he would attend medical school. But by his second semester, he started to display symptoms of schizophrenia and ended up getting suspended from campus. Each week, he would visit with Norma and explain how guilty he felt for shaming his family. He talked of feeling as if his intelligence was getting sucked out of him and of hearing voices. He described the sound to her—like having earphones stuck to both ears and tuned to your least favorite radio station, with no control over the dial or the volume. The description, as Norma told her students, reminded her of when she had been a nurse at the University of Virginia, working the 3 P.M. to 11 P.M. shift and going home each night after her rounds to turn on the television and see various evangelical preachers proselytizing on channel after channel. She couldn't imagine having those preachers stuck in her ear 24/7. In the case of schizophrenics, she said, the station was often tuned to a constant stream of disparaging comments such as "You're ugly" or "That person hates you" or "You smell" or "That person is going to hurt you."

Her schizophrenic patient came to her office one day, and she gave him a shot of Prolixin, an antipsychotic medication that sometimes muted the voices to whispers. He went home and called her to say good-bye again. She hung up and dialed 911 and sent an ambulance to his house. Sure enough, by the time paramedics arrived he had overdosed on asthma medication; he ended up in the intensive care unit for three days on dialysis. He survived that suicide attempt but hung himself not too long after. "For some people," she said, "it's just too much to bear to live like that."

In Norma's profession, you didn't always win—but when you did, it affirmed life. Caitlin wanted that for herself too.

Ever since high school, Caitlin had been thinking about becoming a school psychologist, since one day in ninth grade, when her sister had called Caitlin on her cell phone while she was in class. Looking at her caller ID, Caitlin knew her sister had stayed home from school that day. Worrying that something awful had happened to their parents, she slipped out of class and into the bathroom to take the call.

"What's going on?"

"Mommy's high and they're fighting," her sister said. "I don't know what's going to happen."

Caitlin hung up and wandered into the empty hall, debating whether she should tell a school nurse she felt sick so she could go home. She had never told a soul about what was going on at home. A friend turned the corner, saw her crying, and took her to a counselor's office. With her friend's support, she felt safe with the counselor, who helped her talk about her family problems for the first time. Talking made her feel better. Caitlin knew she wanted to help people, as her school counselor had helped her that day and as Norma helped her students and patients.

"I want to change lives, like on a big scale, like huge," Caitlin said once. "I plan on living an extraordinary life."

Of the death class excursions, the autopsy observation was by far the most popular field trip, right behind the visit to the maximum-security prison, and most students could hardly wait to see a dead body being dissected. Caitlin, who had seen her mother's abused and withering body up close, wanted no part of it. She told her professor and her parents that she was not going. Norma pushed her anyway, told her to get past her fears. There's no way in hell, Caitlin thought. The germs alone would make her want to run away and drench herself in sanitizers and antiseptics.

On the morning of the trip, Caitlin told her father, "I'm not going."

But he looked at her and replied, "You're going." For all of their problems, her parents knew this professor of hers was a good influence. Her dad's words echoed: *Don't be a quitter.*

When Caitlin showed up at the medical examiner's office, she saw a dead person on the table who had died of alcohol and drug abuse. She stared at the swollen organs, the liver, the lungs. She thought of her mother. This is what her body will look like if she doesn't stop. But she did not throw up.

See? Norma said. Caitlin could face her worst fears without chants or pennies or sanitizers and still come out okay.

"It's good to be alive, right?" the professor often told her students after the autopsy, including those who had run outside in tears. "Did you notice how fragile we are? We have no business taking our lives for granted."

As THE SEMESTER stretched on, Norma suggested it was time for Caitlin to visit a campus therapist. As Caitlin had been learning in school, most mental disorders came from a combination of biology and environment, and the professor thought the sessions could help now that Caitlin was beginning to understand the roots of her anxiety and OCD.

Maybe Norma was right, Caitlin thought. Maybe she could conquer her demons, invest in herself, even if her parents didn't seem as though they ever would do the same. She could help others with her background in psychology and get a job working with young people who struggled like her. Maybe she could even get married one day and raise kids in a peaceful home. She could find her own skeleton key buried within.

"As long as a man has the strength to dream he can redeem his soul." She'd heard those lyrics to a song once, and they were beginning to make sense. Caitlin had reason to hope for the future; she was madly in love. The closer she grew to Norma, the more she told her professor about him.

His name was Jonathan, and he was twenty-three, almost a year older than she was. They had known each other since high school, and it sometimes still felt as though they were love-struck teenagers.

She would never forget the day she'd fallen for him. Driving by the high school parking lot one summer afternoon in 2003, Caitlin's best friend had spotted Jonathan talking to the school security guard. Her friend knew him through a mutual friend. Kids usually gathered in the parking lot, even when school wasn't in session, to throw Frisbees or talk about what they could do next on lazy summer afternoons, but on this day it looked as though Jonathan might need help. The girls drove up to Jonathan and his two-door 1997 Firebird Formula. Caitlin's friend asked if something was wrong.

"My car won't start," Jonathan said. He'd left the lights on, and his battery had died.

Wow, he's cute, Caitlin thought. They had the same color eyes, hazel, with flecks of copper and green. Why hadn't she paid more attention to him before?

"This is Jon," her friend said, introducing them. Jonathan Stein-graber.

Their mutual friend called someone she knew who fixed cars, and he showed up minutes later and got the Firebird started again, telling Jonathan to go to the auto shop and pick up a specific part. Caitlin stepped up. "I can go with you if you want."

Jonathan looked at her as if he was considering the offer but then said it wasn't necessary.

Was he being polite? Or was he just not interested? Caitlin couldn't be sure. She handed over her phone number in case he needed help along the way again.

A few days later, she spotted him in the same school parking lot, next to his Firebird like the last time. But his car was not broken that day. As she approached, rain began to fall, and she stood before him, rapidly getting soaked.

"I'm having a party at my house," she said. "You should come."

"Yeah, I don't think I can," Jonathan said to her. "I just broke up with my girlfriend. I'm not in a good mood."

Rejection again? Could his girlfriend have been the reason he'd turned down her offer to accompany him to the auto shop the other day?

"Come on," Caitlin said flirtatiously. "Just come to my party."

He flashed a perfect grin. "All right."

It was the beginning of Jonathan and Caitlin.

CAITLIN COULD NEVER have known that Jonathan had kept his eyes on her all school year. Or that he already knew her name. She would later learn that he'd watched Caitlin from afar for months before they met, mostly passing her in hallways since they didn't share any classes, catching glimpses of her in her baggy sweatpants, tank tops, and Timberland boots. At the time, she was a grade ahead of him. She soon discovered that he had been held back a grade because his own family upheaval had forced him to move around so much. She would also find out that he really didn't need any more convincing that day. Jonathan was surprised that she was coming on to him. He tried to help her realize that she didn't need to be any thinner. He thought her body was beautiful the way it was.

Caitlin felt the rush of love: joy, heart palpitations, constant fantasizing.

But that was all a reaction to her "brain on drugs," as Norma explained the behavior to students in her love lectures. "It's all your mind's trick to get you to have sex and make babies." When a person is attracted to someone, as the professor explained, his or her brain becomes flooded with a cocktail of chemicals—many of the same feel-good chemicals that are released in the dying brain.

Though euphoria might be one characteristic of the brain and body's intense reaction to love, according to one study published in the *Journal of Neurophysiology,* others can include "focused attention on the preferred individual, rearrangement of priorities, increased energy, mood swings, sympathetic nervous system responses including sweating and a pounding heart, emotional dependence, elevated sexual desire, sexual possessiveness, obsessive thinking about him or her, craving for emotional union with this preferred individual, affiliative gestures, goal oriented behaviors, and intense motivation to obtain and retain this particular mating partner."

It is that feeling of "I wonder what that person's doing, I wonder what that person's thinking, is he going to call me, is he going to text me, should I go on Facebook, see if they're on Facebook, if I go here maybe I'll see him again." Norma rattled off the thoughts at high speed. Serotonin, she explained, is likely responsible for the feelings of infatuation, while norepinephrine causes an adrenaline rush (the heart beating faster, blood pumping, loss of appetite), and dopamine can be linked to increased energy, cravings, and intense bursts of utter elation followed by withdrawal symptoms, similar to what happens with cocaine addiction.

Some people become so dependent on these love highs that when such feelings wane in one relationship, they jump into another. Someone experiencing unrequited love may end up acting out with "inappropriate phoning, writing or e-mailing, pleading for reconciliation, sobbing for hours, drinking too much and/or making dramatic entrances and exits into the rejecter's home, place of work or social space to express anger, despair or passionate love," according to the *Journal of Neurophysiology* study.

But real love? That isn't just a conglomeration of temporary chemical reactions. Real love sustains itself on good and bad days, as the professor taught, after the rush of infatuation-stage neurotransmitters have normalized and oxytocin, the cuddling hormone, has become more prevalent.

Caitlin now believed she was way past infatuation-stage endorphins. She loved Jonathan because he was protective and gentle, yet stronger than she could ever be. For most of her life, her dad was the one person in her life who made her feel truly loved. But now, Jonathan made her feel that special too. It had taken years of dating for her to fully comprehend the horror of Jonathan's childhood, which was far worse than all of her combined memories of pills stuffed into socks, Mommy's suicide attempts, stray gunshots, and thrown-up Doritos.

Jonathan didn't talk about his childhood much to anyone. It took a while for him to trust her enough, but eventually he did. Most others didn't know why he had no parents or why, as soon as Jonathan had turned eighteen, he'd adopted his younger brother.

Caitlin's heart broke when she tried to imagine Jonathan as the child he had been before he'd grown into the young man she'd fallen for. The very thought of him at such an innocent age made her want to reach into the past, before his world had severed, and protect that little boy from all of the pain and death to come.

Take-Home Writing Assignment:
Letter to Your Younger Self

If you could speak to yourself as a child, what would you say? What advice would you give?

Write a letter to your younger self. Begin your letter with, "Dear _____, age __," and remember to sign and date it.

FOUR

Little Boy

March 10, 1996

Eleven-year-old Jonathan Steingraber opened his eyes. Some kind of loud noise had jolted him awake. Like screams, he thought. Definitely screams, a woman's screams, and they sounded close, as if they were coming from the living room, or the kitchen. Still in his pajamas, he stumbled out of bed.

Jonathan liked wearing his pajamas, especially the fuzzy warm kind that zipped up the front. He and his two brothers would stuff them with pillows and fight like sumo wrestlers. Wrestling, Super Nintendo, and eating mounds of Cheerios—that's what life was all about, and the boys' lives, so far, had been pretty good, apart from their parents' divorce.

They'd watched a movie before falling asleep that night, and now it seemed really late, maybe two in the morning, though Jonathan couldn't be sure. He glanced at his brothers. Nine-year-old Josh, the youngest of the three, and twelve-year-old Chris were both fast asleep in their bunk beds, oblivious to the uproar beyond their bedroom. Jonathan was the middle child, a take-charge, sports-buff kind of boy who balanced out the sensitive Chris and the stubborn rascal, Josh.

Jonathan followed the screams, breaking into a run down the hall, past his dad's room, past the bathroom, past the living room of the two-bedroom apartment they shared with their dad. The boys had been living here, across from a high school athletic field just off the Garden State Parkway, for about a year. Their parents had split two years earlier, and they had lived with Mom first, but she'd quickly decided she'd had enough of the boys' unruliness. The brothers fought with each other all the time. They drove their mom's new boyfriend nuts.

Once Josh had refused to take a shower. It was nothing new. Josh always refused to take showers. But since Josh was the most ornery of the three, Jonathan knew that neither he nor Chris could calm him when he got into one of his moods. All they could do was deal with the consequences. So when their mom's boyfriend smacked Josh across the face for disobeying, Jonathan and Chris jumped to their little brother's defense right there in the bathroom, pummeling the man with all their might. When the boys visited their father that weekend, they told him what had happened. He flipped out. "I'm not letting some other guy put his hands on you," Jonathan remembered his dad telling them. The next thing they knew, they were living with dad in Roselle Park, a borough of New Jersey ten minutes from Newark International Airport.

It was cool living with Dad. He took the boys fishing at the waterway in Union County's Nomahegan Park, where they caught bass and cooked them for dinner. They played basketball together, and football. He told them not to smoke or hit girls, cooked them fettuccine or made them hot sandwiches, and walked Jonathan and Josh to school each morning. Chris was old enough to walk to school on his own. Jonathan knew their dad was not happy about the divorce, but he didn't seem to show his emotions that often.

So it confused Jonathan when he stumbled into the kitchen that night and saw blood. Lakes of it. He saw his dad, in his work boots, jeans, and white T-shirt, the same outfit he always wore since he worked as a handyman and also in a factory. Why was his dad punching someone in the face? Jonathan looked at the person on the floor. He recognized the long trench coat. He could make out the woman's blood-drenched hair. Jonathan knew that hair. It changed styles and colors often. The person it belonged to worked as a beautician and massage therapist. Her hair was long, wavy, and black. Mom. She was drowning in her own blood.

"Stop it!" Jonathan yelled. "Stop! Get off of her! Don't you know who that is?"

"Yeah, it's your mother. Go back to your room."

Why was Mom here in the middle of the night? Why was she on the ground? The next thing Jonathan knew, his father was wielding a steak knife. It had a black handle, or maybe wooden. All Jonathan could focus on was what happened next. His dad plunged the knife into his mom's chest. Over and over. She'd been stabbed already, before Jonathan even got there.

Jonathan ran over to his dad. He tried to hit him. But his dad shrugged him off. Jonathan bounced back and tried to pull his dad away. But his dad pushed him again. Jonathan looked at the phone on the wall and thought about calling someone, but his dad grabbed him and carried him back to the bedroom, where his brothers were beginning to stir.

"Stay here," his dad told him, shutting him in.

Jonathan opened the door and followed him back into the kitchen. His dad snatched him up again and took him back to the room, then returned to the kitchen to finish off his mom. He stabbed her twelve times in all.

When he was done, he told Jonathan, "Wake up your brothers. We're leaving. Don't put on your shoes, let's just go."

It felt like the inside of a freezer as they made their way to the car outside. Jonathan was barefoot. His dad tramped across ice and snow in his boots, headed toward their mom's car.

This was his chance. Jonathan could make a run for it, zigzagging between parked cars, bolting through an obstacle course of snow-covered bushes and alleys between brick buildings until he showed up at a neighbor's place, panting, heart pounding, banging on the door with his tiny fists.

Jonathan's eyes darted from his escape route to his brothers to his dad, whose jeans shone with blood. Josh was asleep in their dad's arms. Chris trailed behind in a clueless zombie state. Maybe, Jonathan thought, if he acted quickly he could pull Chris aside and whisper in his ear, "Dad stabbed Mom!" He could quietly tell Chris how he'd seen and heard it all. He wanted to convince Chris to run away with him, run as fast as they could. But the sight of Josh asleep in their father's arms stopped him.

Jonathan couldn't do it. He couldn't leave either of his brothers.

Maybe he could convince Chris to run too, but he just couldn't leave Josh behind.

He climbed into the backseat of the car, sitting right behind his dad.

"Don't put your seat belts on," he told the boys. "You don't need them."

Jonathan put his on anyway. His brothers still had no clue what was going on, and they seemed too sleepy to notice the blood smears or wonder why they were getting into their mom's car with their dad in the middle of the night.

Jonathan stayed wide-eyed and awake, as Chris fell asleep in the seat to his right. Josh dozed off in the front passenger seat. Their dad didn't put his seat belt on either. He drove for what seemed like hours. Jonathan stared at the back of his dad's head, his pale blond hair. His dad kept looking back at him in the rearview mirror, and Jonathan couldn't avoid his dad's gaze, the blue eyes and eyebrows light as his hair. "We're going to the hospital," he told him.

Let's just get there, Jonathan thought. He knew he needed to tell somebody what had happened. A police officer. A doctor.

The car approached a bridge. It had metal barriers along its side. Jonathan noticed his dad speeding up, gripping the steering wheel and veering to the right, charging straight for the bridge barrier. Was he attempting to drive right off of it?

The vehicle rammed into the metal, skidding and screeching for about five hundred feet. His dad lost control, and the car spun.

Jonathan grabbed Chris and held him until they came to a halt. The smell of hot metal and burned tires filled the air. Jonathan's hips hurt from the seat belt, but Chris seemed unscathed. When it seemed safe to move, Jonathan and Chris peered over to the front seats, where they caught a glimpse of their dad. His head had a giant gash in it, with blood pouring out of it. His right ear seemed to be hanging off. He kept slipping into and out of consciousness.

"Dad, wake up!" Jonathan shouted.

He saw Josh. His little brother was trapped underneath the dash, wailing in pain about his shoulder. His brothers couldn't pry the mangled door open. It was compressed against the bridge barricade.

"Get me out!" Josh screamed at his brothers. "I'm gonna die!"

Jonathan looked down the road and saw truck headlights coming in their direction.

THE BOYS DID not see their father again until the murder trial, when Jonathan had to give a statement during the sentencing. In the court, he looked at his dad, who was wearing a prison uniform and had chains around his ankles. Jonathan would later remember the people in the court asking him to respond in a letter to questions such as "How long do you think he should be in prison for?" and "How has this affected your life?" Jonathan pulled out his letter and told the court through his tears that there was no amount of time that his father could go away for. Time would not bring his mother back.

When it was over, the judge asked his father if he had anything to say. His dad was weeping too. He looked at Jonathan and answered, "I didn't mean to hurt anyone."

He was sentenced to thirty years in prison, with parole possible after fifteen years.

Jonathan and his two brothers moved in with their aunt and uncle, who like their mother had come to New Jersey from Uruguay, but it was not an easy transition. Their uncle had never planned on staying in the United States forever, and now he was stuck taking care of his nephews. If Jonathan's younger brother had been reclusive and uptight as the youngest among them before his mother's death, he was even worse now, always angry. He would throw dirt into his aunt and uncle's bed. He would wander off and they'd find him hours later, walking along a highway alone.

The boys stayed with their aunt and uncle for two years. When Jonathan was in eighth grade, the brothers moved to Uruguay to live with their grandmother. None of them really wanted to leave their friends and move to a country they barely knew, but it seemed that the aunt and uncle could not handle all of the extra responsibility. Chris seemed the most upset about it. He emailed his girlfriend and called her long distance regularly, and he talked of getting adopted and moving back to New Jersey.

"Yeah, but you're our brother," Jonathan said to him. "Who cares about a girlfriend?"

Chris ended up moving back and living with his girlfriend's family anyway. Then it was just Jonathan and Josh.

They made the most of their time in Uruguay, spending summers on the beach. But when Jonathan turned eighteen, he decided to move back to New Jersey too. He knew he wanted Josh to be with him. The brothers were a trio, regardless of whether Chris kept on ditching them for his girl.

It turned out that Chris agreed with Jonathan, and they petitioned for custody of Josh. They wanted him to finish high school in the United States. He'd have a better chance of getting accepted into an American university. Jonathan and Chris rented a three-bedroom apartment in Linden for $900, and Josh was eventually allowed by the courts to move in.

Josh was seventeen when they adopted him. He had enrolled in Linden High School. They had stepped in to father Josh as best they could, even though Jonathan felt as though he was the most involved with Josh's life, the most protective. Chris had grown closer to his girlfriend and still spent most of his time with her.

Not long after, their dad wrote them a letter from prison, explaining that he had heard that Jonathan and Chris had applied for custody of Josh. He asked the boys to visit him in East Jersey State Prison. Chris chose not to go.

Jonathan took Josh to visit their father. It was an awkward meeting. Jonathan remembered his dad singing a song he had written himself, something about being sorry. They sat in a visiting room separated by glass as their dad belted into a telephone receiver. When he was done, Josh turned to Jonathan and said, "He sings pretty good."

Their father had a job in prison at the time and told his sons he would send them money. But Jonathan made it clear they didn't need his money or his help. None of his sons had turned into drug addicts or delinquents. They had gone to school, held jobs.

"We came here to let you know your kids are good kids," Jonathan told his dad. "We're going to succeed, and we're going to be fine."

Jonathan would make sure of it.

Seven years after his mother's death, the brothers still didn't know why their father had snapped and killed her that night. Jonathan did not ask. Maybe his dad had been jealous of her new relationship. Or maybe he had been stressed about money. Jonathan didn't really care anymore.

In February 2006, a few weeks after saying good-bye to him during their prison visit, Jonathan received a call informing him that their dad had slit his throat with a razor.

And that was that. Jonathan didn't feel too hurt by it. After all, Brett Steingraber was their father, but he had not been a part of the boys' lives for a long time.

His sons had already let him go.

BY THE TIME Jonathan met Caitlin, he had his survival method down to a science: First, don't dwell on the past; don't even discuss it unless you have to. Second, the most reliable person in this life is yourself. Third, know how to fix problems. Others depend on you to set goals, so meet them. That's exactly what he did.

Ever since his father had murdered his mother, Jonathan had figured out a way to negotiate the world with no parents and no road map—all under his own terms. He had learned that there was no advantage to being vulnerable or weak, and he kept that defense up even as he found himself starting to trust this eye-catching girl who had strolled into his life one afternoon in the middle of the high school parking lot. It wasn't easy to be guarded and in a romantic relationship at the same time, but she seemed worth the effort to at least try to strike a balance. Caitlin was beautiful even in her boyish tank tops and sweats. That image of the rain drenching her hair that day as she stood in front of the school and asked him to come to her party was forever seared in his mind.

They lost their virginity to each other, and just as he was her first true love, she was also his. Once when they were cuddled up together, he could remember feeling so connected to her that he couldn't imagine ever feeling this way again with anyone else.

Yet for all his adoration of Caitlin, her anxiety irritated the heck out of him. The random light switch flicking, the fear of germs, the incessant worries about death. Sometimes she would call him on his cell phone and hear sirens from passing emergency vehicles in the background. "Where are you?" she would demand in a panic, assuming he had been hurt. "Are you okay?"

"I'm fine," he would groan.

Caitlin explained to him that she had figured out, after taking classes with Norma, that she had obsessive-compulsive disorder. Jonathan was glad that the professor's lessons had helped his girlfriend get a handle on her "issues." But the truth was, he didn't entirely buy that Caitlin was ill in some way. He didn't really know if he believed in mental illness at all. She just needed to get a grip on herself. There was no reason to worry, he assured her over and over again. No reason at all.

JONATHAN DIDN'T FEEL the need to solve the mystery of why his dad had murdered his mom. He accepted that he had no real answer. There had been no previous signs of depression or even rage from his dad. He couldn't remember his father having a drinking problem.

One day, he found an Associated Press article about his mother's murder on the Internet. The AP story had also been printed in *The New York Times*. But the headline didn't make sense to Jonathan: "Man Who Feared Alien Takeover Pleads Guilty to Killing Ex-wife." The story stated, "Brett Steingraber believed extraterrestrials were about to take over the planet, and he killed his ex-wife, Suraia Sadi, to save her from the pain of the alien takeover, prosecutors said."

It went on, "Sadi, 36, was stabbed 12 times in the chest in March 1996, at her ex-husband's apartment. Steingraber, 39, later drove around with his three sons until crashing his car in Westchester County, N.Y."

Extraterrestrials? What kind of ridiculous story had this reporter made up? Jonathan had seen the murder. His dad had confessed to investigators. But aliens? What an idiotic story.

Jonathan never doubted that his dad had known exactly what he was doing that morning. That was why he had kept staring at him through the rearview mirror before he crashed. If his dad had made up a story about alien invasions to the cops, he was just trying to wiggle out of responsibility for his crime. An insanity plea or something.

That was what Jonathan told himself for all of his teenage years. He kept thinking it right up into his twenties, until the summer of 2008. For weeks, Caitlin had been expressing worries about Jonathan's father and Josh's mental stability. Jonathan brushed her comments off as exaggerated anxieties. Then the couple woke up in Jonathan's bedroom one morning to a loud noise and found his brother wild-eyed in the kitchen.

CLASS DISCUSSION: Homicide, Suicide, and Mental Illness	
DISCUSSION QUESTION: Midterm	
If you could forever eliminate one disease from the planet, which would you choose and why?	

FIVE

Strange Behavior

Summer 2008

If perfection existed, Caitlin imagined it must look a lot like this moment. She glanced around the banquet hall, inhaling the whole scene, the shimmering crystal canopy chandelier that seemed as big as the sun, the Venetian plaster walls, the party revelers clinking their wineglasses and beer bottles. There were mirrors everywhere, even on the cathedral-style ceilings, as if carefully placed to remind everyone at every turn of how much fun they were having.

It was all for her, mostly. Jonathan had gone to the trouble of organizing and planning this elaborate joint celebration for Caitlin, and also for his buddy, since both had just graduated in Kean University's 2008 class. He'd paid for the buffet, rented the hall, brought in a stand-up comedian, and invited all of their mutual friends, as well as Caitlin's family and her favorite professor, Dr. Norma Bowe.

It had been a perfect morning for the graduation ten hours earlier too, with blue skies, warm sunshine, and the greenest trees. "All eyes are on the future!" shouted the keynote speaker, the guy who'd created Monster.com, to 2,100 graduates. Norma posed after the graduation ceremony for a couple of shots with Caitlin. There was the professor in one photo, with her burgundy lipstick smile, aviator sunglasses, and doctoral gown, topped off with a floppy velvety cap. She stood about five inches shorter than Caitlin, who wore a gold 2008 charm on the yellow tassel of her flat cap. A cluster of long ropey cords hung around Caitlin's neck, representing all of the honors she'd received, like for her

3.85 grade point average. Caitlin would later frame that photo and give it to Norma as a gift, which the professor would keep in her office.

Now that she'd earned her bachelor's degree, Caitlin was on track to becoming one of only twelve students selected for the master's program in the school of psychology at Kean. She'd still be able to attend her own therapy sessions with the counselor on campus while working to get control of her anxiety and OCD, and she could visit Norma, who had given her a part-time job as her research assistant, whenever she wanted.

By sunset, everyone including the professor had changed into cocktail party attire and headed to the Galloping Hills banquet hall in a gleaming white Colonial Revival–style building in Union, New Jersey. Caitlin slipped into a white strapless dress with black flowers embroidered along one side. It hugged her tiny waist, flowing out slightly at her hips, making them appear fuller than they actually were, stopping a few inches past her wispy thighs. She'd put on a pair of sparkling dangly earrings and pulled the sides of her blond hair up, letting a long chunk of it droop across her left cheek, while the rest fell down her back in loose ringlets.

Caitlin looked over at Jonathan as he mingled with the guests. Tonight he looked especially good, with his sandy brown hair gelled up at the sides in a short faux hawk and a dress shirt unbuttoned at the top.

Carefully tucked-in pink and blue cloth napkins blossomed like lily petals from the mouths of glass goblets throughout the banquet hall. Caitlin paused to smile for a photo with a friend. Black and white balloons with long ribbons tied to their ends floated around the room like guests at the party. Caitlin posed, hand on her hip, for another photo. Waiters in bow ties glided between tables, carrying trays of fizzy champagne. This party at Galloping Hills, where many people held their weddings, made her feel almost like a princess, right down to the tables with white embossed tablecloths and gold-painted chairs. Perfect.

Her sisters showed up, looking gorgeous as usual. One wore a leopard-print dress, the other a lacy white strapless minidress, outfits that did more than enough to show off their voluptuousness. For some reason Caitlin was the only one who had ended up model thin. She resembled their mother in that way. The three sisters were so close that they each shared pieces of a necklace. Her oldest sister's charm read, "Laugh," while her middle sister's read, "Love." Caitlin's read, "Live."

Someone had hooked up an iPod to the stereo system in place of a live deejay, and R&B tunes bumped in the background. Yet Caitlin couldn't help but notice that the waxy wooden dance floor was mostly empty. No one at her party was dancing.

Her mom, dad, and sisters gathered on the floor to pose with Caitlin for a banquet photo, grinning together, looking like one flawless family. It would be easy for people to look at the attractive clan with envy, oblivious to all the drama that went on at home. But if you saw the party through Caitlin's eyes, you knew better.

She sensed that something else was off too. Caitlin glanced over at Jonathan's younger brother, Josh. He didn't really seem to be talking to anyone. He sat separated from the festivities, in the hallway alone, staring off into the distance with a look of silent detachment or depression. Caitlin thought Josh was a good-looking young man too, but he didn't have his older brother's charm and charisma. Every once in a while, she'd see Jonathan go out and try to coax his brother back inside to join the party, to no avail.

Caitlin knew that Josh didn't care for her. She had always tried to be nice to him, but he'd made it known to Jonathan that he didn't like being around when she was present. This party was probably the last place on earth that Josh wanted to be.

But there was something else about Josh, Caitlin thought, something suspicious, like an illness that she couldn't quite diagnose. Whatever it was, it frightened her. Caitlin knew that Norma could tell something was wrong with Josh too. During the party, the professor had gone into the hall beyond the banquet ballroom and tried chatting with him. But Norma later told Caitlin how despondent he had been.

She smiled pretty for the camera again.

Once Caitlin had told Jonathan's younger brother that he reminded her of Socrates, the way he philosophized in long, hard-to-decipher sentences.

Josh hadn't responded at first.

"Does that bother you?" Caitlin had asked.

"No," Josh had said. "That's a compliment."

But some of his behavior unnerved Caitlin. Josh didn't look directly at people, and sometimes he asked weird, out-of-context questions. "Why do you always listen to Eminem when I'm in the car?" he'd accuse, as if she were listening to the music to intentionally piss him off.

Something about her boyfriend's younger brother alarmed her. She had mentioned her concerns to Norma more than once but didn't dare tell Jonathan. She didn't want to upset him.

SHE HAD BEEN dating Jonathan for five years now, and she often stopped by to visit him in the apartment he shared with his brother. Josh was often up late playing the guitar or surfing the Internet, and he frequently slept in and missed his classes, until one day he had missed too many days and found out he was going to fail a grade.

Josh convinced his brothers that it would be best for him to become a homeschooled student. He had researched the process on the Internet and even found an adult mentor who worked in education to help him organize his transcripts, monitor his homework assignments, and apply for college. Caitlin saw Jonathan's reasoning for going along with his brother's idea at first; maybe Josh was too smart for school and simply got bored.

Josh signed up and began completing assignments. But he complained that the mentor was harassing and pushing him too hard. He asked too many questions and made him think too much. Josh stuck with him anyway, because he wanted to earn a diploma. He made it clear to everyone: he wanted to go to Harvard University. Not Princeton. Nowhere else. Just Harvard. He'd scored high enough on his SATs that he might have even had a shot at Harvard, but a Princeton recruiter requested an interview instead.

Caitlin could see how thrilled Jonathan was for his brother; the two spent hours practicing interview questions together, even though Josh told him again: he didn't care about Princeton, only Harvard. Jonathan drove Josh to the interview anyway. It took place in a huge, fancy house, and he eavesdropped from outside a door. The woman was a psychologist, and Jonathan got her card to give to Caitlin. He recounted to her later what he had overheard in the interview.

"What would you do with your degree?" she asked Josh.

"I don't know," Josh replied. That was all he said. No elaboration. He answered every question with a short answer, sometimes just one word.

Jonathan told Caitlin that his brother had blown it, and he appeared to be right. Princeton did not take him. But Josh received his diploma from his online studies anyway, and to his brothers' surprise, he got accepted into Wesleyan University in Middletown, Connecticut—on a scholarship.

Jonathan bragged about it to all of his friends. Caitlin remained supportive. How could she not? How would that look? Her boyfriend's brother had outsmarted the public school system and made it into one of the best colleges in the nation. She knew Jonathan had never fancied himself an Ivy League scholar, but his brother, as he saw it, must have been a genius. Caitlin didn't want to ruin that gratification for any of them.

She listened to Jonathan's stories about Josh at Wesleyan. He seemed to have made a few friends. When his brothers visited, Josh took them to a campus party, and the three played Ping-Pong in the dorm.

But after a few weeks at Wesleyan, Josh reverted to his usual negative self, complaining about everyone around him, telling his brother, "People suck here. They're so liberal and stupid. . . . They're all rich. . . . They don't know anything." He earned Cs, Ds, and Fs his first semester. Within six months, he dropped out. He'd started reading books about surviving in the woods and decided he wanted to backpack through Europe. He told his brothers he wanted to live in Morocco, Portugal, and Spain, and the next thing Caitlin heard, he'd taken off.

A few weeks later, Josh returned and decided he was moving to Washington, D.C. Jonathan told Caitlin he couldn't figure it out. Josh had no family there. No friends. No contacts at all.

Caitlin's suspicions intensified. The White House was in D.C. The president of the United States. The Pentagon. Some people with mental illnesses, she knew, became obsessed with the government.

Jonathan went to visit Josh in D.C. one weekend, and he later described the trip to Caitlin. He'd found his brother living in a homeless shelter. Josh had acted as if it were normal. He'd even asked him to spend the night there too.

"I'm not sleeping in a homeless shelter!" Jonathan had replied. "Why don't you come home with me? Just come *home*."

Josh had refused. He'd told his brother just to give him a little while. He'd leave the shelter and move into an apartment. He'd work as a waiter—but he wasn't leaving D.C.

Jonathan went home and showed up at Caitlin's house a few weeks later with tears in his eyes. He described a phone call he'd received from Josh.

"Don't do anything illegal," Josh had said to him, sobbing.

"What are you talking about?"

"Don't do anything illegal," Josh had said again, adding "They're watching us."

Jonathan told Caitlin he couldn't figure it out. Had Josh killed someone? Was he running from the law? All he knew was that Josh was coming home this time. He'd arranged to catch a train back to New Jersey.

Caitlin couldn't bring herself to say it to Jonathan, but she wondered if someone could really be watching or stalking Josh. She thought of her psychology lessons, all the warning signs she'd learned, and her conversations with Norma.

Or was he having a delusion?

DELUSIONS, CAITLIN UNDERSTOOD, come up in a mentally ill person's mind very clearly, mostly manifesting in the idea that people are conspiring against you, devising a plan to do something bad to you. Maybe the conspirators are part of the FBI, the CIA, or the White House. Or maybe they're aliens. Delusions are sometimes coupled with hallucinations, such as seeing things that are not there, but more often take the form of sounds, often of voices that seem very real. In extreme manic episodes, bipolar people sometimes experience delusions or hallucinations.

So do schizophrenics.

As Caitlin had learned, schizophrenia is a disease that also usually struck people around their teen and college years. Josh was twenty-one. One percent of the world's population suffers from schizophrenia, and genetics also plays a powerful role in a person's susceptibility to it. Like depression and bipolar disorder, it has been shown to have links to environmental triggers; a particularly rough childhood or high-stress social setting such as college can play a role in setting off schizophrenia in a person who is genetically predisposed to the disease. Paranoid schizophrenics often can't stop believing that people are plotting against them, jealous of them, or spying on them.

Caitlin knew that many mental illnesses are passed on through genes. The more she learned about Josh's behavior, the more she wanted answers about their father, even if her boyfriend didn't feel the need to know.

She worried that Josh might be capable of the same kind of violence as their father. He might even hurt Jonathan.

"I THINK JON'S brother has schizophrenia," Caitlin told Norma. "I think his dad had it too."

"You should tell Jon," Norma advised her. He needed to know if his brother had a mental illness. They needed to get Josh into the right kind of treatment.

But Caitlin was too scared to broach the subject—until one night.

Jonathan and Caitlin went out for dinner together, and on the drive, Caitlin started explaining what she had learned about schizophrenia in school. "I think that's what your dad had, and that's why he killed your mom," she said gently. "Maybe Josh has it."

"You don't know what you're talking about!" Jonathan shouted. He swerved the car, turning around, and headed back home. Dinner was off.

"You're right," Caitlin said. "I'm sorry. I didn't mean it."

"You have no idea what it's like to be Josh," Jonathan kept on, "what his life has been like, what he's been through!"

"I'm sorry. I shouldn't have judged."

She told herself never to bring it up again.

THE LOUD NOISE that woke Jonathan and Caitlin that summer morning in 2008 sounded as if it had come from the kitchen. It wasn't a scream, like the noises that had awakened Jonathan on the day his dad had stabbed his mom, but rather a bang that could have been anything—a door slamming or kitchenware falling. He looked over at Caitlin, now wide awake beside him, her hair tousled. Almost a month had passed since Jonathan had thrown Caitlin the graduation party. The look on Caitlin's face told him she thought the sound was an indication of something worse, but Jonathan couldn't help himself from partially dismissing her fear, again.

He told Caitlin he would go check it out, so she stayed behind in the bedroom. Once in the kitchen, Jonathan didn't notice anything out of order. The apartment was quiet. Josh must have been in his room sleeping, or on the computer as usual.

Jonathan opened the refrigerator and grabbed a bottle of water. He turned around and ended up eye to eye with his younger brother.

Of the three brothers, Jonathan knew he and Josh looked the most alike. They were the same height and shared the same thin-lipped smile, same bushy eyebrows. Josh was a few shadows bulkier that Jonathan but was still fit, and he wore his hair longer, shaggy, and parted loosely down the middle. He didn't invest as much time in his appearance as Jonathan. Josh didn't care about fashion at all, and his face always bore traces of red acne around his forehead and cheeks, a teenage trait he had not yet outgrown by twenty-one. But that morning, Jonathan thought, his brother looked particularly disheveled and out of it, with his chest puffed out and his eyes stretched wide open.

"Josh, what's up?" Jonathan asked.

His brother erupted. "Don't fucking look at me! Don't stare at me. Don't look into my eyes!"

"What?" Jonathan said. "I'm just getting water."

"Look away!"

What the hell was wrong with his brother? Josh had been acting weird for months now, but this was a whole different level.

Josh warned him again. "Don't look at me!"

But Jonathan looked anyway.

Jonathan felt the first punch fly at his face. Another blow to his chest. Jonathan threw up his arms and tried to block his brother's throws. Why was Josh hitting him? What had he done?

He felt Josh shove him into a column in the living room. The impact tore a bloody gash through his arm. Jonathan knew he had to fight back, even though he had no clue as to why they were fighting. He charged toward his brother, tackling him onto the ground.

"Why are you trying to hurt me, Josh? I love you!"

Jonathan loosened his grip and backed away. He watched Josh stumble as he got up from the floor. Then Josh bolted outside toward Jonathan's truck.

Jonathan wasn't an idiot. He knew what his brother was looking for in that truck; he kept a pocketknife in the glove compartment.

BY NOW CAITLIN had made her way into the living room. Jonathan's bedroom door had been left ajar, and she had watched the skirmish unfold. She knew Josh was having a psychotic episode and realized there was no way out of the basement apartment besides the front door, which Josh had been blocking. The windows were too small to climb through. Caitlin had waited for the right opportunity to make a move and prayed. She was going to watch her boyfriend die in front of her. Josh was about to do the same to Jonathan as their father had done to their mother. He might even kill her too.

As soon as she saw Josh go outside, Caitlin ran to the door and locked it. "I'm calling the cops," she said as Josh began banging on the door a few minutes later, shouting for them to let him in.

No cops. Jonathan pushed past Caitlin and unlocked the door. There was no need to overreact. He would calm his little brother down.

Josh barged in, eyes vacant, heading straight for a wooden block that held cutlery ware, which their aunt had given the brothers as a move-in gift. He apparently had not located the pocketknife, so he grabbed one of the cooking knives instead. Gripping it in one hand, he glared at Jonathan, positioning himself in an attack stance.

Suddenly, as if battling with his own impulses, Josh went back into his room.

Jonathan turned to Caitlin. "Get out of here!" he told her. It was an order.

"Walk me out to my car," Caitlin said, knowing that it would be the only way to get Jonathan outside. Caitlin had her cell phone in hand and was wearing no shoes. She didn't want to bring up her schizophrenia theory again, fearing it would set Jonathan off. But she had to get him out of this apartment.

He followed her out for a second and then started to go back. "I'm not leaving my brother."

CAITLIN KNEW JONATHAN might never speak to her again if she called the police on Josh. But he could die in there too. She dialed 911 and sat in her blue Hyundai Tiburon, waiting. She dialed her parents and then Norma. But the professor did not pick up at first, so Caitlin left a frantic message: "Josh is trying to kill Jonathan! He has a knife. Oh, my God!"

Minutes later, she saw Jonathan barreling out of the apartment. He was bleeding but alive.

Jonathan jumped into his truck and drove off, roaring past Caitlin. Police cornered him with their squad car before he made it too far.

She began to drive away too, but the police called and asked her to return to make a statement. She began to worry. What if officers saw the blood on his arm and thought Jonathan was the one she'd called 911 about? The one with the knife? What if they arrested him by mistake? Caitlin raced over to explain the mix-up to the police. It was his brother who had attacked Jonathan, she explained. He was still inside the apartment. Caitlin said she would return only if Josh did not come out.

The cops refused to go inside, unsure of what danger might await them. They asked Jonathan if Josh had a weapon, because if he did they would have to shoot him dead if he tried to attack.

"I'll go in," Jonathan said as Caitlin stayed outside.

His brother was in his bedroom. With Jonathan out of earshot, she told an officer that Josh was "really sick." His dad had killed his mom, and Caitlin believed he might have been a schizophrenic. Josh might too.

Josh didn't need to go to jail; he needed to go to a mental hospital.

"JOSH, THE COPS are here!" Jonathan yelled once inside the apartment. But his brother still didn't come out.

"Get your ass out here!" an officer barked.

Finally Josh emerged. The cops frisked and handcuffed him, then sat him on the couch. He smirked, not saying a word in response to the cops' questions. He seemed as if he was almost snarling at them.

"Is he on drugs?" an officer asked.

"I don't know," Jonathan replied. "I bend over backwards for this kid. I'm trying as hard as I can. I honestly don't know why he's acting like this."

The police told Jonathan they would have to take Josh to jail or a hospital.

The cops took Josh in an ambulance to the psychiatric center at Trinitas Regional Medical Center in Elizabeth.

Jonathan got into the passenger seat of Caitlin's car. "I knew deep down there was something wrong with him," he said.

Sure, Jonathan realized that Josh had not really been responsible in the last year, dropping out of Wesleyan for no good reason, backpacking around parts of the world, becoming homeless, refusing to work, sometimes refusing to brush his teeth. The most Jonathan had allowed himself to believe about Josh until now was that maybe he was depressed. With two dead parents, Josh had enough of an excuse to feel down every now and then.

As they headed to the hospital, Caitlin finally got hold of Norma. The professor advised them to make a timeline of Josh's life—from birth to their parents' deaths to every unusual event that had happened and any odd behavior he might have displayed along the way. It would help the doctors make a more accurate diagnosis and understand how far along any possible illness had progressed.

Josh didn't have insurance, so Norma prepped Jonathan on any questions the medical staff might ask and paperwork he might be asked to fill out. She told Jonathan to meet her at Kean University and to bring his older brother, Chris, along with his uncle and aunt. Her last class ended around 9 P.M., and she would stay late to give the family a crash course on schizophrenia.

When Jonathan arrived at the hospital, a doctor pulled him aside. "He's hearing things," the doctor said. "He's seeing things."

Josh, the doctor told him, had paranoid schizophrenia.

Sometimes when patients with his symptoms ask you not to look into their eyes, it is because they think you are trying to control their mind, he explained.

Jonathan barely knew what schizophrenia was, much less how it was dictating his brother's thoughts or behavior. He just wanted to see his brother.

Doctors let him into the room where Josh was tied to a bed.

"Josh," he asked, "why'd you attack me?"

His brother simply smiled back at him from the bed and replied, "My brother has a tendency to lie a lot. He lies and everyone believes him."

"What did I lie about?" Jonathan asked incredulously, feeling himself getting ready to argue.

The doctor pulled Jonathan aside and explained, "He's having an episode right now."

"All right," Jonathan said, still upset. "But I didn't lie about anything!" he added, storming out of the room.

Doctors asked Jonathan a long list of questions about their family history and especially their father. He handed over the timeline that Norma had advised him to create, documenting the whole tale of his family's fate.

Suddenly it all clicked, as if Jonathan's mind was finally allowing him to accept what he had been denying for so long. Caitlin was right. The doctors were right. Norma was right. Josh had schizophrenia—and their father had suffered from it too. Josh had inherited the disease.

It was a terrifying realization. What did it mean? Had he inherited it too? Had Chris? If they one day had their own children, would they get this mental illness too?

Jonathan contacted his father's sister. He needed to know if she had realized that their father had been paranoid too. The boys had never noticed, they had been too young, but had his sister?

She had. Sometimes, she told him, their father had locked himself in the bathroom for hours, reading the Bible and crying. Or he would guard the door to his sons' room and refuse to let her see them. When she'd asked why he was reacting like that, he'd told her that he was afraid she was going to poison his children.

Jonathan didn't have time to agonize. He had a job to do. He had to fix this problem. Take care of his brother. Get him into the best treatment he could so that he didn't end up dead, like their mom and dad. Jonathan had pledged long ago never to leave his little brother behind.

That night, as Josh stayed in the hospital, Jonathan rounded up the few family members he had left and told them to meet Norma at Kean. He listened along with them as she went over the biological and environmental aspects of schizophrenia, possible treatments, and the dire prognoses.

When the meeting was over, Jonathan turned to Caitlin. "I know how this is going to end," he told her. "Josh is going to kill himself."

He couldn't let that happen. Not on his watch.

He was determined to do anything in his power to protect his brother from this disease, if that meant going into debt, or babysitting him for the rest of his life.

Josh bounced between mental hospitals for weeks after his diagnosis, and his thoughts only seemed to grow more odd. When Jonathan visited him in the psychiatric ward, Josh would tell him that everyone around them was walking like a lizard, even the pigeons and squirrels outside. He said he thought it was a miracle; God was speaking to him and giving him signs through those lizard-walking creatures. Or he would say, "Maybe I'm just really fucked up in the head."

"Josh," his brother would tell him, "you're not Jesus. You're just crazy."

"Yeah," Josh would reply, "you're probably right."

But the next thing Jonathan knew, Josh would be in bed talking about a bright white light—another sign from God. Jonathan would try to reason with him. "If I'm sitting next to you, don't you think I would see the light?"

"No," Josh told him, because God intended it only for his eyes.

Weeks went by, and the hospital released Josh. Once at home, he was supposed to take one pill a day, and Jonathan made sure he took it each morning. Josh didn't want it, but Jonathan lied and told him that the hospital called every day to check up on him, and if he didn't take the pill he would have to go back. That was the last thing Josh wanted, so he took the pill.

Taking care of his brother was a twenty-four-hour-a-day job for Jonathan, and that left little room for socializing or dating. He had no other choice but to sacrifice his personal needs for his brother's well-being. But now he was beginning to realize that he could no longer dedicate the kind of time to Caitlin that she deserved. If she remained a part of his life, she might even end up in danger herself. Jonathan was willing to risk his safety and his life for his brother, but not hers. She would be better off without him.

There was no other choice, Jonathan told Caitlin. He had to break up with her.

And just like that, he did.

MONTHS PASSED, AND summer bled into fall. The weather turned from humid to brisk to bitter. Caitlin fought off the urge to throw up. When she cried, the sheer flow of it would give her migraines. Her OCD rituals had intensified, and her chest throbbed with a penetrating ache. If anything could be considered a precursor to mourning death, it must have been this. Caitlin knew she would never be able to handle the death of a loved one; she could barely survive a broken heart.

One night, Norma convinced Caitlin to meet her at Applebee's. Caitlin sat down and ordered a fishbowl-sized margarita and two shots of tequila. She poured the shot into the fishbowl and gulped the whole thing down with two straws. Caitlin knew that under normal circumstances Norma might have told her to ease up, but this night she said nothing.

Caitlin had been spending a lot of time with Norma, revisiting the anxiety issues she thought she'd dealt with months before. They had returned in full force. Applebee's had become Caitlin and Norma's meeting spot of choice. Norma reminded Caitlin again that it might be wise if she used this time of mourning to refocus on herself, instead of worrying about everyone else and instead of vying for the love of Jonathan or her mother.

The professor's take on Caitlin's struggle went back to her lesson on Erik Erikson's life cycle. Norma had lectured about Erikson's theories in Caitlin's mental health and death classes. It seemed as though Caitlin, at twenty-two, was caught in the fifth stage of life—a period filled with confusion that Erikson had called "Identity vs. Role Confusion" and said lasted from ages twelve to eighteen. In that stage a young person asks, "Who am I?"

To Erikson, those who emerged from the previous four stages of childhood with the right amount of love and nurturing would develop a strong sense of identity that would carry them forward through life's challenges. Norma believed this questioning period extends well into the twenties or thirties, sometimes longer.

"Some people never get out of this stage," Norma would tell her students. "They're never able to form their own identity, never able to figure out who they are."

It didn't mean they couldn't, she said, as Erikson believed that life is a constant change and someone with a weak identity can develop a more confident one later in life.

"To a considerable extent adolescent love is an attempt to arrive at a definition of one's identity by projecting one's diffused ego image on another and by seeing it thus reflected and gradually clarified," Erikson wrote. "This is why so much of young love is conversation."

The next phase of Erikson's life cycle, the sixth stage, which he called "Intimacy vs. Isolation," can last into a person's forties or longer. This is the period when a person is looking for a life partner, true love.

As Norma explained it, adults in this stage learn to value their closest friendships over collecting dozens of peripheral friends, as they might have done in high school. They also look for a person to build a life with.

As Norma summed up this stage: "Until we have an identity separate from our peer group, we cannot have intimacy. We will not know real love until we know who we are."

"You must," she told all of her students, "love yourself first."

"Unfortunately, many young people marry under such circumstances, hoping to find themselves in another," Erikson wrote, "but alas the early obligation to act in a defined way, as mates and as parents, disturbs them in the completion of this work on themselves. Obviously, a change of mate is rarely the answer, but rather some wisely guided insight into the fact that the condition of a true twoness is that one must first become oneself."

Caitlin was caught between two stages. Norma told her she needed to detach and let everyone else sort out their own lives while she seized control of hers.

But the message didn't quite seem to be sinking in.

ONE NIGHT AT home by herself, Caitlin listened to the song "Hurt," by Christina Aguilera, and her thoughts turned to her mother. She began to think about what would happen if her mother died of a drug overdose. What if she never had a chance to tell her how much she loved her? Caitlin knew she often gave her mother an attitude, but it was only because she couldn't forgive her for becoming a hostage to those pills.

She began to write her mother a letter, explaining that she didn't hate her and didn't harbor anger about her childhood. The next day, she handed over what she had written. When her mother read it, she hugged Caitlin and thanked her but didn't cry. Her mother rarely shed tears in front of the family anyway.

Caitlin called Norma and told her about the letter. "I'm happy about this," Caitlin said. "I think it's going to change our lives."

But her professor did not sound convinced.

"What are you talking about? This is great," Caitlin said. "It took me three years to tell her how I feel." Norma was the one who had taught her the idea of writing a "good-bye letter." Caitlin had figured, why wait until her mother was dead to tell her how she felt?

Three days later, her mother swallowed dozens of prescription pills. Caitlin's sister found her upstairs, unconscious and not breathing. Caitlin got the call and headed to the intensive care unit. When she arrived, her mother was hooked up to breathing tubes. When she finally woke up, she was delirious, but she was able to say one word over and over.

"Caitlin, Caitlin, Caitlin."

When her mother finally seemed coherent, all Caitlin could say was, "But, Mommy, I wrote you that letter."

"I know," she replied, barely able to get the words out. "I love you so much."

If she loves me so much, Caitlin thought, why does she keep trying to kill herself? Why does she keep putting her family through this nonstop torment?

For Norma's death class, another assignment had been "Write a letter to your younger self." Caitlin had written to the little girl who had been afraid to speak up in class, "The things that you are afraid of are either out of your control or not an issue. The only things that you have control over are your actions and how you react to the actions of others. You should try to be enjoying the freedom of being young and not having as much responsibility."

The older Caitlin needed to listen to herself now.

Caitlin turned again to her professor that night after visiting her mom in the hospital. She felt bad for unloading so much on Norma. She felt bad for calling her at all hours and dragging her out to meet her at Applebee's long after the professor's teaching day had ended. But Norma never seemed to mind.

CLASS FIELD TRIP: Father Hudson House—The Center for Hope Hospice

TAKE-HOME WRITING ASSIGNMENT:
On Visiting a Hospice

Write a reaction paper on your experience visiting a hospice care facility and meeting patients and staff.

Caitlin

Dr. Bowe

Death in Perspective

Hospice Reaction Paper

There was one little lady upstairs and she wasn't feeling good at all, I wanted to hug her. . . . They are people who have lived their lives, and are probably wiser than any of us, but they're facing death and disease. I can tell that some of them feel embarrassed that they are in that condition and it's so sad. . . . I'm going to spend as much time with [my grandparents as] I can and never miss a chance to tell them how much I appreciate them.

SIX

To the Rescue

One Sunday morning, Norma drove one of her students named Stephanie to Seaside Heights, a two-hour ride from Kean University, to visit the young woman's parents. Stephanie's mother was an alcoholic, and her father had just been released from prison. Both parents had been homeless for most of Stephanie's teenage years, and she had made it to college on her own, working two jobs to cover the tuition.

Stephanie had come into the death class terrified that her mother would die of alcohol abuse, just as Caitlin feared her mother would overdose on pills. Stephanie hadn't seen her parents in months. She wore a fitted bright pink, electric green, and gold T-shirt, tight jeans, and gold hoops for the occasion, bringing along a plastic garbage bag filled with donated secondhand clothes to give to them.

As with Caitlin, as with so many of her students, Norma had a special interest in Stephanie, though she didn't end up growing as close to her over time as to some of the others. While some students stuck around long after graduation, others dropped out of Norma's life after the class was completed, like passing blips in her electric lifeline. But the professor figured she could be of help to Stephanie by providing her with a ride and being there to support her as she reunited with her family. Stephanie's mother had been hit by an SUV a year earlier when she was drunk and was still recovering from her injuries. Stephanie worried that her mom was dying of alcoholism and thought the professor could use her nursing skills to check up on the woman's health.

When Norma's party bus pulled up to the Offshore Motel just after

11 A.M., a bar across the street was already filled with bikers. The professor parked at a meter, and a front-desk clerk glared, craning her neck as the visitors walked past the office, headed to the second floor. Outside room 30, a frail woman with her front teeth missing, a drained face, and a mop of stringy blond hair pulled back by a clear plastic headband smoked a cigarette with a trembling hand. She stood near a rail, peering over a dry pool covered by a blue tarp. She wore an orange sneaker on her right foot and a cast on her left. A distended belly swelled beneath a white T-shirt, which she wore under a faded denim jacket. It was Stephanie's mother. She was already drunk.

"I told you to stay out of the tanning booth," the weary-looking fifty-year-old told her daughter, her morning breath reeking of alcohol.

Room 30 was just big enough to fit two double beds. Pink-and-burgundy blankets covered the mattresses, which matched the sheer pink-and-burgundy blouses that hung over the windows as curtains. Norma stood outside talking to Stephanie's father first.

Meanwhile, a middle-aged man, who said he was a friend of the parents, stumbled into the room, swiped a beer from the minifridge, popped it open, and took a gulp. He wore a stonewashed jean jacket and had bloodshot eyes and stubble sprouting from his cheeks and chin. He asked about the lady he had run into and chatted with outside. "What is she, a doctor?"

"She has all kinds of degrees," Stephanie told him. "Like MS, PhD, all these letters."

"Hey," he said, "I told her I had hep C."

In walked Norma, smiling. She wore an old black sweater over a cotton dress and leggings. Peach-colored toenails peeked from her walking sandals.

"You're the doctor!" the man with hep C said.

"I'm the teacher," she corrected.

Stephanie's mom sprung from the bed and began to pace, looking angered by this woman's intrusion.

Norma approached her to shake hands, but the mom grabbed her hand and yanked it. Hard. "Whoops," said Norma, jerking forward.

"What do you mean, whoops?" the mom said, lowering her eyes, tightening her grip. Stephanie explained later that her mom had always been a good fighter, drunk or not, and now she was in attack stance.

"I thought you were pulling me," Norma said, without flinching, as if to say, It's okay, go ahead. I'm not scared.

Stephanie's mom smiled back mischievously. "I'm Margaret."

"You're strong, Margaret."

"Yeah, I'm strong," she said, not letting go.

The woman gave Norma a look like, who is this nurse-teacher-doctor lady anyway? She leaned in closer, breathing in her face. "So," she said, "what'd you come here for anyway?"

"Listen, Margaret, the reason I wanted to meet you is because I know it's been really hard for you," Norma said, explaining that she thought her daughter was amazing, ". . . and I try to figure out sometimes, even through hardships, how some people—"

"Let me stop you right there," the mom said, backing off for a moment. "Let me tell you something . . . sometimes I pray, and you know God does listen," she slurred. "And my daughter is the only one that's strong. And I thank God that, at least, she got something from me. And I thank God, growing up with an alcoholic parent, that she is still—this kid—with her own apartment, she bought her own car, and she works every day."

Slumped on the bed, the male visitor with the stubbly face muttered to himself, "They're good-looking and they're smart," he said of all three of Margaret's daughters, whose pictures adorned a mirror. "Usually you're smart and you're ugly."

"Would you let me take your pulse?" Norma asked Margaret.

"I don't know. I don't care."

"She's a nurse," Stephanie said again.

Norma reached for her wrist, gently. Margaret's face softened. Her arm wilted between Norma's fingers. Her pulse was up, Norma noticed. Probably the alcohol, she thought. Dehydration. Margaret forgot about her cigarette, which left a trail in the ashtray like a black snake firework. Next, Norma checked beneath the cast on her leg.

"Margaret!" a voice screeched from outside.

"What!" she shouted back.

It was the front-desk clerk, agitated about the visitors. She went to the balcony and leaned over. "It's my daughter!"

"Everybody?" the clerk said, scanning the pack of people who had followed her outside. The dad leaned over too. "That's my daughter," her dad said, pointing, "and this is her teacher."

"You have to understand," the front-desk clerk said, suddenly sweet, as if realizing that Norma might be working undercover for an inspection agency, "if we don't know you, you have to go."

"It's okay," Norma said. "Thank you for checking. We're leaving now."

As they made their way to the stairs, the mother grabbed Norma's hand one last time and squeezed. "Listen," she said, looking the professor in the eye, appearing unsure of whether she wanted to punch her, push her down the steps, or pull her back inside to stay longer. "I'm not a bad person."

Norma squeezed her hand back, tenderly. "I know you're not."

"I'll see you at graduation," the professor told her before turning away.

Outside, Norma stopped in the motel courtyard and watched a little girl pick through a McDonald's bag by a Dumpster. She walked down to the boardwalk and stared at the ocean for a few moments before buying a round of orange custards.

"If I didn't know you, Dr. Bowe, I would be embarrassed," Stephanie told her later, as they walked back to the party bus. "I don't want you to feel sorry for her."

"I don't feel sorry for her at all," Norma said. "Your mom's not going to die tomorrow. I would even say she's going to be alive a year from now. But if she continues on this path, you know you're not going to have her too much longer, right?"

"She'll stay sober for me," Stephanie said, "like completely sober around me, and she'll eat, because I'll make sure. But it's, like, a full-time job. I wouldn't be able to work or go to school."

Stephanie had to stay in school. "That will be your victory lap," Norma said.

"I know," she answered, "but I would feel better if I could give them some money."

"Don't even go there," Norma said. "You give them money, you know exactly what they're going to do with it."

The mood inside the party bus dimmed. Stephanie dipped into her custard with a plastic spoon. Norma slowed to pay a thirty-five-cent toll. They drove for a while, before the professor broke the silence.

"Well, we got to see the ocean today," she said. "It was beautiful."

IT SEEMED AS if Norma had a radar hardwired inside her that could detect whenever somebody within her vicinity might need her assistance—an aspirin, a Kleenex, a letter of recommendation, a spur-of-the-moment therapy session while riding shotgun in the party bus. Students called her purse the Mary Poppins bag. What do you need? Hand sanitizer? A granola bar? A hairbrush? The business card of a good funeral home? She had it covered.

This sixth sense of hers had started as far back as nursing school, but probably even earlier. She could remember feeling it with the first patient who had ever died on her watch, an elderly woman whose body had been shutting down. Norma was still a nurse in training at the time and had been taking care of her for nearly five days.

In the middle of the night, while in her dorm room, Norma jolted awake. The dorms were attached to the hospital, and she lay there feeling frustrated, knowing that she needed to be back on the floor of the intensive care unit to start her shift at 7 A.M. She needed her rest but couldn't fall back to sleep. She couldn't stop thinking about the woman on all the meds. She got out of bed, slipped her blue lab coat over her pajamas, and wandered over to the ICU, only to be greeted by the night-shift nurse, who explained that she was glad she'd popped in because the woman Norma had been treating was dying and two other patients had just coded, so no one else was free to stay by her bedside. Norma went into the woman's room and held her hand, talking to her until she took her last breath.

Norma would witness many more deaths of all varieties, but she never forgot that first one, its serenity, its peacefulness.

Another time, while working as a nurse at the University of Virginia

Medical Center, she noticed an elderly man walking near the hospital while she was on her way back to her apartment. He looked sad, she would recall many years later. He had black marks on his throat, brutal signs of his radiation treatments, and he seemed worn down and lonely, wandering out of the hospital by himself. So she invited him over to her place for lunch with her roommates. Her two roommates were also nurses, and they had all been friends before coming to the University of Virginia Medical Center together. One worked in labor and delivery. The other worked in plastic surgery. The nurse in labor and delivery had even received a free nose job in the department after volunteering to let medical students watch the procedure. Norma worked in neurology intensive care. It was the unit that treated people with neurological disorders, including Lou Gehrig's disease, and patients suffering from brain injuries after roadway accidents. Neurology intensive care had been Norma's first choice. Her roommates didn't seem surprised that she had brought the man over for lunch. But they always joked with her after that, asking which stray she would bring home next.

Whenever Norma's internal helper buzzer went off, she could end up drawn into the most unexpected, sometimes sketchy, sometimes absurd situations—such as inside a women's prison classroom, nearly two hours from campus, where she had decided to teach without pay. Sitting before her during one visit were two dozen inmates. In the second row sat a mother who had drowned her baby in a bathtub. In the back was a transsexual who had shot two Camden County police officers to death. In the front row was a former exotic dancer who had dismembered her girlfriend, scattering her head, legs, and torso across three different cities. Norma's pro bono lesson of the day? Safe sex and STDs.

The professor always joked that she "had no danger button," no clear sense of alarm, to warn her of threats. When it came to her students, she was cautious. When it came to herself, not so much.

Once she took a van full of students on a community service field trip. During a pit stop in Alabama, Norma just about had a heart attack when a student darted off into the night to pet a stray dog. The professor fretted that it might bite her or pass on some God-awful infection.

Shortly after, while back on the road, the professor spotted a homeless man sitting in the dark at the entrance of the highway.

"We're pulling over!" she shouted to the volunteer who was driving. "I think I have some cereal," she said, rifling through the van, hopping outside, and scampering into a ditch to the toothless, shoeless man. She also gave him half of a banana and a small container of soy milk.

"Wait, let me get this straight," remarked another student sitting in the backseat, "I can't pet a dog, but it's okay for Dr. Bowe to give cereal to some crackhead?"

The professor chuckled at the comment later, admitting that it had been kind of ridiculous. But frankly, there was no proof the man was on drugs, and it didn't matter to her anyway because, besides looking frail and weak, he had also looked hungry. She thought the dog, on the other hand, had looked like an attack dog. It was guarding a truck, and Norma pictured calling her student's father to explain why it had ripped the girl's face off, all because she wanted to pet it.

Just as she didn't have much of a danger button, she also had no problem thrusting herself into people's normally private lives.

On that same road trip, during a stopover at a Holiday Inn in Birmingham, the hotel manager broke down crying as she explained to Norma, who'd checked in at a discounted rate, how her dog had just died after nineteen years of life. She was keeping the dog's body in a freezer at a nearby funeral home and planned to hold a burial and funeral the upcoming weekend. Norma held a bereavement session with her students and the hotel manager right there in the buffet breakfast room with cold scrambled eggs and half-eaten English muffins still on plastic plates.

Some considered it her caring curiosity. Others, flat-out nosiness. But I understood her tendency because I'd always had the same habit— no filter when it came to asking personal questions, no limits on poking my nose into stuff people don't naturally talk about or care to share. It had served my reporting career well.

Once the two of us ended up crashing a Buddhism retreat in the woods of upstate New York on a whim because Norma wanted to meet the lama of honor who was running the sessions; she and the lama had a mutual student in common, and Norma had some general questions about Buddhism. But she didn't want to enroll in an entire weekend of meditation and training sessions, and she had no desire to actually *become* a Buddhist. So we just showed up and slipped right in between the chants as the lama started talking about focusing your breath and concentrating on the pit of your stomach. When it was over, Norma cornered the lama and coaxed the woman into meeting her for an organic lunch.

Part of her audacity stemmed from her own childhood, all those stashed guns, fistfights, and mob dinners. But the other part, particularly her extreme tolerance for the maniacal and macabre, had to do with spending years working in neurology intensive care and psychiatric wards. After a nursing career like hers, very little could faze her. She could remember chatting about dinner plans with a doctor as he sewed a woman's eyeball back in place. The patient had gotten into a fight over a guy, and the other woman had bitten her eye out. It had ended up hanging from a tendon.

Another time, Norma saw a patient who had undergone a sex change operation from woman to man, long before it became a common procedure. The former woman had been given a penis made of her own flesh, which could be pumped into an erection by squeezing a scrotal pump. Many years later, on an autopsy field trip with her students, the class walked in to see a naked body on the table with a full erection.

"Dr. Bowe, how can that be?"

Sure enough, she explained, the deceased person had had a penile implant just like the one she'd seen when she was a nurse, complete with a pump.

Nothing was too off the wall for the professor. In fact, the more unusual and the more intensely personal, the more at ease she felt. As if they had a sixth sense too, the people with the most mind-boggling problems gravitated toward Norma.

But the pull went both ways.

ADULTHOOD, NORMA BELIEVED, is about giving back and passing lessons on to the next generation, so that the virtues you work so hard to develop live on even after your death. Norma came to embrace the idea of Erik Erikson's seventh stage of life, "Generativity vs. Stagnation," as she explained in her lectures to students. This period, according to Erikson, comes down to questions such as: What is my legacy? What will I leave behind for the next generation?

If a person never figures out his or her identity and never finds real love or intimate relationships during earlier stages in life, he or she can hit adulthood and become a miserable complainer, she said. "Nothing makes them happy," as Norma explained it to her students. No one is good enough, nothing satisfies them—not even winning the lottery. A life lived in this manner will likely lead to serious letdowns in the final stage of Erikson's cycle—the one before death.

But those who have developed all the virtues Erikson described in previous stages of life, who have come to know, understand, and love themselves, who have found true intimacy and discovered purpose in their career, creative, or community endeavors, often develop a different attitude in adulthood. They work toward goals that will leave something behind for the next generation, whether money, wisdom, creativity, or genes. They often want to make life better for their children, and even if they haven't had children of their own, they work to leave something behind for people around them. This is *generativity*, according to Erikson, a term he coined that emphasizes productivity, caring, and behavior that often involves committing oneself to a cause, people, or a larger universal purpose—and a teacher is in many ways the ultimate example of giving something back and passing it on.

EACH SEMESTER, NORMA took her students from the death class to visit a hospice center, in which residents spend their dying days; in order for patients to be admitted, they have to have been diagnosed by a doctor as having six months or less left to live.

Father Hudson House was a cozy place with creaky stairs filled with nurses, such as the director, Sally, a short, unassuming grandmother with ginger-colored hair lopped off at the shoulders, feathered bangs, and tiny gold hoops in her ears. She wore white hospital staff pants, white slip-on nurse shoes, and ankle socks with pink bow designs.

Sally had been working with the terminally ill since the 1970s, when the public first began noticing that people were dying alone and in pain. Caregivers had been going into the homes of the dying to assist but soon realized that those who were less fortunate didn't even have homes to die in. That was when hospice facilities like Father Hudson House began opening in New Jersey.

Since her career had begun, some of Sally's own family members had died in the hospice center, including her thirty-seven-year-old niece, who had succumbed to a brain tumor. Some people who came to them had no family at all, she said. Her staff members had searched the Internet, even gone to Ellis Island, to rifle through records to track down relatives.

Father Hudson House had been home to a hospice dog at one point and was decorated with wooden mallards and gold and green wall trim, as well as a piano and an old boom box with a crate full of Benny Goodman CDs and sound tracks with titles such as *Strings of Paris, Songs of World War II,* and the sound track to *Singing in the Rain. Jeopardy* blared at full volume from television sets as white-haired folks reclined in chairs, while some hobbled through hallways, clinging to handrails.

On every hospice field trip, Norma stopped in to see a patient named Jim, a ninety-six-year-old who had lost both his legs to diabetes and had outlived the six-month prognosis.

"There's my favorite person!" she would exclaim. Jim seemed to remember her each time. He had a hollow nose, red eyes, and thick, calloused hands from his years of working on a tugboat. The students took a liking to Jim too, sitting next to him in his room, his leg stubs draped in a blanket, listening to him tell stories about his family and life on the tugboat.

After one trip, when back in class, some students said how sad it must be to spend your dying days in a hospice center, no matter how kind the nurses. The place, for all its charm, seemed pretty dreary. It could use a makeover.

"So let's do one!" Norma replied, not entirely sure of what she was getting herself into. But the death class went along with the idea, and within a couple of weeks Norma and her students, including Caitlin, had recruited nearly fifty volunteers to paint the walls in brighter shades, such as yellow, and furnish the hospice facility with bright bookcases, pictures of suns and trees on the wall, a revamped game and recreation room, and a beauty salon. Jim, chipper as ever, chatted with the youngsters about his life on the water as they painted. When done, the place was a rainbow of purples, reds, and greens.

And Jim? He outlived many of his neighbors in that made-over hospice facility, greeting a dozen more semesters of death class students—longer than any doctor could have anticipated.

It had been only a small project, completed in a single weekend. There were no cameras in the room to capture it for a reality television show and no wealthy donors. The students had raised the money to pay for the paint themselves, as well as securing donations of the furniture and decorations. This was Erikson's theory of generativity in vibrant action, a lesson that Norma had learned on her own so many years before from the lonely 110-year-old woman who lived in the trailer with her dog.

After the makeover, the students pitched in to decorate another hospice facility, this one for dying children. Norma kept a sign on her office door, right next to an article about the survivors of the Virginia Tech University shooting. It was a quote from the man whom Erik Erikson had written a 1969 psychobiography about, entitled *Gandhi's Truth: On the Origins of Militant Nonviolence,* for which he had won a Pulitzer Prize and National Book Award. The quote from Mohandas Gandhi read: "Be the change you want to see in the world."

In late 2008, the death class students who had made over the hospice facilities decided to launch a community service group, with Norma as its innovator and adviser.

They would call it Be the Change.

ONE MORNING, KNEE-HIGH banks of dirty snow lined the sidewalks and roadsides like mounds of dirt left over from freshly dug graves around the Crabiel Parkwest Funeral Chapel in New Brunswick, where the funeral for Norma's neighbor was being held. Inside, the men, including Norma's partner, Norman, wore yarmulkes. The couple and their daughter, Becca, sat behind the widow, in the second row.

Paul Griminger, a longtime friend of Norma's family, had lived for eighty-eight years—surviving the Holocaust, outwitting the Nazi Anschluss in Austria, and in 1938 leaving for Palestine, where he had ended up fighting as a British soldier and later being stationed in Egypt. After the war, he had become a professor of nutrition at Rutgers University, settling in Norma's Highland Park neighborhood. But in the fall of 2008, he had fallen ill and been told by a doctor he would need an aortic valve replacement. The procedure would give him the benefit of living probably another year.

His mind was astute, and he still very much enjoyed waking up to his morning paper each day, often writing letters to *The New York Times*. He had four children and nine grandchildren, and he decided that another year would be worth it; he wanted to live even longer than that if he could. But in the event that he might encounter complications during surgery, which he knew was risky given his age and condition, he scheduled the procedure for November 5, 2008; he did not want to miss the opportunity to vote for Barack Obama on November 4. On the day of the election, Griminger and his wife, Olga, drove to the polling station to cast their votes and then went home to prepare for his surgery at New York Presbyterian Hospital.

Complications did ensue. Griminger went into respiratory failure and ended up on a ventilator. Doctors intubated him, and for the next four months, with the emotional support of her neighbors, Olga commuted back and forth to the hospital. He seemed to be doing better until mid-February, when he came down with pneumonia. It was a Saturday night when Norma received a phone call from Griminger's family. They knew she was a nurse who also taught about death. They wanted to know what was going to happen next. She sat down with the family and gave them a lesson on the process of dying, like the one she gave her students. She explained how morphine worked and how to read the signs that would indicate the end was near. Griminger died the next morning.

His funeral had no casket, no cosmetically made-up body on display. Those present seemed almost jovial, as if they were attending a retirement gathering complete with stately speeches, poetic tributes, antsy children, and a woozy white-haired woman who looked as if she was about to doze off in her seat a few rows away.

"This feels like an out-of-body experience," said Griminger's daughter, a curly-haired woman in glasses, standing at the lectern, refusing to cry. "I don't know if every daughter thinks her father is larger than life. But I do. It seems to me that he knew about everything."

The funeral ended with psalms read in Hebrew and English, an e.e. cummings poem, and an open invitation to the family's home for a reception. The mourners rose to leave, lining up to exit out of the back doors and hugging family members.

But the white-haired woman, who had appeared to be nodding off, did not get up. She slumped in the chair like a rag doll in her black-and-white cable-knit sweater with snowflake designs, black polyester pants, and black orthopedic shoes.

"Is there a doctor in here? A medical doctor?"

"Robert?" someone else called out. "Where's Robert?" He was another neighbor and also a radiation oncologist.

A cluster of onlookers stared on, dumbfounded, unsure of what to do. Someone dialed 911. The doctor had yet to be found.

But there was a nurse.

Norma, in her black frilly shawl and turquoise beaded necklace, lifted the woman, who looked to be around eighty-something, from the chair, gently spreading her limp body across the forest green carpet. She kneeled over her body.

Norma Bowe to the rescue. Again.

The woman's eyes had rolled back. Her white ankle socks had slipped down onto the balls of her feet, revealing two pasty pale ankles. Plum-colored veins slithered beneath her parchment skin.

Norma grabbed a pile of beige pillows from a sofa nearby and propped them under her feet so blood would flow to her major organs. She grasped the woman's thin wrist and pressed it between her fingers. That was when she said, "No pulse."

Someone in the funeral home finally tracked down Robert, who was now kneeling on the floor of the funeral home over the unconscious woman alongside Norma, who gave a quick pound on her chest, and Robert gave her mouth-to-mouth resuscitation. Just like that, she woke up.

"Can you squeeze my hand?" Norma asked, looking into her eyes.

The woman could barely speak as she tugged furiously at her sweater, trying to yank it off. Three paramedics showed up and hooked blue and red wires to her ankles, setting up an EEG monitor. "Where do you live?" one asked. "Do you know what day of the week it is?" One of them pricked her finger, and a sliver of blood slid out.

She looked mortified. Perhaps she was embarrassed because several dozen people had been staring at her sprawled on the moss green carpet. Perhaps she realized that amid all of the commotion, she'd wet her pants.

"It looks like she went into cardiac arrest," Norma told one as she stepped away from the scene. The paramedics began loading the woman onto a stretcher as someone said to Norma, "It's a good thing you were here."

Later that evening, Norma arrived at class looking drained and apologizing for being a bit off her game. She'd had quite a day. Students pressed for details, so she obliged with a condensed version of her day. "We need that story in the local paper!" one said.

Another piped in with a possible headline: "Death Teacher Saves Life at Funeral."

The class burst into laughter.

"Oh, my God," Norma said, gasping between her own laughs. It was a pretty wacky situation, wasn't it? She caught her breath. "All right. Anyway, where was I?"

Organ harvesting. Right.

"IN TIMES OF strife and crisis, she thrives on it." That was how Norma's formerly Mafia-affiliated father once described his daughter one afternoon when we sat down for orange juice and coffee in a New Jersey diner. The seventy-four-year-old was wearing loafers and an orange sherbet–colored rayon shorts suit. He wore gold chains around his neck and a diamond ring on his left sun-spotted finger. In the middle of his tanned face was a slightly crooked nose; his eyelashes were whitish blond like his hair, which he wore gelled and spiky like a teenage boy's. His daughter, he went on, for all her virtues, "has to be the one in control."

"That," he said, "is an insight into Dr. Death over there."

He added with all seriousness and cluelessness, "I don't know if it's something about the way she was raised in her life."

LOVE YOURSELF FIRST.

That's what Norma repeated to Stephanie and to Caitlin. That was what Norma had tried to do herself, after feeling, as Erikson put it, as if she wanted to "destroy the eyes of the world."

Norma remembered when she was a teenager visiting a friend's beach house in Long Island and noticing how loving and happy that family seemed, eating and laughing together. "I was, like, 'Oh, wow, no one is breaking anything?'" That was when she realized how far her home life was from normal.

Many years later, she would find herself grieving over the child-hood she'd never really had during a spiritual retreat in upstate New York, when she ended up sobbing to a near stranger. That woman broke down sobbing to Norma too. It turned out that the woman's parents had adopted a chimpanzee when she was a child, raising it as part of a university-endorsed experiment to see if the chimp could learn human language. The chimp had ended up becoming the darling of the family, and the woman had grown up feeling neglected and unable to compete with the chimp for her mother's affection.

Norma remembered comforting the distraught woman and thinking it was time to stop feeling sorry for herself: Okay, she's got me. Nothing I've been through in my life can top that. She had broken their cycle of abuse and replaced the missing love with new love from her daughters, her life partner, her students, and even her father, who, for all his irrita-tion and foul-mouthing, was beginning to show hints of tenderness in his old age.

"I have always wondered, what puts somebody on this path and what puts somebody on that path?" Norma once said. "I think for me it was my grandmother. I just got determined, like I was not going to let this crazy family shake me or define me or make me a bad mother or make me into a person I didn't want to be. School and my grandmother. That's what saved me."

Norma's grandmother Rosalie had been a true southern belle of the 1950s and '60s, a dignified high-society woman, as she remembered her. Born in 1910, and proudly Jewish, she wore high heels with her shell neck blouses, pencil skirts, and full-skirt party dresses that cinched at the waist. She got her hair and nails done every week and always seemed to be dripping in diamonds or pearls as she smoked Virginia Slims and played bridge with the local ladies. She lived in a craftsman home off the Chesapeake Bay in Newport News, Virginia. It sat alongside a tree-shaded creek and had a big wooden deck and a master bedroom that opened into a full bathroom with a sunken tub. The house had deep, turquoise-colored couches and a long black slate coffee table with crystal bowls and figurines on it. To Norma, her grandma's place back then felt like a magic house. A refuge.

Down the block from the house, a series of towering statues of lions had been built on a bridge overlooking a park and the waterfront. Rosalie used to tell Norma that it was *her* bridge and *her* park overlooking the water, because, with her August birthday, Norma's zodiac sign was the lion. The statues stood tall and splendid, with their chests puffed out. Lions commanded authority, with their strong wills and the courage to do whatever it took to survive. The lion statues, her grandma explained, represented her. Norma Lynn. The Lioness.

Norma's grandmother had been raised by affluent parents. They had lived on New York's Central Park West. Rosalie had ended up marrying a jeweler, although they eventually divorced. Many years later, after Norma got out of nursing school, she found out that her grandfather lived in Florida and decided to call him in case he wondered what she'd made of her life.

"Hi, it's your granddaughter, Norma Lynn," she could remember saying on the phone.

She would never forget his reply: "Do you want me to buy you a steak or something?"

"And that was that," Norma remembered. He'd died of cancer not long after.

"She would tell me she loved me all the time, but it was more about how she treated me more than anything else," Norma remembered of her grandmother. "She adored me. My parents were so abusive, but when I went to her house, I just felt bathed in love."

Rosalie pampered her granddaughter as she pampered herself, fancying her up in pretty party dresses and putting bows in her hair. Norma remembered that she'd had her own bedroom in her house, which looked out onto the big backyard where her grandma had built a swing set just for her. Her grandma also had a vanity table and mirror, where she would sit and put on lipstick, shimmering powders, and floral-scented perfumes as her granddaughter watched.

Norma knew her mother and grandmother did not get along. Rosalie didn't approve of Norma's father, but the mother's and daughter's personalities probably would have clashed even without him in the picture. They bickered constantly.

When Norma worked at the University of Virginia, she drove to Newport News on the weekends to spend time with her grandmother. When Rosalie was diagnosed with breast cancer and ended up having a mastectomy, Norma helped her after the surgery, taking her back and forth to chemo and radiation treatments. Her grandmother spent five years in the clear, but then the cancer showed up in her lungs.

By the summer of 1990, Rosalie was about to turn eighty. Norma was working in New Jersey and raising her own family, but she spent three weeks in Virginia, caring for Rosalie as she spent her final weeks in hospice. Her grandma died on August 21, the day before Norma's birthday, and it was as peaceful a departure as the first death she'd witnessed as a nursing student. And just like that time, she held her grandma's hand through her final breath.

Norma's mother didn't come for the funeral, which the professor arranged the next day, her birthday, all on her own. Rosalie was buried the day after Norma's birthday next to Norma's great-grandmother in a cemetery off Chesapeake Bay.

In her will, her grandmother had left Norma enough money to buy a cabin in New Hampshire. After the house in Newport News was put up for sale, most of her grandmother's antique furniture ended up finding a new home in that cabin.

Ever since then, around the same three days each year and feeling the weight of her past, Norma had retreated from the rest of the world completely. She didn't want to feel cherished. She took no phone calls. Answered no emails. Helped no one. She didn't even let her family near her. Her self-isolation started the day before her birthday, August 22, and ended the day after.

Usually she ventured off to the cabin alone. Sometimes she curled up in bed until the days before and after were over. Her family knew better than to push the subject. They had stopped trying to throw birthday parties or bake cakes long before. There was no happy-birthday song. No unwrapping of gifts. Instead, they left her alone. Once she drove off by herself and didn't tell a soul where she was going until she got back. They would have worried more had it not been her birthday week.

As an adult, she couldn't remember her parents ever having thrown her a birthday party when she was young or acknowledging the day at all. Her mother had told her so often that she wished she had never been born that it had become clear that there was no reason to celebrate her life. When her grandmother told her the story of her birth, the girdles, the stillborn brother, she realized how close she had come to never being born in the first place.

"Shame," as Erikson wrote, "is early expressed in an impulse to bury one's face, or to sink, right then and there, into the ground. But this, I think, is essentially rage turned against the self."

As a little girl, Norma had learned how to be nearly invisible. As an adult, she was at her most dynamic when front and center, teaching and helping people.

But every summer, when her birthday came around—two weeks before the fall semester began each school year—she couldn't help it. She found herself wishing to be invisible again.

TAKE-HOME WRITING ASSIGNMENT: Eulogy

Write your own eulogy.

SEVEN

The Trigger

Fall Semester 2008

A day before the first day of class that September, a young man showed up in the professor's office to introduce himself. He was wearing a shirt and tie, with two cell phones strapped to his belt, one for personal matters and the other for work. He stood five feet, six inches and weighed 180 pounds, mostly muscle, only 2 percent body fat, and politely made his plea to be admitted into the death class, despite the waiting list.

His name was Israel, and he rattled off all of his accomplishments, his words colored by a lisp, one he'd spent many days of his youth trying to get rid of. He was working at a boot camp for juveniles and mentoring high-risk youth throughout the community. He'd worked with organizations promoting safe sex and gang prevention. He wanted to learn more about death so he could boost his qualifications on his résumé, maybe end up doing some grief counseling. He flashed a close-mouthed, dimpled smile, careful to hide a gap between his front teeth.

Norma looked him up and down. She would eventually learn all of Israel's stories. She would come to see all that he was ashamed of, all that he wished he could change. The gang members he'd rolled with. The crimes he'd committed.

"There's something about you," the professor said to him that day. "I'm going to let you in."

*   *   *

A WEEK LATER, Israel sat at his computer, contemplating what to write for his first class assignment. Even with his arms extended over the keyboard, his medicine-ball biceps would have appeared clenched to anyone peering into his room, as if they were in a state of permanent tension. He had worked out hard to get them. Seventeen inches around, solid as stone. A tattoo of barbed wire encircled the right bicep. Strong arms were good for many important things, such as lifting weights, picking up girls, or throwing punches. But typing?

There was no getting around it, Israel was a *college student* now—a title no one from his youth would have ever guessed he would hold. He'd traded his street gang affiliations for a college fraternity long before. He wore his Greek letters with pride and lived by the motto "Opportunity for wisdom, wisdom for culture." If only he'd had a sliver of that wisdom in his youth.

"Write a good-bye letter to someone or something you have lost," Norma had told the class on the first day of Death in Perspective. It was just a week ago that she'd given those instructions. "Go to the place that immediately came to mind," she'd said. "Go where it's scary."

Sure, Israel had made his pitch to the professor to let him into the class at the last minute, and she'd taken a chance on him. But this letter had him stumped. Guys like him didn't talk about parts of their past that could give away their weaknesses. One part of his past would lead to another, and another, and pretty soon he'd be wading through territory that talking about could get him locked up or even killed. If he started this letter honestly, there was no telling what might spill out of him.

What would his new professor think about him if she knew the truth about his life? Norma seemed like a nice enough lady, the kind who hugged strangers. She didn't seem like someone who could even for a moment understand the darkness he knew.

*   *   *

Ten years earlier

ISRAEL PUT HIS finger on the trigger and pointed his gun at his enemy's face.

Two words ran through his mind: *Kill him.*

The room began to echo and blur. Israel could hear people screaming and crying and shouting and cursing all around him, but the noise came rushing through him like waves. He felt as though his ears were popping and ringing, but none of it felt real. More like he was inside of a movie. Was he dreaming?

Israel blinked and looked at the young man kneeled before him, body trembling. Israel was seventeen. The guy wasn't much older, maybe nineteen. Israel felt his hands shaking too, as he fiddled with the trigger.

A sound in the room broke through the ringing in his head. It was the only voice Israel could hear clearly, distinctly—the young man's mother. She was crying and begging "Don't kill my baby. We'll move to Puerto Rico. We'll leave. You'll never see us again. Please don't kill my baby!"

How had he gotten here? How had this happened to him? Israel's life, from childhood to now, had been one rapid ride of misfortune, wrong turns, and bad decisions. It had all led Israel to this moment—one that would surely change his life forever, transform him from teenage boy into teenage killer.

His hand steadied around the metal of the gun. All it would take was one shot.

ISRAEL HAD BEEN a scrawny kid, growing up wearing washed-out clothes donated from churches. His skin was so fair for a Puerto Rican that he looked like a white boy living in a neighborhood of dark-skinned Latinos and African Americans. When he was four, he'd moved to New Jersey from Puerto Rico, where his family used to live in a tin shack, after his mother had fled his abusive father. In New Jersey, Israel, his brother, and his mother lived with three others in a studio apartment. Israel barely spoke English.

He'd had no choice but to fight back whenever someone picked on him, and with so much practice he became good at it. By middle school, he'd grown into a street fighter who was recognized around town for getting into boxing matches in alleys and scraps on corners. Once he beat up one guy, a bigger guy would want to take him on. But the bigger and bulkier Israel got, the fewer could beat him. He soon realized he didn't have to wait around for the fight to come to him. He could use his skills to get things he did not have: sneakers, Walkmans, pagers, jewelry, jeans. By fourteen, he was waiting outside schools until kids came out with something he wanted.

By fifteen, he'd moved on from jumping kids after school to picking car-door locks with screwdrivers. Israel and his friends cruised North Jersey for the hooked-up cars—the ones with shiny rims and expensive stereo systems. They'd strip them down, take the valuable parts to a chop shop, and earn $200 to $400 a job. When they were done taking the cars' valuable parts, they'd barrel down some empty road—going a hundred miles per hour—then swerve rapidly until they toppled over. Israel and his friends earned a few bruises that way, as well as broken bones, but man, was it a thrill. After a while, the chop shops started getting closed down, so Israel and his friends moved on to a more lucrative venture: they started selling weed.

But there was a lot of product and not enough profit. A dime bag sold for $10. He could make three times as much if he sold to the white kids in richer neighborhoods, but that was a hassle and riskier. Plus, everyone around him sold weed. It was about as competitive as trying to become a professional boxer. So Israel turned to selling cocaine. The money was good. He showed up at high school in $150 Parasuco jeans, $300 Vortex boots, and thick flat gold herringbone chains. A lot of it came from the addicts who showed up with stereo systems and jewelry in exchange for drugs. His mom was working two or three jobs to make ends meet. Israel would stash his expensive clothes in a bag at a friend's house and change before going to school.

One day a neighborhood gang leader asked Israel if he wanted to get out of street peddling and gain a little more responsibility; he could do pickups and dropoffs. Israel was seventeen now, and it seemed like a good idea. He wouldn't have to dodge undercover cops or local police on the streets or deal with snitches setting him up with fake sales. All he had to do was drive across the George Washington Bridge to New York, pick up a load of drugs, and bring them back to New Jersey. Israel happily started his new job. But he had no idea that if he got caught, his punishment would likely be worse than it would be for selling—he wouldn't find out until later that crossing a state line with narcotics was a felony.

Israel bought a gun for protection. It cost $250 from a guy on the street who was also selling a grenade for $600.

One day, while passing through another neighborhood, a group of three guys from a rival gang cornered Israel's Mustang at a stoplight. One walked up and punched Israel's friend in the face through an open car window. Israel got out to fight. But he saw two more guys come out of nowhere.

"Yo, let's go," Israel's friend said to him. "Don't be stupid." It was just the two of them against five.

Israel got back into the driver's seat and put the car into reverse, trying to hit their attackers. They dodged out of his way. As Israel sped off, he heard gunshots. They'd fired at his Mustang, hitting it twice.

He rushed home and grabbed his gun, calling up three more friends, who also had guns. "We're not going out like that," Israel told them.

Together they went back to the neighborhood. Just after 10 P.M., they rolled up to the house where one of the rivals lived. Two of the guys were on the porch, with the others scattered near their car. Israel and his crew pulled their triggers.

Israel had never fired his gun at anyone before, but now he and his crew were popping off rounds in every direction. The rivals dived under the porch and ran inside. Israel thought he'd seen at least two guys get grazed.

His crew wanted to leave before cops showed up, but Israel wasn't finished. He wanted to do more damage. He grabbed an emergency flare from his car and tossed it into one of the enemy's cars, then sped off. The car blew up.

It was a windy day, and the explosion caused a chain reaction that Israel had not anticipated. Three other cars next to the first blew up. The whole block had to be evacuated. The incident made the local newspaper.

But there was a street code that Israel's crew and his enemies lived by: never snitch. Ever. No one did. And Israel and his friends never got blamed.

They were more than friends by now, actually—they were a gang, affiliated with the Latin Kings. The guys that they'd clashed with were members of a rival gang. And the beef was not over. The others came back for revenge. But this time they went after Israel's mother. She had an office job as a receptionist, and somehow they found out where she worked. The gang members bashed in the glass door of her office and barged in, screaming "We're going to kill your son!"

Israel's mother came home crying. "What have you gotten yourself into? What have you done?"

Israel snapped. They had messed with his family. They had crossed him for the last time. You threaten mine, she thought, I'm going after yours.

WHEN ISRAEL GATHERED up his gang and headed to the rival leader's house that day, he had made up his mind: he was going to kill him.

The guy's dad answered the door, and Israel busted it in, bashing the man in the face with his gun. "Motherfucker, get on the ground!" he screamed.

The dad still tried to stop them, but they pummeled and kicked him until he fell on the floor, his head bleeding. They knocked down his mother and little brother too, as Israel went for the gang leader, beating his face with his gun and then aiming it at his face.

With everyone crowded into the tiny living room, Israel knew this was his chance. The punk-ass had shot at him and threatened his mother.

Besides, Israel had made a real show of it now. He'd always understood: if you pull your gun, you damn well better use it. If he didn't kill the guy, Israel and all of his gang members would be as good as dead, and probably their families too.

But those cries. The wrenching pleas from the young man's mother: "Please don't kill my baby!"

He'd shot in this guy's direction just days ago and could have killed him then. But that was nothing like this, just inches away, the gun to his head, looking into his eyes. Israel noticed the guy's eyes watering. Or were those tears?

"Do it!" Israel heard his crew yelling. "You can't leave him like that!" But he couldn't pull the trigger. He couldn't kill him.

"Naw," Israel said, hitting him a few more times before turning to the rest of the guys. "Let's go."

"YOU'RE FUCKING STUPID," one of the other guys said to Israel on the ride home. "You broke the rules."

Now what? The rival gang would come back for revenge. Israel and his gang would have to look over their shoulder at every turn, grabbing their guns at every knock on the door.

A few days passed. Israel and the rest of the guys jumped at sounds, dodged cars, avoided malls and open spaces. But no one came for them. The word on the street was that the gang leader's family had stayed true to his mother's word. They had packed up and left for Puerto Rico.

Less than a month later, Israel had resumed his duties under the leader of his gang, driving to New York, picking up drugs, and bringing them back. The gang leader leased a car for Israel to drive under the boss's name.

One afternoon, Israel visited the gang leader's house and decided to walk to the corner store two blocks away. On his way back, he noticed cop cars swarming the block. They had surrounded the house and were raiding it. Officers had discovered the arsenal of weapons and mountains of drugs, and the gang leader was arrested. The leader took the rap for everything. He could have pointed the finger at his workers too, but he didn't do it. He was sent to prison. Again, the rule of the street—no snitching—had saved Israel from getting caught too.

Israel owed the gang leader big time. Israel looked up to the man, who'd started at the same low level as he and progressed up the ranks. He went to visit him in prison. The gang leader knew that Israel had been messing up in high school. School counselors had referred Israel to attend a boot camp for juvenile delinquents. But Israel didn't want to en-list and considered going AWOL. He had a job to carry on in the streets.

The leader came out of his cell in a jumpsuit, officers escorting him. The two sat across from each other in the prison. He looked at Israel gravely and said, "You're a smart kid. You've got a lot going for you. You don't need this life, this gang."

Go to boot camp, he told Israel, get out of the gang. He had his permission—his blessing.

Israel shook his head in disbelief. Was he acting all weak now because he'd gotten locked up? This didn't seem like the same hardened man he'd looked up to. Besides, everyone knew there was no getting "released" from a gang. You got killed before you got out. But the gang leader insisted. He gave him his word as the leader, the boss—he was letting him go.

"Okay," Israel said, uncomfortably. But he didn't know what to think. Go and do what? Israel had always just assumed that he would die young living the gang lifestyle. That was all he knew. He went home and thought about what the gang leader had told him. He thought about how close he'd come to killing a man. He wondered if he had any good left in him anymore, if he really could change.

A few days later, Israel decided to try to find out. He checked in to boot camp.

He stayed for the next six months, earning his GED, and after he got out, he felt new. "Change places, people, and things." That became Israel's new motto. He would treat his life as if he were a recovering alcoholic or drug addict.

He decided to go back to school.

ISRAEL ENROLLED IN a community college. But it was located in the neighborhood of the rival gang that he had crossed, the turf of the guy he had nearly shot in the face.

One night, Israel was walking near a McDonald's across from campus when he noticed a burgundy Honda with tinted windows slowly rolling by. Israel had not lost his jumpiness since the last incident involving him and the gun, seven months earlier. He started walking toward the parking lot, when he saw the window lower. He heard someone shout, "Get 'im!"

Israel took off, dipping between cars as gunshots pounded behind him, hightailing it back to campus, barging into an office, where he jumped over a desk and hid behind it. He waited in a safe place for a long time and then called a cab when he felt enough time had passed, leaving his own car in the parking lot to pick up another day in case they were waiting for him near it.

That was his last day of community college.

Maybe, he thought, school was not for him anyway. He tried working instead. He found a job at an HIV clinic as a peer educator and worked his way up the ranks to coordinator. The clinic sent him to counseling training in Los Angeles, Chicago, and Las Vegas. Israel finally felt as if he was doing something worthwhile. A few years had passed. He began to rethink his decision to quit school. Perhaps he could handle college after all, just not so close to his old enemies?

He went to speak to a counselor at Kean University, after a mentor suggested he try to get in through the school's Exceptional Educational Opportunities Program, which relied on state funding to help at-risk students who might not be accepted based on their SAT scores or grades and didn't have the money required to pay for college.

It took some effort on the part of the counselor, but one day Israel received his official notice: he had been admitted to the university.

As ISRAEL SAT contemplating what to write for Norma's first class assignment that day, a name came to mind. A young man he'd once known. The name sometimes cracked in his throat when he said it out loud.

Israel had never had the chance to say good-bye to him.

Before he knew it, Israel's fingers were flying over the keyboard, as if they knew what he needed to say better than he did.

When Norma called on Israel to share his good-bye letter in front of the class, he said he didn't want to read it. She urged, but he refused. When she called on him again the next week, he still flat-out said no.

He wasn't ready to go there, to disclose his shame and guilt. Not yet.

CLASS FIELD TRIP: Northern State Prison

TAKE-HOME WRITING ASSIGNMENT: The Death Penalty

Research a current death row case. Take a stance. Write an essay arguing for or against the death penalty based on your research.

EIGHT

Despair

Each semester, Norma took her students to a men's prison. It was a death class requisite. She usually spent the class period before the field trip running down the list of dos and don'ts: no keys, IDs, pens, notebooks, cash, coins, cell phones, ChapStick, belt buckles, or underwire bras. "You can't wear blue, red, orange, or khaki. Don't wear tight clothing. Don't wear anything that says your name on it. You can't have anything in your pockets, not even a piece of gum."

The prison visit would take about four hours. "There may be times when there is a code," she added, "and we'll just have to wait it out. Everybody goes running, and you have to jump against the wall."

Students would see the insides of cells, the gang unit, the psychiatric center, the infirmary, and the administrative segregation section, which was like a jail within the jail. Northern State Prison was the second largest prison in the state, originally built for 1,000 prisoners, now straining to house 2,700 to 3,100. It also held the most notorious gang members in the region. Norma used the trip to launch a discussion on capital punishment, sometimes held with inmates themselves. After being led through the facilities by corrections officers, everyone would gather in the prison law library, where, as Norma explained, "You will be face to face, sitting at the table with murderers."

For the next hour and a half, students would meet arsonists, serial killers, robbers, sexual offenders, kidnappers, and men who had shot, stabbed, strangled, or beaten people to death. There would be no bars between them, no glass partitions, no handcuffs. The inmates would rotate tables so everyone would have a chance to talk.

"You will be able to ask them anything you want about their life, about what they did, about what they think of the death penalty," she said. "You can ask about remorse. Anything."

Norma looked around at the thirty-six students in class, some of whom sat in stunned silence, eyes wide, jaws dropped, some smiling incredulously or dumbfounded. Apparently not everyone had heard about her field trips before signing up for the course.

She heard the under-the-breath mutters: "Oh, my God."

"Now," Norma would reply with a chuckle, clasping her hands together, "anyone wanna drop?"

ISRAEL COULDN'T HELP but feel a mixture of anticipation and foreboding when Norma announced she was taking his class to the prison that winter of 2008. What if he ran into someone he knew from his past life?

Two of his former gang affiliates had been locked up in the years since he'd left—for shooting people in a drug deal gone bad. He believed they were housed at Northern State. And there could be others he'd crossed paths with. How would it look, his old friends, acquaintances, or perhaps even enemies on one side of the bars, Israel the college student on the other?

Still, he could not pass up the opportunity. He had not been able to forgive himself for the wrongs he'd committed in his life, and he didn't even know if he deserved forgiveness in the first place. He didn't know why he'd been given second, third, and fourth chances. Maybe in prison he'd find some answers.

Israel's class met in the lobby of the prison, which sat across from the New Jersey Turnpike and the airport, sharing a long, lonely street with a Holiday Inn and a ditch filled with cattails. The prison opened in 1987, on a landfill. Before that, the site had been used for a petroleum distribution center and a plant that produced formaldehyde. Though built to relieve overcrowding, Northern State had become one of the most congested prisons in New Jersey.

Some of the region's most notorious killers had served time at Northern State, including Robert Zarinsky, sentenced to ninety-eight years for the 1969 murder of a seventeen-year-old girl on her way home from a corner store, where she had gone to pick up a carton of milk. Or Christopher Righetti, a bald, bearded man with a tattoo of the word "animal" on his body, who was serving a life sentence for kidnapping, raping, and stabbing to death a young woman who had gone to buy shoes at the Paramus Park Mall in 1976.

The students lined up and passed through metal detectors as the doors to the yard opened. They walked into a cell block and through another set of bolted doors, and a guard unlocked an electronically controlled sliding door to a cell. Israel took his turn as students were allowed inside two at a time, as the inmates who lived in the space were kept in a separate holding space. At eight by ten feet, each cement cell was about the size of an elevator and had been designed for one person. But the guards explained that the inmates slept two per cell, sharing a stainless steel sink, a metal locker, a toilet, and a bunk bed barely big enough to fit Israel's burly frame into. There were not enough cells to house everyone, so trailer-style bungalows had been installed in a lot across the grounds to sleep 140 men, with 14 men in seven bunks per wing.

In some cells, pieces of cardboard covered the toilet, and rows of Sprite bottles and cartons of lemonade ice tea lined the sink. Inside one cell, an inmate had set up an outdated, yellowing computer monitor and keyboard. It did not receive the Internet, but the prisoner used it as a word processor. Most prisoners received their meals on trays handed through slits in their cells. Many had small televisions, on which men watched *ABC Nightly News*. Among the men's favorite shows: *America's Got Talent*, *Lost*, and *CSI*.

Some inmates woke just before the third shift ended, arriving in the kitchen at 6 A.M. to report for duty, while others worked as electricians or in sanitary jobs. Some prison jobs could go on for twelve-hour stints, for which inmates could earn $1.25, or $4 a day in the kitchen. That was how they paid for goods such as plastic televisions the size of small computer monitors. But when it snowed, guards woke the inmates from their slumbers and told them to shovel, for no pay.

The guards quickly ushered out Israel's class, and they were on to the next stop: the gang unit.

By the late 1990s, state prison officials had hatched a plan to squash the growing power of gangs in lockup across the region. One morning, nearly three hundred incarcerated gang members from a dozen prisons across the state were awoken by guards and carted away in buses and vans to Northern State, where a new two-tier, 160-cell unit had been established for 320 inmates. The inmates placed there had to meet three of eleven criteria proving their gang affiliations, such as tattoos, participation in gang-related crimes, and affiliations with other gang members through, for example, cell phone contact lists or possession of gang paraphernalia.

When Israel walked through the outdoor courtyard of the gang unit, he noticed that there were no basketball hoops, no open areas through which to roam. Instead, the recreation area was filled with clusters of metal cages not much bigger than porta potties. The men housed in the gang unit were not allowed to mingle with members of other gangs. Their outdoor time consisted of being released from their cells into these outdoor cages in rain, snow, or sweltering heat for two hours every other day, while separated from their rivals by the fences. "This is a dog cage within a prison," a guard liked to tell the students. "I got two pit bulls at home, and their dog house in my backyard is as big as that." The unit was known as "PC," for protective custody. But the officers called it Punk City.

The door was unbolted, and into the unit Israel went, glancing up to see inmates staring down from their cells, pressing their noses against glass windows, and peering through slits, like spectators in a gladiator stadium. This, Israel knew, was exactly where he could have ended up had he pulled the trigger that day in the living room. He looked at the prisoners kicking and pounding violently on their cell doors during the class visit, overexcited by the young specimens before them. Some inmates dropped their pants and masturbated in plain view. Handwritten signs posted on the front of each cell spoke to their allegiances: Bloods, Crips, Aryan Nation, Five Percenters, Latin Kings. This could have been his life.

* * *

HIS CLASS CIRCLED back to the law library, through another metal detector, past a corridor with a barbershop, past walls painted with images of the Statue of Liberty and Muhammad Ali. A sign on the wall announced, "Learn to read and you will forever be free," a quote from Frederick Douglass. The library was filled with legal books and ratty paperbacks that looked like leftover titles from someone's garage sale. Paintings of dolphins, hammerhead sharks, pink jellyfish, and schools of fish floated across the rear walls. The students took seats as a dozen inmates strutted and scuttled into the room, standing before the class as if in a criminal investigation lineup. Israel looked them up and down. They were dressed head to toe in khaki jumpsuits.

One freshly shaved man with broad shoulders stood five feet, eleven inches tall. He had pink cheeks, a square jaw, and a helmet of dark, closely cropped hair. He introduced himself as Carl, and he looked approachable, as chummy as a neighborhood postal worker. His chin dipped inward beneath his lower lip in a pout, and a faint dimple emerged in his left cheek when he smiled, along with traces of wrinkles in his forehead. He had red-rimmed ears and brows that arched into accent marks above his hazel eyes when he smiled.

Unlike most of the other inmates, who blamed their fate on unfortunate circumstances and dirty prosecutors, Carl made no excuses for his crime in front of Israel and his classmates. Instead, he gave the students the same explanation that he had once written in an essay: "I beat a man to death in my sister's kitchen in a failed attempt to steal his inheritance. It was brutal, senseless, intense, messy, tragic, and absolutely without justification. It was the most terrible thing I have ever done, by far, and the one thing I can never take back."

One by one, the men sat at one of the nine tables, two prisoners facing three college students. The two COs monitored from the perimeter of the library. The encounter began with uneasy greetings. No handshaking allowed. First names only. The obvious questions hung in the air. Why? How? Some students charged right in. Others didn't know how. Awkwardly, they tried to strike up a casual conversation. "So, what's it like living in here?" or "Do you get conjugal visits?" A prison supervisor strolled between the tables, eavesdropping. Israel sat across from a Mafia hit man and an arsonist.

When the small-group sessions ended, everyone formed a large circle, inmates interspersed with students. Carl told the students to remember that some of the men before them would be paroled one day. "We could be your neighbors." Unlike the inmates, Carl said, the students could contribute to the world with their college degrees and careers. He urged them to support rehabilitation, education, and job training for prisoners.

As the men filed out, Israel watched them nod good-bye to the students before being led back into the trailers and holding cells he'd been standing inside of earlier. The funny thing was, Israel thought, he'd spent so much of his life believing he would die young, probably by a gunshot wound. He had lived his life with a target on his back and a finger close to the trigger. As he'd learned from talking to Norma and the inmates, many men died inside Northern State—of cancer, by hanging themselves with bedsheets, or by setting a mattress ablaze inside a cell. One old inmate had dropped dead in the middle of the prison courtyard under a blue sky as guards and prisoners stood over him. Even now, Israel was not entirely sure why his own life had been spared after all those close calls. But seeing those men, Israel realized that he had dodged not just a gunshot but a life of inescapable despair.

NORMA HAD KNOWN Israel only a few weeks, but she knew enough to have a hunch that he needed to visit the prison. She'd read his essays, even if he had not wanted to share them aloud with the class. Norma had been visiting Northern State Prison with her students for the last five years. The men who spoke to her classes in the law library, like Carl, were part of a speaker's forum handpicked by prison staff. To participate, the inmates had to show a track record of good behavior in prison, but their crimes were no less serious than those of any of the other men serving time in Northern State.

There was Donald Paul Weber, for example, who on December 18,

1977, at age nineteen, had attempted to rape an eighty-year-old neighbor, then he slit her throat, killing her. At Northern State, Weber worked in the kitchen, learning computer skills, culinary arts, and Spanish, going to therapy, and taking part in group counseling and self-awareness programs, including one called "cage your rage," in addition to the speaker's forum. During one of Norma's class field trips in 2007, Weber was one of the inmates who backed up a challenge put to Norma: why not teach a university-level class for the inmates? They did not have much more than vocational education and a GED program, but to learn from a professor with a PhD would be invaluable.

She mulled over the inmates' request. As vicious as their crimes had been, the men at Northern State had given her students an invaluable experience, talking so openly about their lives semester after semester, teaching them about prison, crime, guilt, punishment, life, and death. She thought of her father's life of crime. Some of these men could have been students in the Newark school system back when he was extorting from it for the mafia. This, she thought, could be her way to atone for her father's wrongdoings. The least she could do was volunteer her time for a semester. Norma wrote up a proposal for the prison directors. She would teach one course—public health—that was it.

A dozen men ended up on her roster. She'd met most of them before on the field trips. As with her classes at Kean University, she had a waiting list. She did not ask for what crimes they were serving time. Unless they wanted to tell her, she did not feel the need to know.

Weber recruited other students and showed up for the first couple of classes. Then, to Norma's shock and the rest of the community's, he was let out of prison by the state parole board.

The idea of a man who had murdered a grandmother now suddenly free, and so familiar with her name and face, could have been enough to convince Norma to give up the volunteer teaching experiment and the prison field trips altogether. Paroled or not, some of the men had deeply evil streaks inside them. Some might never have been capable of reform, and who was she to think she could even begin to help them along that road? But even if no one else seemed worth coming back for, Carl did. He'd been locked up since 1990, with a projected parole eligibility date of December 16, 2020, and he was known around Northern State as a poet, a mentor to younger inmates, and a devoted practitioner of Buddhism.

Somehow it seemed to Norma that amid all of this death and drear, he'd actually figured out a way to lead a decent life. Whenever her students met him, they came away feeling touched by him. "He just seems so at peace," one student said in front of the class after returning from the prison. "And here I am still floundering."

Norma decided that if she could be of service in Carl's self-improvement endeavors, even in the slightest way, she would. And Carl appeared to look forward to Norma's classes, pondering the lectures while in his bunk, holding study groups for exams in the library, looking up whatever information he could add to bolster her lessons, and writing thoughtful essays as homework assignments. In one, he told of the time before he'd been locked up when he'd taken a feral kitten home. He raised the animal, and it learned to trust and love him, often purring on his chest. One day Carl had been forced to relocate, so he put the cat, which he'd named Kitty-Kitty, in a pet carrier. But the move terrified her, and once he opened the box, she jumped out and ran away. Carl spent four hours with a flashlight in the woods, looking for her, but never saw her again.

"In the years since then, staring at the different prison ceilings above my head, this cat has helped put my own past into better perspective," Carl wrote. "I mean, this animal ignored every instinct it had and learned to trust me. In the end, the trauma of having her world turned upside down by the very one she so trusted is probably what drove her to hysterics. My own life has many parallels with that."

Not long after Norma read that essay, Carl stumbled across a gray, white, and orange stray calico cat that had wandered onto the prison grounds. It looked beat-up, with wounds and matted fur. Carl helped clean the cat and fed her scraps of kitchen food. He made a bed for her in a kitchen shed. But he worried that the guards would dispose of it if they found it.

The guards did discover the cat. Norma herself had a fondness for these furry creatures, maybe as a reaction to her father, who she remembered once lit a cat's tail on fire. She found out that a guard would be removing the cat at 3 P.M., where it would be taken to a pound. She assembled a "Kitty Rescue Team," sending a student to the prison with a milk crate, who waited to intercept the cat on its journey. The student then transferred the cat to another student, who dropped the cat off with Norm, who took it to their home. Ever since then, around Norm and Norma's house the animal came to be known as "Prison Kitty."

What, she wondered, had happened in Carl's past to lead him to this place? She did not have a hard time believing that the other men she'd met had committed horrendous crimes, no matter how much they denied it. But Carl? He could no longer even harm a cat.

Before she knew it, Norma had pitched an idea to teach a second class in prison: Community Mental Health.

And then a third: Death in Perspective.

She taught her prison classes with a scattering of stackable plastic chairs in a cramped room near the law library. A green banner ran across one wall, with the alphabet: "Aa Bb Cc Dd . . . ," along with a poster of a surfer riding a wave and the word "Courage" and another of the R&B singer Brandy holding the Dr. Seuss book *The Cat in the Hat*. There was an old green school chalkboard, and two shelves held tattered paperbacks and hardcover novels with spines ripped off, with titles such as *Birdsong: A Novel of Love and War*, by Sebastian Faulks, and *Before You Sleep*, by Linn Ullmann.

In her classroom, everyone could speak comfortably because she taught inmates with the door closed—and a guard stationed on the outside. Since the men in this particular death class would not get to go on field trips, she would bring the field trips to them, inviting guest speakers, such as hospice and funeral workers, bringing in autopsy videos, and sneaking in copies of *Tuesdays with Morrie* donated by Kean University students. She would require the men to write their own eulogies and share them aloud.

As the inmates filed into the classroom, they knew Norma's drill and always began scooting their chairs into a circle immediately. There was the tall man with gray dreadlocks and a long, droopy face who had been locked up since 1985 for kidnapping, rape, robbery, armed burglary, and weapons possession. He usually greeted the professor with: *"Hola! Cómo estás?"* There was the wiry man with stringy gray hair who seemed fidgety, his eyes darting around, sitting with his knees and toes pointed inward, smiling like a little boy; he was serving his seventeenth year of a thirty-five-year sentence for rape. And there was a glazed-eyed middle-aged man serving a life sentence; he'd killed his mother and father with a hammer and a walking cane.

She had hoped that by attending Death in Perspective, some of the men would develop some victim reconciliation, some reflection on their own crimes. So far she didn't know if it was working with most of the inmates, but her hunch about Carl had been enough for her to keep trying. He was no sociopath, she believed. Rather, she saw a man trying to hold on to his humanity in a place filled with violence, misery, and death. She felt the same defensiveness for Carl as she did for students like Israel. Carl helped her believe that redemption and forgiveness were possible. If he could do it in prison, she had no doubt Israel could do it on the outside.

Norma had traced Carl's narrative from his class essays, discussions, and one-on-one conversations with him and his mother, a soft-spoken woman reliant on a walking cane, whom the professor chaperoned around one weekend when she came to visit her son as a birthday surprise.

From what the professor came to understand, his mother had raised seven children, Carl her third. He was so close in age to two of his sisters that he'd grown up practically a triplet—his mom had given birth to the three of them within twenty-three months. As a child he'd watched his father beat his mother and shove a gun into her mouth. Once his dad had shoved a loaded gun into Carl's face and threatened to kill him. Carl had run away the next night. Within eight hours, he had been arrested for his first felony: burglary. He was eight.

He broke into schools and stole electronics. He broke into trucks and stole radios. He stole cars for joyrides.

One day his dad took off with the family to Florida. But Carl ran away his third day in the Sunshine State. During one of his truck stop raids, he found a gun under a seat. He used it to rob a radio store and got caught. That time, a judge slapped him with charges for possession and use of a stolen firearm. Carl was twelve.

He was sent to a group home with a dozen other delinquent boys. He arrived on the day Elvis Presley died, August 16, 1977. All the boys crowded around a television with sullen faces as they watched memorials to the singer. A piss yellow bus came each day to pick up the boys and take them to school. But the supervisor was as drunk and abusive as Carl's father, and within a year of his arrival the group home shut down and Carl was sent back home. But he was thirteen now and bulky enough to take on his dad—and anyone else, for that matter.

Carl's dad was working in a plastics factory, running machines that shredded up and recycled old pieces. Once again, Carl went to work with him. One day, his dad, who was hovering right up close to the blades, gave the wrong signal to another worker, who turned on the machine too early. Three of his dad's fingers were nearly severed. His dad drove to the hospital, maneuvering the car with his fingers hanging off at the bone. The doctor patched him up, but he couldn't work for the next year. Before the accident, he'd been a drinker. Now he became an all-out drunk.

One day, Carl's father ordered the kids outside, locking them out of the house and telling them not to try to come in for any reason. When his mother returned, the boys flocked to her, complaining. She wanted to know who had been in the house with Daddy. They said it was Carl's fifteen-year-old sister. The sister confessed: their dad had been raping her. It had been going on for about two years. It turned out that he had raped his nonbiological daughter, Carl's half sister, and molested Carl's younger sister too. His mom called the cops. Carl's dad was sent to prison.

But all of the events had worn Carl down. By fifteen, he had his own criminal charges chasing him through Florida. More robberies.

Carl decided to say good-bye to his mom and siblings. This time, he wouldn't be coming back. He gathered up a small bag of his belongings and hitchhiked his way back to New Jersey.

Ten years later, Carl found himself crumpled on a grimy floor of the Camden County Jail eight days before Christmas.

THE MAN CARL had confessed to killing was a thirty-five-year-old named Stephen with brown hair and a receding hairline, according to police reports. On the day he died, he was wearing dark corduroy trousers, a long-sleeved T-shirt, a green sweater, and orange swim trunks beneath.

A month after the man's disappearance, Carl's sister walked into the police station and fingered her brother and his twenty-two-year-old friend in Stephen's death. Both men confessed in recorded interviews, explaining that they had known Stephen and discovered that he inherited about $12,000 and was keeping the money in the trunk of his 1982 black Chrysler, which he was living out of. They looked for him for a few days, planning to rob him, but they couldn't track him down and soon gave up—until Stephen showed up at Carl's sister's house to watch a football game. Carl showed up later, along with his accomplice. His sister put the children to bed and fell asleep after midnight.

When she was asleep, as the twenty-five-year-old Carl confessed to police in recorded interviews, "I hit him once in, in the side of the head and his head bounced and then he lifted his head again, and I hit him a second time and his head dropped." Carl said he dropped the heavy statue made of wood, which was from Jamaica, after its top broke off. He backed away. But the guy was still breathing. That was when Carl got the vacuum cord. "I tried to strangle him with it, but I couldn't hold the cord, my hands kept slipping."

He still had not stopped breathing. "I took the plastic bag and put it over his head to try and stop the bleeding," Carl told police. Then he fastened the bag with gray duct tape. The men found about $200 in Stephen's pockets. They searched the car trunk and found "magazines, clothes, shopping bags full of junk." They found a drafting kit in a blue case, a tan suede jacket, a thermal sweatshirt, thermal underwear, stacks of flyers, a marijuana pipe, two bottles of cologne, a white plastic hairbrush. But no inheritance.

The men folded Stephen's body into the trunk in a fetal position using duct tape and wiped up the blood on the floor with an orange tablecloth.

After Carl's confession, he led police and a German shepherd named Buffy to the spot where Stephen had been buried. About 1,250 feet into the woods, Buffy began to bark. They spotted the shallow grave, about three feet wide and three feet deep.

Carl had covered Stephen's torso with leaves and dirt but had left his head exposed: according to police reports it was sticking out above ground.

When Norma eventually learned the details, it didn't make her feel "all warm and fuzzy toward Carl," she said. That was for sure.

But she knew the person he was now, not the person he'd been at twenty-five.

In prison, Carl returned to the religious values that his mother had tried to instill in him during his youth. He signed up for mail-order courses from Christian colleges and Bible study classes in prison. He could debate religion and quote scriptures for hours. To prove his restored devotion, he became born again. "I convinced myself that my failure to live a Christian life was the reason why I was in prison, and that only my devotion to the Lord would get me out," Carl once wrote in an essay. "So I went all in for the Lord." But by forty, Carl was beginning to realize that believing in the power of the Lord wasn't going to be enough to change his predicament.

Carl wanted to learn about other religions without being required to commit to a single one. He also realized that of all the spiritual systems, aspects of the Buddhist tradition seemed to make the most sense to him. It was more like a philosophy or a way of life than a religion. So Carl asked his pastor in prison whether he minded if he studied Zen Buddhism. The pastor wasn't enthusiastic about the idea, but he allowed Carl to get in touch with a teacher from a Zen Buddhist school, who agreed to begin conducting classes at the prison.

His spiritual studies had been progressing nicely until one day in 2003, when a guard told Carl, "Get your stuff." The next thing he knew, Carl was shackled and put onto a bus, leaving his comfortable prison community, where he had his own cell with a desk and took classes learning skills such as carpentry and upholstery making. He wasn't informed why he was being transferred or what had prompted the move. He soon realized he was headed upstate, to Northern State Prison.

Upon arrival, guards sent him straight to the medical unit to get a checkup, but during processing Carl looked around and saw the guards take off running. One locked Carl in the medical unit. He watched officers bring in an inmate who looked as though half of his face had been torn off. It turned out that another inmate three floors up had dropped a heavy metal shoe locker onto the guy's head. The guards gave Carl a pillow, blanket, toothbrush, and miniature tube of toothpaste.

It turned out that the prison did not have Buddhism or meditation classes. Within days of showing up, Carl asked if a Buddhist teacher could come in to work with him and other men, but his repeated requests were ignored. He asked if he could talk to a clergyperson about the idea, but again, Carl said, he was refused. Finally he wrote a letter to the Liberation Prison Project, which connected inmates to volunteer Buddhist teachers. He also threatened to file a federal civil rights action lawsuit. That seemed to get the prison officials' attention. The prison notified him that it was accepting applications from volunteers, and within six months it had found a teacher, a well-known spiritual teacher and meditation instructor, Dean Sluyter.

When Dean walked into Northern State Prison in 2005, three men greeted him for the first meeting. "The other two guys weren't quite sure what was going on," Dean later remembered. "But Carl? He was very clear, very precise. Clearly had been reading and practicing." Every Thursday night, Dean would show up at 6 P.M. Prison officials would call out for Buddhist studies, and the men would emerge from different wings, meeting in a chapel for the hour-and-a-half-long sessions. The group soon grew to include eighteen regular attendees. Carl became the cornerstone of the Buddhist community at Northern State. Dean called him "the deacon."

During each session, the men would sit unflinchingly as prison announcements roared out of the overhead speaker above their heads four or five times an hour. They became masters of meditation, Dean explained. "The Buddha said, 'Practice like your hair is on fire.' And those guys practiced like their hair was on fire. They recognize the urgency;

for them this is not some weekend workshop at the yoga retreat. It's survival. This is life or death, sanity or insanity."

Carl kept a forty-five-page yellow booklet, *The Thirty-seven Practices of Bodhisattvas*. He'd placed a yellow Post-it note on page 6, with the lyrics of the Tibetan yogi Milarepa:

Fearing death, I went to the mountains.
Over and over again I meditated on
death's unpredictable coming,
and took the stronghold of
the deathless unchanging nature.
Now I am completely beyond all fear of dying.

Norma knew that Carl had forgiven his father in the years since he'd learned of the sexual abuse of his sisters. Even though he still got upset about it from time to time, he had found it within himself to call his father from prison from prison every once in a while, hold a conversation with him, and even tell him "I love you."

When asked why, he simply replied, "How can I ever expect to be forgiven if I can't forgive?"

It seemed to Norma that Carl was navigating through the stages of Erikson's life cycle, despite his horrible mistakes. The final stage—the eighth one, before death—as Norma taught, came down to reflection. Erikson called this stage "Integrity vs. Despair."

"If you can look back at your entire life and at the end of the day and say, 'You know? My life was good. I'm pleased with how it all turned out . . . and if I could do it all over again, I'd be happy to'—those people have integrity," Norma told her students.

She knew Carl might not, in the end, end up "happy" about how it had all turned out, but he was trying his hardest with the time he had left to put as many good deeds as possible on the ledger.

Based on Norma's own experiences, when the end came, people who have made it through every stage and its difficulties satisfactorily, people who have developed a strong sense of Erikson's *generativity*—meaning beyond themselves—can face their death with less fear and discontent.

She said they can simply let go. If they die a natural death, it usually comes peacefully, without violent resistance or pain, like that of the first patient Norma watched die when she was a nurse in training; she ended up holding the patient's hand as the last life blew out of her body and never forgot how serene it all seemed.

"Wisdom, then, is detached concern with life itself, in the face of death itself," Erikson wrote. ". . . Only such integrity can balance the despair of the knowledge that a limited life is coming to a conscious conclusion, only such wholeness can transcend the petty disgust of feeling finished and passed by, and the despair of facing the period of relative helplessness which marks the end as it marked the beginning."

Those who look back and realize that they are unhappy, unfulfilled, who leave behind a trail of ruined relationships, a broken family, or maybe have never experienced the feeling of real love or never figured out who they really are—their lives could end on a harsher note. When death arrived, Norma told her students, "Oh, my God, they hang on and hang on. They're in pain."

"Those people," she said, "die in despair."

The professor had witnessed many such deaths. Scared people who were simply not ready to let go.

"Despair expresses the feeling that the time is too short, too short for the attempt to start another life and to try out alternate roads to integrity," Erikson wrote. "Such a despair is often hidden behind a show of disgust, a misanthropy, or a chronic contemptuous displeasure with particular institutions and particular people—a disgust and a displeasure which . . . only signify the individual's contempt of himself."

"It's hard to watch," Norma told her students. "They have a lot of unfinished business, and the clock has run out now. There is no way to go back."

The hardest death Norma had ever had to watch had happened two years earlier. It was her mother's.

LINDA HAD BEEN living in California since she'd split from Norma's dad, and by December 2006 she was suffering from lung cancer. Even though Norma had barely spoken to her mother for more than a decade, she ended up flying back and forth to California while juggling her classes at Kean to help Linda through the chemo treatments, as she had done when her grandmother had been treated for lung cancer.

In her final days, Linda could no longer move, swallow, or respond to people around her, and she had been on a ventilator for days, medicated with morphine. Doctors had managed to remove her tumor, but the cancer had devastated Linda's body, and she had developed a MRSA staph infection that was eating her insides. She needed a tracheotomy, but doctors warned she could die on the operating table during the procedure. Linda was 67, and would no longer be able to swallow or eat. Norma was her medical proxy. In her classes, Norma taught her students that a medical proxy was someone named in a person's living will—the document that specified end-of-life care—who would make medical decisions on behalf of an individual in the event that he or she could no longer make them. Norma always handed out copies of living will forms to students. There were checklists about issues like whether the person wanted feeding tubes or resuscitation. Linda had specified in her living will that she did not want to be kept alive with tubes and machines.

Norma's brother, a musician, was overseas on tour with an orchestra at the time. Linda had split from her most recent husband, an older man whom she had met after divorcing Norma's dad for the second time. Now she was running a high fever and the infection was not getting better. Antibiotics had not slowed the infection. Norma had to wear a mask, gown, and gloves around her so as not to contract MRSA. The doctors said they would give her mother two days to turn around, and if she did not get better Norma would have to make a decision whether to have her mother extubated.

Linda had always been a well put together woman, particularly attentive to her hair and makeup. The movie *Must Love Dogs* seemed to be the only distraction keeping up her spirits through the first rounds of chemo. Now that she could not speak, Norma thought her mother would have hated to see herself in such a sorry state. Even if she survived the surgery, she might have to relearn to walk and talk and swallow, but doctors were not hopeful that she would get that far in recovery.

"Okay, you've really got to fight," Norma told her mother. "Give me some kind of sign about what you want, because if nothing gets better they're going to do exactly what you had written down."

Norma went out into a waiting room and began to cry, knowing she would have to make the call to take her mother off the machines—to end her life.

An elderly woman approached Norma. The woman was slight, with curly silver hair, orthopedic shoes, and spectacles. She reminded Norma of Mrs. Claus. Norma figured she was a hospital volunteer. She tried to comfort Norma, who explained to that stranger the tubes, the directive, the decision she faced.

The woman explained that she had recently made a similar decision about her husband. She took Norma's hand and told her to come along to the lobby. People had written the names of loved ones on ornaments and origami cranes. Family members were lining up to hang them on a Christmas tree. The woman helped Norma make one. She hung it on a branch. Her mother's name dangled alongside all the others.

"It's going to be okay, dear," the old woman said to her. She asked for her phone number and continued checking in for the next few days. Norma would not see the woman again after her mother passed away. But she would not forget the comfort she had felt in hearing the gentle tremble of her voice, the kind of comfort she had felt in the presence of only one other person in her life: her grandmother.

"Do you want us to do it tonight?" doctors asked.

"No, not tonight," Norma replied.

She returned to her mother's home that evening, stripping down at the door, tossing all of her clothes into the washing machine with bleach and hot water to disinfect them from any trace of MRSA. She took a long, steaming shower and stayed up most of the night going through old photo albums.

Hospice care has its own version of a life review, as Norma knew. Workers and counselors sometimes conduct it with terminally ill people— like an oral history. Some write down their stories. Some record them on tape. Some use music to stimulate buried memories. Some invite friends and family members to talk about old times.

There were even forms, in some cases, that offered life review guidelines with prompts: Who took care of you as a child, and what were they like? Who was your first love? Who were your closest friends in college? If you were going to live your life over again, what would you do differently? The same? What was the unhappiest period of your life? What did you learn from it? What was the happiest?

Norma knew that her mother was not alert enough to engage in her own life review, so sitting alone in her home that night, she did one for her. She thumbed through photographs of her mother on vacation in Thailand and China with the last man she had married, a man Norma had never known.

When her parents had divorced a second time, Norma had been an adult. As Norma remembered it, her mom had been having an affair with a bridge partner, and when her father had found out, he'd threatened to have the guy killed. Her mother had called her father's place of work and ratted him out, telling his bosses that he had been giving their contracts to the mob. From what Norma understood, the "big boss guy" sat Linda down, gave her money, and said, "We never want to see you or hear from you again. Let this be a warning to you."

Norma could remember her mother crying and saying, "They're going to kill me." That was when she moved to California.

It was the second time Norma's father had come close to getting arrested, and he decided to get out of town and lie low.

The sixteen-year estrangement from her mother had been triggered by a series of serious incidents. One of the first occurred when Norma was at the apartment of her mom's cousin in Brooklyn one Fourth of July. She'd walked out on the balcony and saw her drunken mother dangling her daughter, Melissa, who was a little girl at the time, over a railing on the forty-eighth floor. Norma thought, Wow, this woman can't hurt me now, but if she were to hurt my kid, that would be something I couldn't get over. Not long after, Linda tried to take Melissa out of ballet class, and another day, she tried to sign her out of school, both times unannounced and without permission. That was when

Norma told her, "Don't come near me. Don't try to call." Her mother
did not see Melissa again, and she would never know Becca.

In the final months of her life, Linda had come close to making some
kind of apology to Norma. One day when Norma was driving her to get
chemo, Linda looked at her and said, "I wasn't the best mother."

Norma didn't reply. She just let it hang in the air, knowing that was
probably the closest to an apology she was going to get. After a few seconds of silence, Norma told her mom, "It was a long time ago."

That night of the life review in her mother's California home,
Norma knew her father would have to go on living with his own upsets
and mistakes after her mother's death. She knew that the eighth and
final stage of life was also about "the acceptance of one's one and only
life cycle," Erikson wrote, "and of the people who have become sig-
nificant to it." Despite their feuds, everyone in the family knew that her
parents' love for each other, twisted and violent as it had been, was real.
Norma's father would have to go on living with all that had been unsaid.
The next morning she called her father. "They're going to extubate her
today."

"I want to talk to her," he said.

In the hospital room, Norma held the phone to her mother's ear.
She hoped her father wouldn't start cursing and getting inappropriate,
saying things like "You owe me money," as he had been known to do.

"Linda," she heard her father say, "I've loved you since the first day
I saw you."

Maybe this will be okay, Norma thought, moving the phone closer.

He went on. "You were the love of my life."

Her mother's eyes began to flutter.

"Thank you for two beautiful children," he said. "I'm sorry you're
so sick. I don't want you to leave with any regrets."

Norma thought she could hear her father crying.

"We had so many good times," he continued. "I want you to remember the good times, not the bad."

She let the phone call end as her father said his last good-bye. Then
she told her mother, "They're going to take the tube out. I'm going to
stay with you the whole time."

Norma climbed into the hospital bed with her mother and wrapped her arms around her. She could hear her panting.

"I'm here," she told her. "It's okay."

Norma had brought a portable CD player to the hospital. She slipped in a CD of her brother's classical music. The doctor arrived with nurses. One held her jaw, another pulled the tube out through her mouth; it slid like a long, ribbed milk shake straw out of her trachea and throat.

She could not breathe without the tube. Norma climbed into the hospital bed in her mask and hospital gown. Medical staff turned up the morphine, which stunned Norma. It seemed like too much. But her mother hung on.

Norma cradled her until it was all over. But her mother's last moments had not been as graceful as her grandmother's or as those of the woman from nursing school.

"I can't even imagine what she thought," Norma said while recounting the story. "She did struggle, she was gasping for breath, and I was playing the music, and she looked a little panicked." Norma paused, her eyes red from crying. "It was really hard."

At one point Norma felt as though allowing the doctors to take out the tubes had been the wrong decision, even though Linda's wishes had been specified in the DNR. She considered stopping it all. But it was too late. The clock had run out.

ISRAEL'S TURN TO share his essays with the class arrived yet again. Each time the professor had called on him before, he had declined. But this time he changed his mind. The visits with the inmates had lingered with him. His old friends from his gang, some of whom now lived at Northern State, haunted him. He could tell that too many inmates still didn't take full responsibility for their crimes. But a rare few like Carl seemed to be making steps toward redemption and integrity. Pulling out his good-bye letter, Israel hesitated.

"Dear Jason," he began.

Jason was a teenager Israel had met after he'd landed a job working at a boot camp for troubled boys, like the one he'd graduated from, he explained to the class. Israel had been twenty-four at the time, going on six years of leaving the gang life behind him, trying to find some way to make amends for his past but unsure of exactly how. Jason was still entrenched in a gang and told his new mentor that he wanted out for good. Israel gave Jason his word: he would help him escape the gang life.

When Jason graduated from boot camp, he fibbed to his fellow gang members, telling them that Israel was his probation officer. Every time his friends were about to go out and do something stupid, he would call Israel, who would drive by and call out, "Jason, come here."

"Yo, that's my probation officer," Jason told the gang. "I gotta go."

Israel was no officer, just an older-brother type who took Jason to the gym with him or out for meals, and helped him get a job at UPS. He told him what he'd learned, how getting out of the gang life was like being a recovering drug addict. For the next year, Jason followed his mentor's advice.

But one night, while Israel was seeing a movie in Manhattan, he got a phone call from one of the teens he'd met at the boot camp. He'd always told the youngsters he worked with to reach him on his cell at any time if they needed him. The teenager told Israel that something had happened to Jason. He'd been walking down the street when two guys had approached him from behind. They'd shot him twice. He hadn't survived.

Jason's killers, Israel would later learn, had been members of his own gang.

Israel blamed himself. He had tried pulling Jason out of the gang too fast. He'd kept on pulling and pulling, thinking he knew what was right, thinking Jason could get out without paying a price. He had let his street senses slip—and look what had happened.

"You always get one you get attached to," Israel said. "He was my kid."

Almost a year had passed since Jason died when Israel shared his story with the class. The two suspects had been arrested and were facing trial. But they were still alive and probably also housed at Northern State Prison.

Norma listened. The others did too. Israel admitted that he'd held a gun to another young man's head. That was why he'd felt so strongly about helping Jason and so tormented that he had failed him.

ONE WEEKEND, BEFORE his semester in the death class ended, Israel went to Burlington Coat Factory, and, after riding down an escalator, he came face to face with someone he recognized from ten years earlier: it was the guy he'd nearly killed. He'd come back from Puerto Rico and was a grown man now. Their eyes met. Israel remembered those dark eyes, the way they had watered, the terror they had held. He remembered the mother's screams.

The two men stood in the department store, staring at each other. Israel noticed he had a baby stroller and a woman by his side. His thoughts raced. You got a family now? It looked as if his old enemy had moved on with his life. Settled down. Israel wondered if the guy had heard that he'd left his old life behind too. After all, they'd crossed paths at Burlington Coat Factory, not on some street corner. Now here they were, two men who'd both received a second chance at life.

Israel wanted to apologize. But how could he start? I'm sorry I beat your dad and you down with a gun and put a gun to your head with your mom on the floor.

No words came out. None was needed.

Instead, both men stood there for what felt like several minutes in silence. Then both turned and walked away.

CLASS FIELD TRIP: McCracken Funeral Home
TAKE-HOME WRITING ASSIGNMENT: Funeral Homes
After speaking to funeral home directors and embalmers, write a reaction paper about your visit.

NINE

Brothers

November 2008

After the hospital released his brother, Jonathan had no time to worry about his breakup with Caitlin. He didn't know how often she had been turning to Norma at all hours in tears, coping with her mother's suicide attempts. Jonathan was too busy making sure Josh took his daily pill. His brother seemed to be getting better; he was brushing his teeth again and taking showers. Jonathan figured they needed a break from New Jersey. Josh had seemed sane enough lately, so Jonathan booked them a flight to Uruguay to see their grandmother. It would be good for Josh to hang out on the beach and relax as they'd used to when they were kids.

The white sand, the clear water, and Grandma's cooking seemed to do the trick at first. Josh seemed happy in Uruguay, almost his old self again. He even put on deodorant and a nice outfit and told Jonathan, "I want to go out."

"Okay," Jonathan replied. They spent the night out at the bars and dance clubs, like two college-age guys with no worries in the world.

But by the time they had been in Uruguay for nearly a month, with their trip almost over, Josh began complaining that he wasn't feeling well.

One morning, Jonathan gave Josh his pill. But he could tell his brother had hidden it in his cheek, then gone to the bathroom and flushed it. Jonathan confronted him.

"You don't understand how the medicine makes me feel," Josh told him. "I'm having suicidal thoughts. I'm having thoughts of killing you when we're sitting at the dinner table and I have a knife in my hand. I feel like stabbing you."

"Okay," Jonathan said calmly. "Well, you didn't stab me. Maybe if you were not on the medication you would have stabbed me. Let's worry about it when we get back. We'll set up an emergency appointment with the psychiatrist."

ONCE, WHEN JONATHAN was fifteen, he was running along a beach in Uruguay when he noticed a pack of six dolphins swimming and playing together. Jonathan ran alongside them for a while and then glided straight into the water, where he swam next to the dolphins as if he were a part of their family. They were enormous, and he was so close to them, he even touched their skin. Jonathan was exhilarated and thrilled but not the least bit scared.

When Jonathan was a little boy, watching his father stab his mother as his brothers slept, he didn't feel fear—confusion and anger, maybe, but not fear. Even when the car crashed into the bridge and they hauled his dad off to jail, he was not afraid. Jonathan just figured out what needed to be done next, and did it.

He had never felt real fear—until now.

He knew Josh was capable of killing him. He had even come to expect that his brother would do it eventually. It was just a matter of when. Jonathan decided to draft his will.

In their grandmother's house, the rooms were dark. Jonathan's bedroom door was open, and he could hear Josh pacing up and down the hall, over and over, all night long. Did he have a knife?

Jonathan did not sleep.

TEN DAYS AFTER returning from Uruguay, Jonathan found himself buckled over on his knees in the shower. His arms and chest were covered in psoriasis. When he had it checked out, a doctor told him it was from stress.

Jonathan couldn't talk about it with anyone else, but he felt he was failing both himself and his brother. He'd lost Caitlin, the only girl who really seemed to understand him. He was exhausted and deeply in debt from paying Josh's medical bills and living expenses. The flexibility of his job had helped provide time to care for his brother at first, but lately work at the real estate firm was going to hell, and there just didn't seem to be any way out of the mess.

He knew Josh would never be 100 percent better, but even if he improved just 50 percent, he might have a shot at living a good life. Maybe he could go to community college, finish school, and get a part-time job, or they could move back to Uruguay for good and Jonathan would support him.

Some nights, Jonathan stayed up late after working all day to listen to Josh play the guitar or sing and play along with him. But his brother would get mad. "You're copying me," Josh told him. "You're acting like me. You're doing that on purpose to try to control me. You never wanted to play the guitar before, you never even liked the guitar."

Jonathan was trying to *help* him. He'd thought singing together would be *good* for him. Jonathan started doubting himself. How am I going to help him if all of the things I thought I was doing right are wrong? How am I going to do this?

A social worker came to visit shortly after they returned from Uruguay. She told Jonathan to face facts. "You can't spend all the time you spend with him, you're hurting your life. You can't do this forever."

After Josh's diagnosis, Jonathan had written him a letter. He figured maybe written words would sink in better than a face-to-face conversation, since there was no telling what Josh was hearing these days:

> Josh I love you so much and I don't give a fuck what I have to do to help you but I will even if it's against your will. I want you to talk to me and tell me what you think about everything and what you think about yourself and what's been going on lately in your head and in your life. . . . You're the smartest kid I know and after everything that has happened to us this is the last thing you need. But at the same time it will bring us together if you let it. I want to be there for you but I can't do this shit alone I need you to trust me.

He went on:

> I'm not against you, I'm on your side I'll always be on your side. No matter what Josh, like I told you in the car that day that you came back from Washington. I wish it was me that was going through it instead of you. . . . The most important thing you need to know about me is that I feel alone. I always feel alone, even when I'm around a lot of people. I've felt like that since what happened with Daddy and Mommy and the only time I don't feel alone is when I'm with you, or with Chris or Caitlin. I can't lose you Josh and you can't lose me, no matter what.

Jonathan had never been a religious person. But in the shower that day, he began to pray. "Please let Josh be strong," he said, crying. "Please make things better for him."

The next day, Jonathan and Josh waited in the psychiatrist's lobby. They were called in together. The man turned to Josh and said, "So you're having suicidal thoughts?"

Josh said yes, and he was hoping the doctor could lower his medication.

"What kind of thoughts are you having?" the doctor asked.

"I would jump in front of a train or a bus or shoot myself."

"So what's stopping you?"

"I'm scared of what happens after death," Josh replied.

The doctor nodded, scribbled some notes and agreed to change his medication, and said, "I'll see you in one month."

The appointment had lasted ten minutes.

The brothers walked out glumly. The doctor wasn't much help at all, Jonathan thought. He could tell Josh was disappointed too.

"Are you hungry?" Jonathan asked his brother, trying to cheer both of them up. They could eat lunch at the sub shop, and maybe they could go out to dinner later that night at the pizzeria with their older brother, Chris, and his girlfriend.

"Sure."

At lunch, Josh seemed like he felt a little better. The psychiatrist had altered Josh's meds and added an antidepressant. Josh said he would try it, and the two went to the pharmacy together.

Jonathan dropped Josh off at home while he went to run more errands. He told Josh he'd be back in an hour or so.

On the way home, he gave Josh a call to check up.

Jonathan listened to the phone ring. No answer. That was nothing new. Josh always lost his phone or forgot to charge his battery.

By the time Jonathan made it back to the apartment, Josh was not home. He left a note on the stairs: "Josh, I'm trying to call you, you're not picking up your phone."

Jonathan called Chris. Had he heard from Josh? Chris said he had not, but he'd go back to the apartment and wait in case Josh showed up.

Jonathan drove around the neighborhood. Maybe Josh took a walk.

A few minutes later, Chris called. He was crying. He had gone into Josh's room and found a letter tucked into the strings of his guitar, with the light of a lamp pointed to shine directly on it. It was a will.

Jonathan's mind flashed to the doctor's question earlier that day:

What kind of thoughts are you having?

I would jump in front of a train . . .

There were tracks by the apartment. Jonathan sped toward Linden station.

THE CLOSER JONATHAN got, the more ambulances and police cars he saw. He stopped his truck and jumped out, asking people what was going on.

Police officers were trying to get a crackhead off the bus, someone replied.

Thank God, Jonathan thought. It wasn't Josh. But he still needed to find him.

"I have an emergency. I'm looking for a twenty-two-year-old kid. He has brown hair," he said when he approached an officer. "It's my brother. He wrote a will. He's going to kill himself." He had to get to the train tracks to stop his brother.

The officer wouldn't let him through. "Stand over there," he told him.

Desperate, he ignored the command and started to run toward the tracks, but another cop grabbed him. "I have to tell you something," the officer said.

"You don't understand," Jonathan replied. "I have an emergency."

The officer paused.

Jonathan looked at him. He could read his face. "My brother's dead, isn't he?"

"He killed himself an hour ago."

Witnesses had described a young man smoking a cigarette near a platform. A New York–bound train had stopped at the station. As it had pulled out, Josh had laid his head down on the tracks. The train driver had not had a chance to stop. Josh had been decapitated on impact at 5:47 P.M.

Chris appeared at the train station and saw Jonathan's tear-streaked face. They fell into each other's arms. He had Josh's suicide note: "We spend our entire lives fearing death but know this . . . that from this day to the end of time I will have conquered pain, sorrow, and love. I hope the human race also conquers Death. Good bye my friends I love you forever."

He'd left his guitar to Jonathan. Into the side of the instrument, he'd etched these words: "Jon brother I love you."

CAITLIN'S PHONE RANG that evening. She looked at the caller ID: it was Chris's girlfriend. Caitlin got goose bumps; she knew something was wrong.

"Hello?"

"Caitlin?" she was crying. Caitlin panicked. Had Josh killed Jonathan? "What is it? What's wrong?"

"Josh killed himself."

"Oh, my God!" Caitlin screamed. "Where's Jon? Where's Jon?" She had not spoken to him in weeks. She called Norma, hysterical. She couldn't even speak coherently, she was just sobbing and stuttering.

"Caitlin! Caitlin!" Norma screamed. "Stop!"

Caitlin stopped.

Norma told her to take a few breaths; she couldn't understand a word she was saying.

"Josh is dead."

"What?" Norma screamed, nearly dropping the phone. She told her to meet her at their usual spot, Applebee's. She put on a pair of ripped boots, threw a coat over her flannel nightgown, and bolted out the door.

The Applebee's waiter took one look at Norma's nightgown and Caitlin's swollen face and seemed to realize they needed some alone time.

Caitlin had to try to calm down, the professor told her. She was shaking and rambling. She was going to have a panic attack.

But Caitlin didn't know what to do. In her heart she just wanted to make sure Jonathan was okay. How was he going to handle this? She wanted to hold him and shut out the rest of the world. Where was he? Who was he with? Who was there for him?

Caitlin pulled out her phone and started calling everyone Jonathan knew. She found out that Jonathan was with a friend and they were on the way back to the friend's mother's house. The mother told her, "Just come here, Caitlin."

"I don't know," Caitlin replied. "I don't know if he wants that."

"Men never know what they want," she replied.

Caitlin turned to Norma. Should she go?

Yes, Norma told her. Go and be there for him.

When Jonathan walked through the door of his friend's home later that night, Caitlin was waiting. Jonathan was carrying half of a sandwich wrap. His friend had taken him out and tried to get him to eat something, and Jonathan had brought back half the wrap, as he usually did when he went out to eat, to share with his little brother. But he'd forgotten. He didn't have a little brother anymore.

Jonathan took one look at Caitlin, too exhausted to express surprise at her presence. Instead, he held out the sandwich and asked sheepishly, "Do you want this?"

He didn't need to say anything more.

Caitlin went with Jonathan back to the apartment where Josh had left his guitar. When they walked in, she saw Jonathan's note still on the steps. The lamp in Josh's bedroom was still on. Caitlin switched it off.

They fell asleep together that night side by side. It had been three months since they had been this close to each other.

Caitlin made sure there was space on the bed in between them, so that he didn't feel like she was trying to force her way back into his life. She just wanted to be near in case he had trouble falling asleep or awoke from a nightmare. She listened to his breath slow and thought about Josh and all that had happened today.

Caitlin had barely dozed off when she felt Jonathan reaching for her. He pulled her into his arms, nuzzled her close to his chest, and hugged her tight.

TWO DAYS LATER, Caitlin's mother overdosed again. It had not even been a full month since the last episode. This time Caitlin received a call from her father while she was on campus. Her mother was still conscious and lucid, and her father had said to her, "Caitlin's on her way home. She's not going to let you get away with this."

Caitlin raced home, but this time she wasn't scared. She was furious. How could her mother pull a stunt like this now? She knew that Jonathan's brother had just killed himself.

Caitlin's parents adored Jonathan, and they had met Josh. He'd been to her parents' house at least three times, and they'd met at her graduation party. She got on the phone with her mother's psychiatrist. Why had he prescribed her more pills when he knew she had a drug problem?

"She's your patient," Caitlin said. "You need to do something."

The doctor told Caitlin to bring her mother to his office. Just as when they had been children, her dad refused to call an ambulance. He didn't want other emergency personnel to find out their family secret.

When Caitlin got home, she tried to drag her mother into the car. But she kept squirming and fighting her off. Caitlin began to cry. "How the hell could you do this right now?" she demanded. "Josh actually did kill himself!"

Caitlin collapsed in her room and began to sob. It was too much, it was all just too much.

Finally, Caitlin and her sisters persuaded her mom to let them take her to the psychiatrist's office and then to the emergency room to get the drugs flushed out of her system. Caitlin was on her way to the hospital with her sisters when Jonathan called. He wanted to know if she could help him put together a slide show of photos of Josh for the funeral. Caitlin turned to her sisters.

"Go with Jon," one told her. "He needs you more."

It was true. Caitlin knew she could not keep giving up everything for her mother. She told him she was on her way.

THE SERVICES FOR Josh were scheduled to be held at McCracken Funeral Home on Morris Avenue, down the road from Kean University, where Norma took her students each semester on field trips. It was a pristine white building with a plush green lawn made of the kind of grass that you find on a golf course, since its founder, Bill McCracken, had been an avid golfer. In the spring, the grounds were covered with several thousand red and yellow tulips, purple hyacinths, and yellow daffodils, such a beautiful sight that high school students often took their prom photos in front of the funeral home garden.

The directors had always been kind and accommodating to Norma, allowing students to glimpse a wake or funeral if it happened to be in progress on their visit. During one field trip, the body of a forty-four-year-old father who had died suddenly at his job was laid out. The director said the man's wife and twelve-year-old daughter had been staying with the body for hours at a time and had nearly spent the night there because the girl did not believe her father was dead.

On each field trip, the directors let Norma's students browse through the selection of urns and caskets in the basement. As an assignment, Norma made each student select the style in which he or she wished to be buried or cremated. There were silver and rose, stainless steel and metal caskets, cherry or maple wood. There were personally engraved nameplates, cream or pink satin beddings and pillows, and ornaments such as baseballs, flags, crosses, and even golf clubs. For urns, there were black enamel, cast bronze, butterfly designs, and nickel-plated brass with silver doves. Norma often pointed out that she had chosen the dove urn for her mother's ashes.

Once a mortician took the class into the embalming room, which had no dead bodies laid out, and talked everyone through the step-by-step preservation process, for which he always wore an apron and gloves but no mask. Standing near a tray of facial powders, shampoos, and lipsticks, he described his routine of setting the features, closing the eyes by placing caps under the eyelids, and keeping the mouth closed so it didn't hang open. Sometimes he used a suture string on the mouth. "A needle is passed under the gum and out the nose, under the lip, and around the bottom inside the mouth. That's one way of doing it." The other way was with an injector gun, he said, which drove the needle, attached to a piece of wire, into the lower and upper jaws. "It's like a barb on the end, so it goes into the bone, six snaps from bottom to top, it's tied shut."

He went through the embalming chemicals and aspiration process, adding that when those parts were done "I thoroughly cleanse the body, wash the hair, wash the body entirely down, dry it off. . . . I have a lot of respect for the person that lies on this table. . . . I always cover the person's genitalia during the embalming process. This is a very sacred thing that happens here."

The funeral directors at McCracken once arranged a complimentary service for the child of one of Norma's students; her baby had died at birth. The directors had even helped Norma coordinate a service for her own mother two years prior.

After Josh's death, Norma had told them she needed their help again. Jonathan had spent the last of his money paying Josh's medical bills and apartment costs and trying to feed and clothe him. He had nothing left in his bank account. But he wanted an open-casket funeral for Josh; he wanted his head to be sewn back on, so he could say goodbye to his brother and remember him the way he'd looked before. Could McCracken help?

The directors agreed to do the favor. They would give Jonathan's brother the service he deserved for as little cost as possible and do their best to make Josh look presentable.

It came to $1,200, and Jonathan's remaining family members split the cost. Josh would be cremated.

In his suicide note, Josh had asked for his ashes to be scattered with his father's. But the boys had never managed to recover their father's ashes from the New Jersey prison system. Jonathan told himself he would save Josh's ashes for the day they could.

ON THE DAY of the wake, Jonathan went into the room where Josh's body lay in his casket. No one else had arrived yet. It was the first time he had seen his brother since he'd died. The embalmers had reattached Josh's head and artfully covered the marks on his neck with makeup. Jonathan had bought his brother a brown turtleneck that Caitlin had helped him pick out at Macy's and found a pair of pants that Josh had borrowed from him before—that was how he knew they would fit— along with a pair of Jonathan's black Aldo dress shoes. His shaggy hair had been trimmed and gelled, and he had a goatee.

Jonathan stared at Josh. He looked sad, Jonathan thought, but he looked pretty good for being dead. He touched his skin. It felt cold.

"I love you," he said. "I promise you will be remembered. Something good will come out of this."

Then he said, "If you hear me, show me you are okay."

He sat down and suddenly felt two distinct chills course through his body. Goose bumps broke out all over his flesh.

Jonathan smiled. Okay, he's all right, he thought. He's just fine.

Something good *would* come of this. But Jonathan had no idea how he was going to begin to keep that promise.

PART

II

Life Lessons

Jonathan Steingraber

Josh Steingraber's Funeral

Good-bye Letter Read at McCracken Funeral Home

I can't explain to you in any way how much Josh was suffering because Josh couldn't even explain it himself.

So, instead of trying to explain to everyone how sick he was . . . I've decided to share with you the Josh I will always remember . . . we had our best times in the past three and a half months. We would drive in the car singing at the top of our lungs shutting out the world and all of our problems. He was a great guitar player and . . . he kept trying [to teach me]. . . . He was a deep thinker and behind all his madness and stubbornness he was trying to save the world.

TEN

Reclamations

January 2009

The Tower, the independent student newspaper, welcomed students back from a three-week winter break with this editorial:

> We have just entered our spring semester in the midst of an economic recession, rising prices, impending budget cuts, and the growing realization that jobs and money are scarce. Whether you are a freshman or a senior, you are affected by this economic crisis and many watched the swearing in of Barack Obama as a sign of hope for the future—our future. Seniors who are graduating this semester are realizing that they are walking out of Kean and into a job market that is in trouble. They are competing with experienced older workers who cannot afford to retire and are looking for work too because many have lost their jobs.

Talk of furloughs, layoffs, and 10 to 20 percent tuition hikes had many in the campus community worried. Some of Norma's students worked two or even three jobs while taking full course loads. Her classes included PE teachers, bartenders, hairdressers, UPS workers, prison guards, bank tellers, day care staff, beer and hot dog vendors, insurance agents, accountants, and even exotic dancers. She taught single parents, middle-aged divorcees, and late starters who hadn't had jobs or enough money in their twenties to pay for college, so they'd decided to give it a go a decade or two later. Many were barely scraping by.

Some talked of parents whose homes had been foreclosed upon. Others had been laid off from their jobs.

In the first Death in Perspective class that semester, Norma went around the room to mark names off the roster and asked each of the students why they had enrolled in the class. Some students glossed over the question. Others proved again why the death class attracted a certain brand of student: they needed to process a personal experience with death.

A skinny, pointy-eared guy in a brown beret took his turn. "Uh, I lost a few friends, so you know, I have trouble talking about that."

"You lost a few friends?" Norma asked.

"On my twenty-fifth birthday, I found my friend dead. We were drinking the night before, and he was dead. And that was rough." He paused and swallowed. "You can see I'm choked up already." The room fell silent, tense. He cracked a joke. "I'm also here because I owe lots of money, so I've got to get a degree to get a better job."

As the months trudged on, the mood on campus darkened along with the early evenings, shifting away from those upbeat first days back to school around President Obama's inauguration, when he had stood in his patterned red tie, his right hand raised, and been sworn into office. Clusters of students had crowded around to watch in Kean University's auditoriums and lounges, clasping their hands together in prayer, raising their fingers high in peace signs and waving them from side to side like lighters, or pumping both fists in the air.

"In the year of America's birth, in the coldest of months, a small band of patriots huddled by dying campfires on the shores of an icy river," the president said in his speech that day. "The capital was abandoned. The enemy was advancing. The snow was stained with blood. At the moment when the outcome of our revolution was most in doubt, the father of our nation ordered these words to be read to the people: 'Let it be told to the future world . . . that in the depth of winter, when nothing but hope and virtue could survive . . . that the city and the country, alarmed at one common danger, came forth to meet it.'"

By March, some students had reached the breaking point, trying to juggle midterms, jobs, bills, and stressful home lives. Some gave up on classes altogether. The temperature plummeted; it was too cold for anyone to stay outside long. The bare branches of the trees outside Norma's classroom windows looked like bony fingers pressed against the sky. Her students needed something to inspire them in the depth of that icy New Jersey winter, when salt crystals had turned the granular snow on campus sidewalks a strange shade of blue.

ONE AFTERNOON, NORMA attended a conference on prison issues, where she met a preacher who ran nondenominational services for homeless and drug-addicted people in Newark; he introduced her to someone working with abused women, who told her about a homeless shelter just eight miles from the Kean campus that housed all teenage girls. Norma couldn't believe she'd worked so close to it for the last decade and had had no idea it was there.

Norma got ahold of the address and hopped into her party bus to pay the girls a visit. She turned down the street and spotted the two fenced-off homes on a mostly dirt-lawn block in East Orange, in a neighborhood where it seemed that every fourth front porch revealed windows and doors boarded up with plywood.

Red-lettered signs hung on telephone poles down the street with the words AVOID FORECLOSURE. A corner bodega sat shuttered at midday. Empty lots had been taken over by weeds and were littered with wrappers, crumpled cans, and loose flyers. Men slept on street corners nearby, and graffiti scrawled on one wall read: "RIP."

The professor would later learn that murder and aggravated assault rates in the neighborhood were four times the national average, and most of the young residents inside the two structures that made up this homeless shelter, known as Isaiah House, had been abused and thrown away. Some had parents who had died of AIDS. Two of the girls were pregnant.

These particular houses were identical and side by side, three stories high, eggshell-colored with brown trimming and pointy roofs. Walkways connected them to each other. Burly trees shielded them like windbreaks, as if insulating the nine teenage girls who lived inside from whatever threats might be whirling through the blocks beyond.

The professor climbed the paint-chipped steps of the house, approached the front door, and knocked.

THE RESIDENTS OF Isaiah House didn't really know what to make of the cheery woman with the high-pitched voice who showed up at their door unannounced one afternoon, suggesting that maybe she could be of assistance. She told them she'd decided to drop by and introduce herself, that she was some kind of doctor or something. "Dr. Bowe."

The girls had grown accustomed to a revolving door of do-gooders dropping off used clothes or recycled gifts at their doorsteps. Sometimes the bags sat in piles for weeks, unopened.

"You know how people come and donate stuff?" a seventeen-year-old resident, Nicole, asked one day. Nicole was the sixth of nine siblings born to a mother who was a heroin and crack addict, and she had been in and out of the foster care system since fifth grade. "People come in and out of your life, you see them every once in a while, but Dr. Bowe just really, really stayed."

Norma kept coming back, sometimes just to hang out or talk. She brought nurses to give them checkups and students to tutor them.

During one of those early visits to the Isaiah House, the professor asked each girl if she could redecorate her room, what would it look like? The walls were now mostly bare, drab yellow and gray, with peeling paint. Some rooms had no rugs on the wood floors. Some windows had bars and no curtains. Living here was certainly better than living on the street, the girls said. Counselors and staff cared for them well. But the decor was pretty plain.

One girl said she wanted a giant black rose on her wall. Another requested bright pink walls, and a third said purple. One preferred one pink wall, one green.

Norma rallied some of the same Be the Change students from the previous semester who had redecorated the hospice facility. The group had been attracting fraternities and sororities across campus wanting to get involved in service projects too. She recruited her Death in Perspective classes, her mental health classes, and her students from past semesters.

With Norma in the party bus leading the caravan, Be the Change went to Isaiah House one weekend in late March in droves—more than a hundred students in all—and unloaded a dozen truckloads of sofas, shelves, desks, and hundreds of buckets of paint donated by Home Depot and Sears. Courtyard by Marriott donated hotel rooms for the girls to stay in while the students set to work.

All weekend, paint-splattered students worked away as hip-hop and reggaeton music blasted from a stereo. Jonathan, three months after Josh's funeral, pitched in to help deliver donated furniture. Norma had been trying to convince Jonathan to visit her death class and share his experiences with his mother's, father's, and brother's deaths with them when he was ready. He wasn't yet.

Meanwhile, one tireless young man seemed to have thrown himself into the home makeover project with particular ferocity. He stayed from the early hours of the morning into the night, lifting, hauling, scraping, painting, polishing, and cleaning. He'd driven to faraway donors' homes to pick up sofas, dining tables, and televisions and returned to unload everything from the truck into the Isaiah House. He'd single-handedly ripped out old carpets and hoisted bookshelves over his head.

It was Israel.

He had learned a few lessons since his induction into the death class, such as how much he still had inside of him to give back to a society to which he used to believe he didn't owe a thing. And lately, if his professor needed anything—anything at all—Israel was one of the first to drop what he was doing to step in and help, like the day a young woman from Isaiah House had become a student at Kean University. With no parents or friends around, she needed someone to accompany her through her orientation on the first day. Norma, who was scheduled to be in class, called Israel.

He took off work to show the freshman around, stand by her side as a friendly face, as if letting her know without having to say it: I know it's scary, and it might feel like you don't fit in here. I used to feel that way too.

The girls from Isaiah House were greeted after the spring makeover with a chalkboard on a wall and the words WELCOME HOME. Some burst into tears upon returning to their bedrooms. The walls now gleamed with shades of yellow, pink, green, purple, and orange and images of flowers, butterflies, and clouds. They walked through a spruced-up, brightly painted telephone center, office area, and dining and recreation rooms. The handprints of the volunteers decorated an olive-colored wall—splotchy turquoise, red, and lavender silhouettes of fingers and palms.

Israel walked over to the wall and pressed his palm and fingers against one of the dried handprints. He nodded in Norma's direction and grinned.

March 2009

ISAIAH HOUSE FILLED Norma with a different kind of satisfaction from prison, an unpolluted optimism. Each time she went to the newly beautified shelter in East Orange, Norma met another girl who she believed, with the right dose of attention, could climb her way out of homelessness and into college.

The professor decided it would be her goal to get as many girls from the Isaiah House as possible enrolled as students at Kean University, where she and her Be the Change students could mentor them, and New Jersey would cover tuition since they were wards of the state.

One afternoon a week after the makeover, Norma returned to the Isaiah House with her younger daughter, Becca, a free spirit who resembled her mother, with her long cinnamon hair in loose natural curls, thick eyebrows, and feet that nudged outward when she walked. At sixteen, with two PhD parents who specialized in mental health, Becca seemed to have no doubts about her identity. "Don't shrink me!" she would say whenever her child psychologist father tried to psychoanalyze her.

Becca was a vegetarian and creative soul who collected sound tracks to musicals and had been cast as an actress in theater shows such as *You're a Good Man, Charlie Brown*; *Carousel*; and *Pippin*. Her parents paid for her to attend a high school in Chester County, Pennsylvania, called Upattinas, which encouraged free thinking and "communication over rules." Each summer, Becca attended camps, such as the Wayfinder Experience, which offered adventure games and improvisational theater. But her sense of self-assurance and adventure had been apparent even in childhood, when, at age twelve, she had felt emboldened enough to hop on the train all by herself to get from New Jersey to her acting classes on Eighth Avenue and Forty-third Street in Manhattan.

When Becca was thirteen and her sister, Melissa, was twenty-one, Norma took both daughters to India for three weeks, where she was speaking at a women's conference. Almost immediately, Norma recalled, Melissa yearned to head home, but Becca seemed perfectly at ease. She learned to be a good ambassador in all the out-of-the-way places her mother sought out in New Jersey.

Now, three years later, Becca had helped with the homeless shelter makeover too, and this time during their visit, she noticed a familiar face. The girl looked about Becca's age but was at least six inches taller than she was and slender like a runner, with skin like polished obsidian.

Becca stared at the girl, who wore a barely visible silver stud in her nose. She had not met this resident during the makeover. The girl must have just moved in.

The girl looked at Becca too, as if she'd felt her eyes. She gave a curious look back, like, How do I know you?

"I'm Becca," she said in a scratchy voice.

"Isis," the girl replied. Her voice was low and quick, as if she were spitting out her syllables.

They were the same age. Sixteen.

Isis had just moved in, the Monday after the makeover. She'd missed the Be the Change volunteers with their paint buckets and sorority letters but had been assigned the room with pink-and-white sponge-painted walls. It looked nice and all, but the truth was, she hated it. She hated the fact that she was back living in a homeless shelter again.

"Where are you from?" Becca asked.

Isis said she'd moved around a lot. She'd gone to thirteen different schools.

But she didn't tell Becca all of the sordid backstory, such as how she'd once lived in a motel across the street from a truck stop. The motel had been filled with cockroaches, prostitutes, and drug addicts and smelled so rancid that her mother had made her steal air fresheners from restaurant bathrooms. Her mom had also stolen candy, makeup, and meals. They'd cooked food from cans on a hot plate in the hotel room. Isis spent as much free time as she could at a Starbucks where her aunt worked. When Starbucks threw out food, her aunt gave her the discards.

"Did you ever live in Highland Park?" Becca asked.

"Yeah, when I was young," Isis replied. Before everything took a turn for the worse. "Do you remember the school with the purple dragon?" she asked Becca. That was the mascot. "I used to go there."

"Me too!" said Becca.

It clicked for them both: they had not just been classmates, Isis used to come over to play at Norma's house. Isis and Becca had been childhood friends. What Isis remembered most about being a child around Norma and Becca was how perfect their lives seemed, how happy, living in that two-story house with a big yard, and Becca having both of her parents and an older sister to look up to. To Isis, they were the kind of family she saw in the movies or on television. She remembered thinking, Why is my life not like that?

Living in the apartment down the block from Norma's house in Highland Park had been the best time of Isis's life, even though she sensed that something about her childhood wasn't quite right.

As a child, Isis liked being at home in Highland Park, in their second-floor apartment, across the hall from an African lady who used to let her try on her wigs. Isis's mom decorated the apartment with a long white couch and stemmed lights. She kept the place real nice, paid for, Isis later learned, with drug money. Isis had never met her real father, but she remembered another man, a towering truck driver of at least 250 pounds, who would come and go. On bad days, he beat up her mom, but he never laid a hand on Isis or her two siblings. Isis would remember that when she was around five she tried to fend him off her mom by hitting him with a bat.

Her mom sold drugs. She used drugs too—ecstasy, weed, crack, cocaine, heroin, and prescription pills. Isis even recalled being given a marijuana joint. Isis was four and sitting in the bathtub, and she remembered that her mom put it in her mouth and told her to smoke. "I had asthma, and she was sitting on the toilet, laughing," Isis said. She would get contact highs off her mother's smoke. "The hot box," she said, "that's what you call it, in the car, when you breathe in marijuana."

Isis prayed a lot back then. "Thank you, God, for waking me up today," she would say. She recited the Lord's Prayer daily.

But as she got older her conversations with God changed. "I used to pray for me just to either disappear off the face of the earth," she said, "or for my mom to find another kid and replace me. Or to just take me, to not have a life anymore."

At four, Isis was diagnosed with a rare cancer of the kidney known as Wilms' tumor. About one in 200,000 children get the disease, usually around the same age. She remembers the CT scans and MRIs and drinking the "nasty" hospital orange juice. For her, happiness came on days when she was not hospitalized.

Surgeons removed one of her kidneys and her appendix, leaving her with a scar starting at the dip below her neck, circling all the way around her chest, down to her pelvis, and running perpendicularly up her stomach and chest—in the shape, as she described it, of a Mercedes logo. She hated it and never stopped wearing high-collared and crew-neck shirts to cover it; she would never be caught in a bathing suit or even let a boy get close enough to her to see it. Even as her high school friends fooled around with guys, Isis remained a virgin.

She'd beaten cancer. There must have been some reason her life had been spared, she thought. But she could not figure out what it was.

Isis remembered staying in the first hotel with her mom after the surgery. From there her mom disappeared for long stretches of time, depositing Isis with her aunt. She told Isis she was going on vacation, but Isis later learned that vacation actually meant jail.

She bounced around with family members from state to state, and when her mom got on her feet she would take Isis back. Her mom held jobs too, but not for long because she would lie on her application: *Have you ever been convicted of a crime? No.* She was usually charming enough to land the job through an interview, like the times she got hired at

Kentucky Fried Chicken or Taco Bell, where she worked her way up to manager real quick.

Her mom was pretty like Isis. She wore her hair in different styles of dreadlocks, short, long, blond, or black with orange streaks. She bought makeup from Sephora and Estée Lauder with her checks and lined her eyes like those of a cat. But each time she landed a job, after a few weeks or months of working, she would end up getting fired when the results of the background checks came back.

They moved in with Isis's grandmother for a period, until her grandmother decided she didn't want to take care of her daughter and her kids and kicked them out. Isis was in eighth grade when they moved into a homeless shelter for women and children in Edison, New Jersey. She could remember walking into the two buildings with more than thirty rooms—one per family—each just wide enough to fit a bunk bed. Everyone had to share the showers on the same floor. It was a mix of residents, clean and dirty, rude and nice. Some people were addicts. Some of the women had been abused; others had been homeless for years. For the first two weeks, Isis curled up on the bottom bunk alongside her mom and cried herself to sleep each night.

She enrolled in school, determined not to let her classmates know she was homeless. She started wearing her mother's makeup, applying liquid eyeliner, mascara, foundation, and eye shadow.

In school, she could reinvent herself. Each time she moved to a new shelter, motel, or group home, she enrolled in another school and became the new girl. She could be mysterious. Intimidating. Bold. With slouchy necklaces, fat bracelets, big earrings, high heels. The kids at school did not have to know what she was hiding beneath her spunky exterior, all that makeup, all those high-necked Forever 21 clothes, which she paid for by working three jobs. On the bus ride home, she would feel the familiar dread weighing on her, the feeling of going home to the shelter. Sometimes she'd avoid it altogether, spending the night at a friend's house and waking up to go to school from there the next day. But most shelters had rules. If she didn't check in by a certain time, she could get kicked out.

The kids at school didn't know that she sometimes did not know where she was going to lay her head at night or what she was going to eat, often a donated bread-and-butter sandwich, or a packet of Oodles of Noodles ramen. They didn't see the Mercedes-shaped scar hidden beneath her vintage-style blouses and blazers. By the time Isis was in tenth grade, she had followed her mom from the shelter to a transitional living home to a motel on Route 1 in North Brunswick. "One of those dingy motels you might see in a movie or drive right by and look past because you don't want to stop there," she said.

Her mother's drug use didn't stop. Once Isis came back to the room and saw a woman in their bathtub shooting up. Her mother got angry that Isis had barged in. Her eyes looked possessed. She took a baseball bat and beat Isis with it.

She survived that beating, but her mom hurt her on other days too. Isis had a habit of sucking her teeth. One day, her mother kicked her in the ribs for it. Isis fell off the bed and onto the floor, and her mother got on top of her, punched her in the eye, wrapped her hands around her neck, and began to squeeze. Isis didn't fight back. She never fought back. Even after all of that, she loved her mother.

"I hate you!" her mom screamed at her. She told Isis she wanted her to die, and Isis believed it: her mother was going to kill her.

But when her mom's rage had finally subsided and Isis was bleeding but still breathing, she started to apologize and cry. "I didn't mean to do this to you. I love you, Isis, you're my life."

Her mom said things like "Maybe I should go away from here" and "I'm tired of my life" and swallowed a load of sleeping pills in an attempt to die of an overdose. Isis curled up in the corner of the motel room until she drifted to sleep.

The next morning her mom was awake. No school bus came to the remote motel, so Isis's aunt usually picked her up instead. That morning, her aunt noticed her eye, swollen and bloody. Her mother had hit her so hard, it was going to leave a scar. Another one.

"Isis, I can't do anything for you anymore," her aunt told her. "You're getting older. If you want to get out of this, you need to speak up."

Later that day, when Isis came home from school, she saw her mother peeking out of a stranger's motel room nearby. Isis pounded on the stranger's door and a man opened it, his eyes red and his body twitching. "My mother's in there!" Isis shouted. He slammed the door, and Isis began to kick it, crying. Her mother never came out.

Isis called 411 and asked for the 1-800 number for the New Jersey Division of Youth and Family Services.

"My mother's abusing me," she told the social worker. Isis went to her aunt's house, and a caseworker showed up, arranging to keep Isis at her aunt's for a while. But her aunt soon had a baby and decided to move down south. "I was holding her back," Isis said.

Her caseworker put her into the Isaiah House.

"Get me out of this place," Isis said on the phone to her caseworker, days after she moved in. Isis had never been to East Orange before, and the other girls seemed to sense her foreignness. As much as Isis had invested in her wardrobe, she knew she was an easy target for getting into fights or getting robbed.

Isis used her $81-a-month check from the New Jersey Division of Youth and Family Services to buy a pair of UGG boots. She wore a matching Juicy Couture necklace and bracelet, which a friend had given to her. She also got a job working off the books for $5 an hour as a clerk at a beauty supply store near the shelter, which also helped fund her vintage look. She wore ankle booties and shopped at more affordable stores such as Urban Outfitters, H&M, and, of course, Forever 21. Sometimes she felt preppy, splurging on button-up shirts from J. Crew and Ralph Lauren. She bought herself a $60 bed comforter with pink, green, and white circles on it from Walmart.

Within a few weeks, her UGGs had been stolen. Her Juicy Couture jewelry had disappeared too, along with her stash of cash. Isis got into a fight with another girl during chores. She was "shaking her butt in my face; aggravating and annoying me, so I pushed her to get out of my face. And she hit me with a broom."

She felt disgusted being at the Isaiah House. Even worse, her mother's life had only deteriorated after Isis left. She had been arrested for robbing an elderly woman and stealing credit cards, and ended up getting locked up on two charges of robbery, an eleven-year sentence.

Isis was furious—with her mother, and with all the relatives who had not stepped up to take her in. In Egyptian mythology, Isis was the goddess of rebirth and protector of the dead. Isis didn't think she belonged in a homeless shelter, yet she kept on ending up in them.

It didn't happen right away, but another resident, Nicole, took a liking to Isis, and Isis to her. They had a lot in common. Nicole's mother had also been a drug addict. She was shorter than Isis and wore her hair in a flip. Nicole kept talking about this woman named Norma. How she and her college kids had fixed up the house. How she was going to help get the girls into college too. How she was going to help all of them get prom dresses.

"What is she? Some kind of *goddess* or something?" Isis asked skeptically.

That day when Norma showed up with Becca, Isis flashed back to her childhood, the house in Highland Park, the happy family she envied. She knew this woman everyone seemed to adore.

Norma remembered her too. She stayed late that night talking to Isis on the porch. Isis told her all that had happened since they had known each other when she was a little girl, the motels and the beatings. Norma gave Isis her phone number and explained that her childhood hadn't been so totally different from hers—only in Norma's case, the state had never taken her away. She told her to call anytime.

Isis did call. Week after week. "I miss you," she would say on voice mail messages. Norma always called back. At first Isis really didn't believe this woman would remain part of her life for the long haul. Calling her was almost like a test, to see if she would really follow through with her word. Was she spending time with her for community service? Or was it real? Did she actually care?

But months passed, and there was Norma, still showing up, still calling back.

Isis met other students from the professor's Be the Change group at Kean University, including a young man named Israel with a bodybuilder frame who walked around in button-up shirts and slacks, with two cell phones attached to his belt. He visited the shelter one afternoon to share his life story with the girls. He told them about his life running with a gang. He told them about his unconventional road to college. He was so smart, so motivated, she thought. Isis had never really considered college. But Israel's story set off a little sparkle inside her.

Norma had become the most stable force in her life, and Isis did not know what she would do if she ever lost the professor.

One day in December 2009, Isis called Norma and didn't receive an answer. She called again. Left messages. But there was no return call. That wasn't like her, Isis thought. She asked Nicole if she'd heard from Norma, but Nicole hadn't either. Isis had a bad feeling, the kind she got when she knew her own life, or her mother's, was in peril. Something was wrong. Christmas was coming in a few days, along with a snowstorm, and the professor was probably out running errands before both came.

She dialed Norma, but again it went to voice mail. Isis would soon find out that her hunch had been right: Norma had been hurt.

The professor who seemed invincible to Isis and so many others had been crushed inside the party bus by an oncoming truck, her ribs cracked, her brain bleeding, and paramedics on the way.

What religious or spiritual practice do you believe in, if any, and how does it impact your beliefs about what happens when we die?

ELEVEN

Jonathan

April 2009

The pledge that Jonathan had made to his brother while standing before his casket felt as if it were still lodged in his throat in the three months since Josh's suicide. Something good will come of this, he thought. He had not figured out what exactly "good" would be.

Jonathan and Caitlin were not officially back together. Though they had been spending most nights together, they did not refer to each other as boyfriend and girlfriend. Yet night after night, Jonathan would bolt awake in a sweat from a nightmare in which he was again trying to rescue Josh or trying to save his mother from being murdered by his dad, and Caitlin would be there to calm him, to cradle him back to sleep.

Caitlin was there for him again one April afternoon, when Jonathan came to Norma's death class to tell his family's story for the first time. It was during that time of the year when, according to Norma, many depressed people who tried to hang on through the holidays began to give up. She called spring "the season of suicide."

Jonathan took a desk in front of the circle, his hair gelled, wearing polished dress shoes and a button-down shirt, looking as if he had come prepared to give a business presentation to clients. Sitting behind Jonathan, Caitlin doodled on a piece of paper, avoiding eye contact.

Jonathan's story came spilling out of him as Norma's class sat riveted. That snowy night when he was a boy stumbling into the kitchen and his mother in a pool of blood, the barefoot car ride as his father stared him in the eye in the rearview mirror, the bridge crash, little Josh trapped under the dashboard with a broken collarbone, their father's talk of alien abductions, his suicide in prison.

He spoke of Josh's brilliance and paranoia. The homeless shelter. The knife attack. Shouts of "Don't look into my eyes!" Uruguay. A suicide note. Josh's death on the train tracks.

Some of the girls in the class wept. But no one spoke. So Jonathan kept talking. Now he couldn't stop. As he remembered, the morning after Josh died, he had popped out of bed and called Norma on her cell phone, explaining that he wanted to confront the psychiatrist who had sent Josh home after such a short session. "I was, like, 'That fucking psychiatrist, I'm gonna kill him,'" Jonathan told the class.

Norma had tried to calm him that day, suggesting some legal and medical questions he could ask the man. Jonathan had hung up, grabbed a tape recorder, and headed to the psychiatrist's office with plans to sue him for malpractice and negligence. With the recorder secretly running, the doctor had not seemed to remember much about the session with Josh. When he had come around to recalling the schizophrenic patient with suicidal thoughts, Jonathan jumped in: "Well, he killed himself, like, an hour after he left this office."

The doctor, as Jonathan remembered, had put his head in his hands. But Jonathan didn't think he really cared. "He didn't even remember my brother's name."

Jonathan went on. "'Just take another pill.' I think that's how my brother looked at it. 'They're just going to dope me up, and I'm never going to get anywhere.' It's like he ran out of options."

Norma's students remained silent, still riveted.

"What has your life been like since that time?" Norma asked. "Being a suicide survivor twice over now?"

"You can be pissed off," Jonathan said, "get depressed, push people away, do a million things, but at the end of the day it's either you're going to move forward or you're going to move backward."

"What are you moving forward toward?"

"I said, 'For the rest of my life I'm going to be taking care of my brother and I don't care what it takes, how long it takes, I'm going to take care of him no matter what.' . . . I had to put him first. He was a priority to me, just like if you have a kid," Jonathan replied. "Then he took his life. And I got my life back. Which is kind of weird. So if I did nothing with my life, if I was depressed all the time and didn't accomplish great things, then him dying is for nothing."

Caitlin rose, preparing to leave class early. She had folded a piece of paper into a note, which she left with Jonathan before slipping out of the room. On it, she had written, "I am so proud of you."

Interview someone whose religious or spiritual views are
different from your own. Write an essay about what you
learned based on that interview.

TWELVE

Caitlin

A week after Jonathan shared his story with Norma's class, Caitlin's mother was admitted to the hospital again after overdosing on prescription pills—her third suicide attempt in six months. Caitlin received the call on her cell phone while at work on campus. Her caller ID said it was her dad.

Oh, God, oh, God, oh, God, she thought, taking a deep breath. This is going to be bad.

"Hello?"

"Listen," her dad said, "I'm calling Mommy. She's not answering the phone. Something must have happened."

I could leave right now, Caitlin thought. Her boss was in a seminar somewhere on campus. She could track her down. Tell her it's a family emergency. I need to go home. She paused. But I don't want to find my mom dead.

Caitlin hung up and started calling her sisters and friends, anyone else who might be able to check on her mother, get there quicker than she could. Finally she reached a friend who agreed to go to the house. Caitlin stayed on the phone with her as she entered, walking upstairs to her mom's bedroom. "The door is locked, I can't open it," the friend said. She tried picking the lock and eventually made it inside.

Caitlin heard her friend gasp.

"What's going on?" Caitlin shouted.

"Her wedding picture . . . she drew on it . . . I think she's . . . I have to call 911."

With that Caitlin dropped work and rushed home. When she arrived, she discovered that her mother had colored and scribbled all over a giant painting of herself in a wedding gown before overdosing on drugs. Caitlin used to love that image of her mother, forty years younger and beautiful. It was destroyed.

Her mom was admitted to the hospital again. And again she was released. Not even a week later, Caitlin was preparing to take a shower before meeting some friends when she heard her parents screaming and yelling at each other, and she raced downstairs to intervene. All of the years of yelling, threats of divorce, death, foreclosure on their home, couldn't they just shut up and love each other like normal parents for once? Caitlin picked up a cup off the counter and threw it at the wall. Then she punched in the glass on a framed picture on the wall. Her blood spurted onto the floor.

"Leave!" Caitlin shouted. "Get out of here! Go away! You guys can't be near each other."

Her parents grew silent for a second. Then her father ran out of the house into the rain. Caitlin chased him outside in her socks, telling her sister, "Watch Mommy and make sure she's not killing herself."

Hours later, after the chaos at home calmed, Caitlin fell asleep and into a nightmare. She woke up and couldn't breathe. Her nightmares were common. She often awoke with her jaw locked shut. She'd been in a minor car accident in high school, which had banged her up enough to cause temporomandibular joint disorder, or TMJ, which caused her jaw to sometimes slip out of place, especially during nightmares. It always took a while for her to pry her mouth open again.

The next day, Caitlin came to school with her long blond hair looped through the back of a baseball cap, its front emblazoned with a symbol of a hand with its middle and ring finger raised, thumb, index, and pinky curled down; her favorite comedian, Dane Cook, called it a "superfinger." Caitlin's own fingers were wrapped in white bandages like a boxer's wrap.

Day after day, Caitlin found herself walking around campus feeling like a zombie, surviving on minimal sleep, trying to keep up her graduate school grades and job, all the while losing track of what day or month it was.

She turned to Jonathan for solace. He accompanied her to the hospital to visit her mom when she overdosed and to Norma's office one day to talk to the professor. Caitlin trembled in the hallway and tried to hide her puffy eyes with sunglasses. Jonathan pulled her into a stairwell and hugged her until she stopped shaking.

But she could tell that her distress triggered thoughts of Jonathan's not-so-distant past. He was trying to put the pain of his family's deaths behind him, but Caitlin's family chaos wouldn't let him.

CLASS DISCUSSION: A Handout—"Instructions to the Funeral Director"—Excerpted from A Time to Prepare

1. I would

a. like to be buried

b. like to be cremated

2. I would

a. like the service held at a funeral home

b. like the service held at a church or temple

c. like to have only a graveside service

3. I would

a. like the service to be public

b. like the service to be private

4. I would

a. like flowers

b. not like flowers

5. I would like donations in my memory made to _____

6. I would

a. like to be buried in a shroud

b. like to be buried in street clothes, specifically _____

THIRTEEN

To Serve

Summer 2009

Norma Bowe often said she believed there was a wonder in unleashing your story, horrible as it might be, out into the world. She told her students that speaking it aloud releases a different kind of power from writing it down on paper or typing it on a computer screen. Give it voice, and you never know what kind of gift might find its way back in return.

". . . man *needs* to teach," Erikson once wrote, "not only for the sake of those who need to be taught, and not only for the fulfillment of his identity, but because facts are kept alive by being told, logic by being demonstrated, truth by being professed. Thus, the teaching passion is not restricted to the teaching profession."

Jonathan had felt the truth of that lesson in Norma's classroom that day. He needed to tell his story now, and his story needed a happy ending. So he went in search of one.

Jonathan spent the next several months tagging along with Norma's students on field trips to places such as Northern State Prison, where he saw the psychiatric unit, with its white-brick painted walls and a restraining chair.

"This chair will break you," the guard told the students that day. It was black, with shackles attached to the bottom to hold ankles, and to each armrest. Two straps crisscrossed over the chest of an inmate who found himself in the seat. Those who refused to take their meds or had psychotic breakdowns, violent fits, or tantrums were confined to this chair for four-hour intervals, after which time a guard would enter the room and release one of their hands to allow them to scoop food into their mouth. They were permitted to use the toilet, briefly, before being shackled to the chair again. But if the inmate couldn't hold it until the next stint, well, "too bad, he'll just have to shit himself right in this chair and smell it for the next four hours," the guard said. If the restrained inmate got an itch, got irritated by a fly buzzing around his head, or felt too hot or cold, there was nothing he could do to ease the discomfort. The guard talked of one inmate with "666" tattooed across his forehead; he'd stayed in the chair for four days with no bathroom break. "That guy," the guard said, "was my hero."

No wonder his father had killed himself in prison, Jonathan thought. If that was how the mentally ill were treated, that might have seemed the best option.

He also went with Norma and her class one afternoon when they visited Trenton Psychiatric Hospital. Jonathan's father had been housed there. So had his brother. It looked much like he remembered from his trips there to see Josh: a constellation of buildings located on a vast rolling green meadowlike space. The brick wards stood four and five stories tall and were mostly vacant. The hospital, as Jonathan learned, now served 440 patients on site—but at one time the wards had had 3,800, as a staff member who had volunteered to be the tour guide explained. The buildings had been deemed no longer livable, due to lead paint and asbestos. The guide pointed out buildings in which insulin shock therapy used to take place. Ivy crawled up the exterior walls, and some of the windows had been boarded up. Jonathan trailed behind the students, who tried to peer through cracks in the boards. Spiny brown spheres fallen from sweet gum trees crunched beneath his feet as the class headed toward a neighborhood of cottages, group living facilities, where residents stared from front porches and lawn chairs.

A bearded, shaggy-haired man walked with his hands clasped behind his back, looking giddy, releasing his hands to wave eagerly to the students. Most others just stared vacantly. One man, irritated that the commotion had disturbed his sleep, stumbled away with a grunt. A young blond woman with two braids in her hair, who looked to be in her mid-twenties, sat on a stoop, looking sad, while another man sat inside a telephone booth, not talking on the phone, just sitting. Norma's group passed a gigantic magnolia tree in full bloom. Summer's fading bursts of whitish-pink blossoms stood out against the dull sky and carpeted the earth below.

The hospital tour guide told the group that most family members did not come to visit very often. Jonathan remembered how he had driven the two hours to Trenton every time he could to visit Josh while he was being treated here. The patients looked lonely, he thought. Some of the faces reminded him of his brother.

Many of New Jersey's treatment centers for the mentally ill had shut down in the last three decades, the guide told the group, including the largest one run by the state, Greystone Park Psychiatric Hospital in Parsippany. It had been closed down under Governor Christine Todd Whitman after she said in 2000 that the 613-patient home did not meet "the model of modern psychiatric care." Hundreds of patients across the state had also been reevaluated and deemed to no longer need long-term care. As Jonathan learned from Norma, many of the mentally ill had since ended up on the streets or in prison. The Trenton Psychiatric Hospital guide added, "The system in corrections went up in their population of mentally ill people in prisons and jails. It's horrendous because they don't get the treatment, they're often abused there."

Jonathan was realizing how few people seemed to care about the mentally ill in America. No one seemed to understand that individuals living with schizophrenia and other mental illnesses had family members and people who loved them. Sometimes family members gave up on the mentally ill too.

When the psychiatric hospital field trip was over, Caitlin joined Jonathan, Norma, and a group of students at Applebee's. Jonathan and Caitlin sat side by side, holding hands, as he described the field trip to her. At one point, Caitlin leaned her head against Jonathan's shoulder and rested it there. He ducked toward her face and kissed her. At the end of the table, Norma ordered a mug of Samuel Adams and smiled at them. The weather had heated, and Jonathan and Caitlin's relationship was warming too. Caitlin seemed to be getting serious now about wanting to leave her family's drama behind her; she was moving toward her master's degree in psychology, realizing there was little she could do to change her parents' behavior. For so long she had told Jonathan that she thought living in their house would allow her to monitor her parents, make sure they didn't kill each other or themselves. Now she was talking to him of moving out.

Winter 2009

JONATHAN HAD RESUMED his rigorous pace at his real estate job, setting financial goals, trying to repay debts and replenish the savings he'd spent caring for Josh. He told Caitlin and Norma that he wanted to start a mental illness awareness group. He created a Facebook page for it and attracted more than a thousand members in a matter of weeks. One woman, who said she was a "functioning schizo-affective" living in Oregon, posted a quote on the page about living "in the shadow of the ignorance of the world." The flood of interest invigorated him. Jonathan decided he would hold a brainstorming meeting for the mental health awareness group in November. Norma reserved an auditorium for him at Kean University.

Jonathan spoke into a microphone at the front of a half-filled lecture hall. On an overhead screen flashed a photo of Josh smiling in the sand, wearing a floppy wide-brimmed hat and giving a thumbs-up, and the words "Brainstorming Session: How to Change the Mental Health System and Build Awareness. In Memory of Joshua Steingraber."

Caitlin's father and sister sat at the back of the auditorium behind Jonathan's surviving brother, Chris, his girlfriend, and the brothers' aunt and uncle, the same couple who had first taken the boys in when they were orphaned.

"We need your help," Jonathan told the audience, "and that's why we are here."

Caitlin joined him at the lectern. She'd put her graduate research skills to use by pulling together studies and statistics in a PowerPoint presentation. She rattled off dizzying statistics, like how people with schizophrenia have a fifty times higher risk of attempting suicide than the general population and how suicide is the number one cause of premature death among people with schizophrenia—with an estimated 10 to 13 percent killing themselves and approximately 40 percent attempting suicide at least once. Twenty percent of Americans in prison were seriously mentally ill, far outnumbering the number of mentally ill in hospitals. She cited a 2002 New York study that had found that 70 percent of prisoners who committed suicide had a history of mental illness. She added that approximately 200,000 individuals with schizophrenia or manic-depressive illness were homeless.

In the days that followed the mental health meeting, it was decided that the first order of business would be to organize a clothing and blanket drive for the mentally ill and homeless. Be the Change would team up with Jonathan's mental health group for the event, which would take place the weekend before Christmas. As Jonathan envisioned it, they would hit up streets, alleys, train stations, parks, beaches—anywhere the homeless were living and sleeping—to provide food, clothes, and blankets.

But the days of planning and trying to coordinate a group of people for a common cause brought on head butting between Norma's group and Jonathan's. Norma told Jonathan that she didn't want her students roaming unprotected through streets in the cold trying to find the homeless—it could be dangerous, and she couldn't risk jeopardizing them in that way. Visiting shelters and train stations would be enough.

But how else would they find the most needy homeless? Jonathan demanded.

Norma suggested visiting the shelters, but Jonathan figured the people in shelters already had warm blankets and food. What was the point of helping people who already had help? He wanted to find the mentally ill who were sleeping on the streets, whom no one else had reached out to, the ones who were too sick or alone to seek shelter.

If he felt so strongly about it, Norma let Jonathan know, his group could do it his way, but Be the Change would have to do it its way. She warned him not to attach her name to his project if the volunteers were going to go to unsafe spots, since anything that could put young people in danger could also get her into trouble as the professor advising the undertaking.

But it seemed to Jonathan that Norma was trying to run everything according to her rules and under the banner of the Be the Change group, with their matching T-shirts. It wasn't just the professor who was rubbing him the wrong way lately; some of her Be the Change student leaders seemed to want to boss him around when it came to conducting the project too. This had all started from his idea, his desire to help. It was not about T-shirts or sorority and fraternity community service brownie points. It was in memory of *Josh*. It was for everyone like him. Real, lasting change had to come from it.

What had started as a collaborative community service endeavor eventually ended up splintering into two separate projects.

Take-Home Writing Assignment:
Write Your Living Will

Use the document to express your wishes to your family and physicians concerning your health and medical treatments at the end of your life in the event of an unforeseeable circumstance in which you would be otherwise unable to make medical decisions, such as being in a state of permanent unconsciousness. This includes your directions for handling decisions to provide, withhold, or withdraw life-sustaining measures.

FOURTEEN

Roadblocks

December 2009

It was a Monday, with Christmas a little over a week away. Norma had much to do before then, as a snowstorm was charging toward New Jersey. Forecasters predicted that the sky could dump twenty inches in some parts. There were still stamps to purchase for Christmas cards and dozens of papers that needed grading. She still had to give her students their final exams. And she had to make a stop at the Marriott Hotel near the airport to pick up two hundred blankets for the homeless drive. She had a list of shelters plotted out for her students on a MapQuest print-out on her seat. Her backseat overflowed with donations for the events: fleece blankets, comforters, even a mink coat donated by a student's mother and stuffed into a garment bag. There were groceries to buy and cookies to bake, not to mention her father's impending Christmas visit, which only added another layer of stress. She would book him a room at the Holiday Inn again.

The list of tasks revolved in her mind as she waited at the intersection of Wooding Avenue and Highway 1 in Edison, New Jersey, just past the CVS drug store. She had just dropped Becca off at school, and she was tired since they had been up late the night before, visiting a friend who had returned from overseas.

It was morning rush hour as the temperature dragged itself past the 40-degree mark. Her hands rested on the steering wheel, her radio off. If Norma had known that in a few minutes she would be stripped down and put onto a stretcher, she would have at least thought to put on underwear. Or combed her hair or put on a touch of makeup. But instead she had walked out of the house that frigid morning wearing yoga pants, a T-shirt, and a winter coat but no undergarments. Sitting at a stoplight with the seat belt drooped across her upper body like a sash, she was just glad she had managed to brush her teeth.

A quarter mile down the road, a man driving a white SUV zipped westward along Highway 1. One set of stoplights would soon turn red, sending traffic at the intersection to a halt, and the hurried man in the white SUV would have to stop too. The light ahead of Norma would turn green, and her van was the first vehicle in line to proceed. There was a post office a few blocks away. She would stop there to get stamps for Christmas cards, she thought, sipping her Dunkin' Donuts iced latte.

Inside the party bus, a stack of essays from women lay in a folder on the backseat. She had other inmates on her mind now. Unbeknown to the men at Northern State, Norma had also started teaching once a week in the Edna Mahan Correctional Facility for Women in Clinton, a forty-five-minute drive from Kean University. Some of the women in her new class had murdered too. But already she felt they responded to her discussions more genuinely than the men at Northern State did.

One of the women she had met at the facility was a bespectacled Chinese-American woman whose essay began "I was in the bathroom over my dead baby girl's body." At thirty-four, she had drowned her own child. "It began when I was first hospitalized for depression when I was twenty-four," she had written. "I was struggling with my thesis paper, taking care of my schizophrenic mom, who's been this way since she was sixteen." The woman had been hospitalized and tried to jump in front of a subway train. She had drunk nail polish remover. She had even jumped off a bridge.

"I took the time to fill the bathtub with water instead of the baby tub, just high enough with warm water to submerge her," the woman wrote. ". . . At first she noticed I was distressed and nuzzled me with her face, but seeing that I couldn't be consoled she decided to play with the dinosaur I put in. Then I said to myself I must do it now or I will never do it . . . when it happened I was relieved. It felt like a great burden pressure or responsibility was taken from me."

Norma thought maybe she could make more of a difference with those women.

The light turned green. Norma pressed the accelerator and rolled into the intersection. From the corner of her left eye, she noticed a flash of white.

Norma turned in time to see the SUV tearing through the intersection, heading straight for the driver's side of the party bus. She heard the SUV's wheels scream. The driver must have been slamming on his brakes, trying to stop. She heard his horn honk, a slow, blaring howl. She had one last clear thought: I am going to die!

She heard the grind of metal on metal, like giant claws dragging across a chalkboard. She didn't feel the nose of the SUV impaling her door as if trying to skewer her body. She felt only the violent quake and heard the deafening blast. Her iced latte seemed to explode. Her head slammed against the glass.

She lost consciousness.

WHEN NORMA OPENED her eyes, her head was throbbing and she could barely breathe. She was trapped inside the party bus. It felt as though the seat belt was crushing her chest. Ice cubes had scattered over her lap, onto the seat, into her hair, onto the floor. Her thoughts moved at rapid speed, but she felt as if she were wading through a murky dream.

She looked at the ice. How are Dunkin Donuts' cubes so cold? she wondered. Why do they always take so long to melt? She blinked. It took her a moment to absorb what had just happened. The SUV had T-boned Norma's vehicle. Its front bumper was now inside the party bus. She remembered her last thought before the SUV careened into her driver's-side door: I am going to die!

The cops would arrive soon. What if she was bleeding internally? She was still alive, but she might still die on the scene. I need to find my driver's license. If they needed to identify her body, the police would need her license, she thought. The party bus plates were registered under Norm's name. She had to tell him she'd been in a car accident.

She reached onto the floor to retrieve her phone. Ouch! Overwhelming pain. She fumbled for the phone and grabbed it.

"I'm in an accident!" she shouted, breaking into tears when Norm answered. "I'm really, really hurt."

"Where are you?"

She told him Wooding Avenue and Highway 1, next to the Skylark Diner. He called 911, and within minutes a sheriff's deputy was outside the party bus shouting "Are you hurt? Are you okay?"

The deputy tried to pry the door open but couldn't. Norma pulled what was left of the handle and tried to push the door open, but the SUV had trapped her inside.

Her shoulder ached, but her chest hurt the worst. Trauma workers rushed up and began cutting away pieces of the vehicle. "Am I having a heart attack?" she kept asking when they finally made their way inside. "I think I'm having a heart attack."

Paramedics rolled Norma like a log onto a hard wooden spinal board, used for patients who are believed to have neck or back injuries. They strapped her down with a neck brace and head block immobilizer. The inability to move made her pain feel even worse.

Norm looked panic-stricken when he arrived a few minutes later, offering to ride in the ambulance with her, but Norma told him not to. She told him to drive his car and follow the ambulance so they could ride home together later that day. She had survived so far. The pain in her chest didn't appear to be a heart attack. Her injuries must not have been that bad. She figured it wouldn't take long to get treated in the hospital and go home.

The paramedics began cutting away her yoga pants and shirt. She tried to make an awkward joke. "You know how your parents always tell you to wear clean underwear in case you get in an accident?" Well, she said, "I'm not wearing any underwear!" It didn't matter to them. A paramedic told Norma they were taking her to Robert Wood Johnson University Hospital. She knew it was ranked as a Level I trauma center by the American College of Surgeons, which meant it was equipped to treat the widest scope of the most serious injuries. I don't need a Level I trauma center, she thought.

"You'll be okay, sweetie," a paramedic told her.

Stop calling me "sweetie," she thought.

At the hospital, doctors still wouldn't remove the excruciating spine board or head immobilizer. They had to make sure her back, neck, and head were not injured. They rolled her on her side to examine her back. She grimaced and moaned in agony. Clear. No major injuries. Her neck. Clear. Then they put her through a chest X-ray machine at the hospital: she had five broken ribs.

But what about her heart and her head? Neither had been cleared yet. A nurse came in with the X-rays. "You need another CT scan."

Why another? They had done an MRI already. She tried to refuse. This time, medical staff would inject her with radioactive contrast dye to enhance images so they could see all of the vessels pumping and the inflammation. She knew the dye would make her feel like she was going to wet herself on the table. She didn't want that. "I'm a nurse," Norma said. "Just tell me what is going on."

The nurse had such a serious expression on his face that it made Norma nervous.

"Your aorta may have been dissected."

She felt her stomach turn. Dissected aorta. She knew exactly what that meant: it was a tear in the aorta's wall, the main part of the heart that pumps blood through the arteries to the rest of the body. A severe rupture would result in catastrophic blood loss. More than three-quarters of people with aortic ruptures die, and such an injury is the cause of nearly 20 percent of auto accident–related deaths. If the diagnosis was true, she had about thirty minutes before she bled to death. If they rushed her into open-heart surgery immediately, surgeons might have to crack the rest of her ribs to try to repair the aorta. It was a perilous procedure.

"I need you to get ahold of Melissa," she said to Norm. Her older daughter was still in law school near Philadelphia. "Have her start coming this way."

And Becca? Her younger daughter had been in the middle of taking a high school final that morning, and Norma and Norm had not disturbed her with news of the crash yet. But Norma thought it looked as though they would have to now. Norm dialed Melissa, whose boyfriend agreed to drive her to the hospital. Then he called Becca.

"How was your final?" he asked.

"Fine."

"Good," he said. "Mommy's been in an accident."

"What?" Becca shouted.

Norma got on the phone. "My car got bumped," she said, not wanting to worry her too badly yet. "I'm a little dizzy. But I'm fine."

"You're crying," Becca said.

"I'm not crying. Does it sound like I'm crying? I'm fine."

The nurses came back and whisked Norma away and into the CT scan again. When it was over Norma and Norman waited in the trauma unit for results.

The doctor had both good and bad news: it was not a dissected aorta; it was cardiac compression and myocardial contusion, or heart bruises.

Norma exhaled. I am not going to die.

But the doctor said he was concerned about her head scans.

What now?

He told her she had a small subarachnoid hemorrhage—bleeding between the brain and the tissues covering it. If it got worse, she could end up with vomiting, disorientation, seizures, loss of brain function, stroke, and again, death. More than half of people who suffer from subarachnoid hemorrhages die, and many who survive battle life-changing mental and motor impairments. Norma had seen what happened to such people who were her patients. Little by little you lose the ability to think and speak; I could be drooling on myself for the rest of my life, she thought. They might have to do neurosurgery. I'm going to have a hole in my head.

It all depended on the size of the brain hemorrhage and the amount of swelling.

The brain bleed was small so far, the doctor told her. If it shrank, she might recover without serious complications or surgery. They would have to keep her in the hospital for however long it would take to be certain she was not at great risk. It could be days. Or weeks.

* * *

NORMA WAS SUPPOSED to give a final exam at Kean that night. When she failed to appear, students tried calling her cell phone with questions about the weekend's homeless drive. No answer.

Isis from the teen homeless shelter called, checking in as usual, and becoming distraught after Norma didn't call back.

The next morning, Becca posted a message on her Facebook wall: "Mommy got into a car accident yesterday . . . her ribs are broken, she has a small bleed on the outside of her brain and her shoulder may be broken as well."

By evening, word had spread across Kean University about Norma's accident. The men and women in prison were notified too, as were the girls from Isaiah House. Isis broke down in tears.

A steady stream of students, neighbors, faculty, and friends began showing up in Norma's hospital room, bearing flowers and cards. Entire fraternities and sororities flooded the hospital. Be the Change volunteers dropped by in clusters. Others left dozens and dozens of messages. Norma felt as though she were on an episode of the old television show *This Is Your Life*. The only two people who did not show up at the hospital were Jonathan and Caitlin.

Norma posted on Facebook, "I was discharged from the hospital late Thursday and now home recuperating from 5 broken ribs, a cardiac compression injury and head trauma. I can't even express how thankful I am to be okay and for all of you in my life who inspire me every day. I am so lucky!"

The mental health homeless project went on without Norma, and that was fine. In the days that followed the accident, Norma had not seen Jonathan and Caitlin, but she wasn't worried. More than anything she was tired: tired of mitigating clashes over a community service project and even more tired from her injuries. Her family had convinced her that this was the one time in her life she needed to concentrate on helping herself. She needed to focus on getting better.

Do you believe people have the right to die? Defend your
answer. Give case examples and support your argument.

FIFTEEN

Parting Ways

Spring 2010

Jonathan still thought of his brother at every New Jersey turn. When he drove his truck past the apartment complex in Roselle Park where their father had killed their mother or past the water where they'd used to fish with their dad in Nomahegan Park, or when he crossed the tracks in Linden where his brother had last laid his head—each place brought its own bittersweet memory, and lately they seemed more bitter.

Now again, his faith in Caitlin's transformation and the future of their relationship was fading. It was becoming clear that Caitlin might never break away from her parents' drama. Jonathan worried that she was unable to let go of the need to try to stop her mother's desire to die.

"Her relationship with her family was driving me crazy," Jonathan explained. "I would be in her house sometimes and all this chaos was going on, and I would feel like throwing a table out of the window. I couldn't deal with her family. It killed me. It brought back all this stuff— my head was not right."

He had started coaching others to become financially independent, explaining that without the flexibility of his real estate career when his brother had been ill, he would not have been able to care for him or take days off to take him to doctor's appointments or to Uruguay. Jonathan was thankful for the independence his career had granted him in those last months with his brother. In his financial coaching, he had begun sharing his life story with thousands of people, traveling between San Diego and New Jersey to Chicago, Dallas, Atlanta, Seattle, Anaheim, and

Los Angeles, giving presentations to crowds interested in getting into the real estate field while weaving in his own family's story and his journey with Josh and ending on a positive message of hope. Some rooms in which he presented held between 180 and 300 people, and many came up to him afterward to share their own family stories of mental illness and death.

"My mission is about bringing awareness into the world about mental health," Jonathan said. "But it's broader than that now. It's about life and being positive and overcoming adversity. It's about the changing purpose in your life. . . . I've learned that as your life changes, your purpose changes too."

On one of those business trips to San Diego in 2010, Jonathan found himself enchanted by the ever-sunny skies, blue-water beaches, warm winters, and year-round open-air cafés. It was all so different from his home state. It felt free and full of promise, not at all like the noose around his neck that New Jersey was becoming.

"I just went with my gut," Jonathan said. "I said, 'I'm going to move out here.'"

"You didn't even consider me in this at all?" Caitlin cried when he told her.

"No," he replied. "You're right. I didn't."

"Please, can't you reconsider this? Let me be a part of it."

But Jonathan's mind was made up. "The fact that I didn't think to put you as a part of it must say something," Jonathan told her. He needed to take care of himself, just as she needed to take care of herself first—not her family and not him.

"Her life is her life," Jonathan said, "and she doesn't have to spend it saving other people." He'd learned that already the hard way. "She was fixated on worrying about her mother, worrying about her father. A lot of the mistakes I made I tried to teach her not to do. I tried to save Josh . . . I don't take that back, but she was on the same path: to the point of no return."

None of this changed his feelings for Caitlin, though. The two had talked about Caitlin moving to California after grad school. They tried to make it work long distance for the first year, but the talks fizzled. What would she have done out here? Jonathan asked. She had no friends in San Diego, no family, no firm job prospects. She would have been miserable, he added, especially since he traveled every couple of weeks to give presentations.

But even if she was far away, he said, no one could take her place. He knew no one would ever understand him the way she did. Just as he had written in the letter to Josh when he found out Josh had schizophrenia: "The most important thing you need to know about me is that I feel alone. . . . and the only time I don't feel alone is when I'm with you, or with Chris or Caitlin."

Caitlin had braved her fear of flying on planes and traveled with him to Uruguay when he had taken Josh's ashes there to spread over the sea. Even though it had been his decision to move, Jonathan admitted, he felt heartbroken too.

"I love her to death," he said, shaking his head, as if even he had surprised himself by leaving her.

Jonathan had not spoken to Norma since his move to San Diego. Lately, she had not replied to emails from him or Caitlin. He sent the professor an email on Facebook: "Hey Dr. Bowe, I know we've been out of touch. . . . For whatever reason the project we did split us all apart and we never talked about it. All I know is that you've helped me in the hardest time of my life and I will never forget that. I would hate to not be able to call you or email you and vice versa. I want to thank you for bringing out the best in me."

TAKE-HOME WRITING ASSIGNMENT: Bucket List

If you had a year left to live, what would you want to do
before you died? Compile your bucket list.

Caitlin

Dr. Bowe

Death in Perspective

Bucket List

- *Fly on an airplane*
- *See Niagara Falls, Grand Canyon, Pyramids, Hollywood sign*
- *Visit London, Uruguay, Italy, Amsterdam, Japan, San Diego, Las Vegas, and Chicago*
- *Go skiing*
- *Go to a Yankees World Series game*
- *Run a marathon*
- *Go to Disney World with Jon*
- *Road trip across the country*
- *Swim with dolphins*
- *Meet Billy Joel*
- *Update the education system . . . big time!*
- *Get a Doctorate*
- *Go parasailing*
- *Drive a backhoe*
- *Become a personal trainer*
- *Live in another country*
- *Learn how to cook (really well)*
- *Open an animal shelter (so nice that they won't even want to leave)*

- *Open a school for children with learning and behavioral disabilities*
- *Get through the autopsy! Haha*
- *Learn how to surf*
- *Sing karaoke*
- *Meet David Wright*
- *Go camping*
- *Become closer to God again*
- *Have a family reunion on a cruise*
- *Go to the Statue of Liberty (can you believe I haven't been there yet?)*
- *Take a trip with just my sisters*
- *Learn how to dance*

SIXTEEN

Epiphanies

"I never left his side," Caitlin said one day, sitting in a booth in a New Jersey diner after Jonathan moved to San Diego. "Even when I was still dealing with my own stuff. Never once. He knows that."

There was something different about Caitlin as she jabbed at her salad, rain falling in fat drops against the windows. Her words had an edge now, a kind of self-assurance mixed with exasperation.

"I begged him not to break up with me. But he wanted to go, and there was nothing I could do about it," she said. "No matter what I did, it wouldn't change that. He's very focused on his career. I've always made him first. I love him. That's what you do when you really do love someone, you start to put them before you every time, and that's what I started to do. Even in ways I totally shouldn't have."

Jonathan had walked away from Caitlin during the hardest time in her life. She had been trying to stay afloat, juggling five graduate school classes and her thesis while trying to earn money working as a nanny and still trying to save her parents from financial ruin and her mother from committing suicide.

But Jonathan had abandoned her before, and this time she was done begging. Maybe one day, they would be back together again. "I don't want him to ever be hurt in any kind of way. He's my favorite person in this world. We've seen each other through hell."

For now, she would focus on herself, her needs, her career. She had come to a conclusion about her mother: "If my mom wants to die, she's going to do it."

Her mother had been hospitalized for suicide attempts and overdoses twelve times in the last two years. The doctors kept prescribing her pills.

During one of the those attempts, Caitlin had succumbed to her fears when she and her sister had opted to take her mother to the doctor's office, after deciding that she needed a brain evaluation to see if her destructive behavior might have been due to a neurological problem. Caitlin sat in the passenger seat as her sister drove, and their mom sat sobbing in the backseat. They pulled onto the highway, and her mom asked for Caitlin's bottle of water. She passed it back and when her mom returned it, Caitlin noticed two pills in the bottom of the bottle.

She looked back at her mother and realized that she had sneakily gulped down as many pills as she could hold in her mouth. She couldn't even swallow them all, and some were still on her tongue. She toppled over, unconscious and drooling on the seat.

"Should we call the ambulance?" her sister asked.

"Keep driving!" Caitlin shrieked.

They pulled up to the doctor's office, jumped out, and started yelling at everyone around, "My mom is in the backseat! She needs a doctor!"

Nurses took her into the emergency room and pumped her stomach. She vomited and defecated on herself, and a nurse asked Caitlin to help her clean it up.

"I'm sorry, Caitlin, I can't do this," her sister said, walking out of the room. Caitlin cleaned up the mess the best she could.

Again her mother was admitted to the ICU and then the psych unit. But Caitlin had reached a point where she no longer felt the kind of mind-consuming agony that she once had. Her OCD, fears of her mother or father dying, it all seemed to fade away. All of the craziness, she said, "pushed me into not being so anxious about it anymore."

The family house ended up going into foreclosure, and Caitlin's mother separated from her father, moving into her own apartment. On a recent night, Caitlin had gone over to visit after her mother stopped answering her phone. She prepared herself to find her mom dead inside. She unlocked the door, but the chain lock had been fastened across it. Caitlin put her foot through the door and tried to pry it open; she slid her body into the slim crack, trying to push the door open with the back of her shoulder and break the chain. She kept pushing and pushing, and pretty soon she noticed she had slipped right through the crack, into the apartment. The chain was still intact.

"I was, like, how did that happen? I was so confused," Caitlin said, bursting into laughter as she explained how ridiculous the whole situation was. Who knew being thin could be so handy?

Once inside, she found her mother knocked out, unresponsive. Caitlin called an ambulance. When Caitlin arrived in the ER, she didn't cry. Instead, she lectured her mother after they pumped her stomach: "You would have died if you didn't have a daughter that ran to your apartment and broke through the chain."

Caitlin told her that her three daughters and husband have been by her side through everything, yet she made all of them feel as though their love was not enough to make her want to live. "We've been mistreated," Caitlin continued. "We've done nothing wrong. We didn't create this problem for you. You're making it our problem."

"I never thought about it that way," her mother replied through tears.

Caitlin still loved her mother, as she still loved Jonathan. But she was done trying to make them show her that they loved her back. "I have always felt totally comfortable loving other people with all my heart," she said. "But I never felt comfortable loving myself. That wasn't even a thought in my mind."

Not anymore. Norma's lessons finally made sense. Caitlin revealed her right hand. This time there were no bandages or bloody cuts. Instead her wrist revealed a newly inked tattoo: a skeleton key. Her dad, who first helped her begin collecting the keys, was finally beginning to recover and let go of his broken marriage. He had accompanied Caitlin when she got the tattoo. Her dad had always told Caitlin never to give up, and now he was following his own advice by trying to move on too. The tattoo symbolized all of the doors Caitlin had open to her now. Only she had the magic key. She was in control of her own destiny.

Caitlin had graduated from the Kean master's program in psychology two months earlier—and with her stellar recommendations she had already been offered a job. She would begin her new career as a middle school psychologist in the fall, and now she was working toward a PhD.

"I can't change everybody," she said. "I can't change what happens. I can't change what decisions they're going to make. The times I accomplish the most is when I say, 'I have to do what I have to do.'"

JONATHAN AND CAITLIN'S love story would not end there.

By 2011, they decided to try to make their relationship work again. It started long distance. Jonathan flew back to New Jersey every couple of weeks. Caitlin made trips to San Diego. But the distance took its toll as both realized how much they did not want to live without each other.

After more than a year apart, Jonathan returned to New Jersey.

By 2012, Jonathan and Caitlin moved into their own place together.

But each of them felt like they were "waiting for things to turn back into the amazing relationship we once had," Caitlin said. "It never did."

They broke up again, and Jonathan moved out of their apartment.

Through it all, embracing her own trauma, Caitlin had realized, had only helped her professional life. "I watched Dr. Bowe that way."

Caitlin and Norma had stopped speaking for months after the car accident but ended up reuniting. Caitlin had not realized how severely Norma had been injured, and their disagreement over a mental health project was not worth losing each other. The professor, as far as Caitlin could tell, never once apologized for who she was.

"Everyone admires her because of that. But that is not an easy thing to do. You have to be brave to do that," Caitlin said. "And she has shown me how to be brave."

PART
III

Final Exam

SEVENTEEN

Road Trip

After the car accident, Norma was forced to rest. People waited on her, catered to her, coddled her. Her bedroom at home was upstairs, and she was too dizzy to maneuver the steps, so Norm helped make a resting place for her on the couch downstairs in the living room next to the fireplace. He brought extra blankets and pillows and slept on a couch next to her, in case she needed him.

But she hated feeling helpless. She felt as though she was wasting precious time restricted to the sofa, thinking of all the things she could be doing with her days, the lessons she was missing out on teaching, the students who needed her back at school, the Be the Change projects that needed guidance. She thought of her own volunteer endeavors, how she had only just begun working with the incarcerated women before the accident, and already she was missing in action. She didn't want them to feel abandoned.

Her daughters went to classes. Norm went to work. The new school semester began without her. Life went on outside while she was trapped at home. She felt her impatience and urgency bubbling up inside of her. What could she possibly do from the couch? She watched the televised devastation of the January 12 earthquake in Haiti, a magnitude 7.0 with hundreds of aftershocks. The natural disaster killed 230,000 people and injured 300,000.

I am a nurse, she thought, I should be in Haiti helping! She had been involved with a Caribbean medical mission; now she contacted a local nursing organization with links to Haiti and tried to arrange a trip with

them. But the project did not pan out, and Norma begrudgingly realized, at her doctor's urging, that her health was still too fragile to travel
overseas and parachute into a disaster region, no matter how much
training and goodwill she had.

That week, she spoke to a filmmaker friend named Preston Ran-
dolph, whom she had met through a student she had taken on a field
trip to a sweat lodge. Preston had been working on a documentary about
the poverty-stricken Native Americans living on a reservation in South
Dakota. He told Norma that many of the thousands of residents could
not pay their heating bills and had no ability to cook without propane.
A January blizzard had hit, and many were at risk of freezing to death in
the cold winter weather, particularly the children and elders.

Preston had gathered hundreds of coats, gloves, blankets, and boots
on his own and loaded them into a U-Haul trailer for the residents. He
wrote a letter about these dire conditions he was trying to get the word
out about, urging the same Americans who had reached out to Haitians
after the earthquake and to the people of New Orleans after the levees
had broken to turn their eyes to Native Americans who were suffering.

Norma called over her neighbor Chris Rodda, a blogger for the
Huffington Post, who agreed to write a blog about the Native Americans
in South Dakota. Her item ran on the *Huffington Post* on January 27. In
it, Rodda also posted Preston's letter, along with the address of the propane company where people could pay directly for a resident's propane,
which ran $120 minimum per delivery. Rodda mentioned that she'd
learned of the story from her friend Norma Bowe, who had already paid
for three propane deliveries herself.

Another blog, Daily Kos, reposted Rodda's item on January 29 and
continued reporting on it. Producers on *Countdown with Keith Olbermann*
on MSNBC read the blog entries and assigned the show's own reporters
to check it out.

On February 8, Olbermann mentioned the tribal situation in a thirty-
second segment on his show. He mentioned it again the next night. His
show's website linked to the Cheyenne River Sioux Tribe Storm Relief
Emergency Assistance. Within twenty-four hours, people had donated
approximately $185,000 to help. By February 12, tribal officials reported

that 95 percent of the power was back on. Olbermann told viewers, "Your contributions to Cheyenne River Sioux Tribe Storm Relief Emergency Assistance are now at about a quarter of a million dollars."

Rodda and the bloggers at *Daily Kos* received a message from Olbermann, thanking them for bringing the Native Americans' predicament to his attention.

NORMA RETURNED TO teaching in mid-February 2010. It had been two months since her accident. She'd replaced the totaled party bus with a sporty black Hyundai Touring hatchback. She still didn't feel as though she had fully recovered physically, but that did not deter her. After sitting at home for so long watching parts of the world crumble before her eyes on television, she came back to her students as vigorous as ever, wanting to bring her lessons about life and death to as many people as she could.

She continued monitoring the news. More tragedy followed in the months after the January 12 earthquake in Haiti. There were more deadly earthquakes, in Chile and China. Plane crashes in Libya, India, Russia, and into the Mediterranean Sea, killed 447 people, including the president of Poland. There was the story of a professor who had walked into a biology meeting at the University of Alabama on February 12 and shot six faculty members, killing three of them. Not to forget that by the end of March, 133 soldiers had already been killed that year in Afghanistan.

On April 20, the anniversary of the 1999 Columbine school massacre, the BP oil-drilling rig *Deepwater Horizon* exploded in the Gulf of Mexico, killing eleven men. At Kean, Norma's Death in Perspective students discussed the oil worker victims as reports trickled out about the children, wives, and other family members they had left behind. The students talked about the suicide of William Allen Kruse, an Alabama charter-boat captain who had been found dead from an apparent gunshot wound to the head. He had been helping with oil-spill cleanup duties, and family members told the media that he had been deeply troubled by all of the devastation along the Gulf Coast. The class discussed those deaths and the possible effects of oil pollution as another form of mass death. Weeks passed as thousands more barrels of oil gushed into the sea. Reports of devastated marine, wildlife, fishing, and shrimping habitats dominated newscasts.

There was no way people from other towns, cities, or states could enroll in her death class at Kean University. So, Norma decided, she and her Death in Perspective students would take some of the lessons to them.

They would spread the virtues of *generativity* from Erikson's seventh stage in the cycle of life, the period when "the instinctual power behind various forms of selfless 'caring,' potentially extends to whatever a man generates and leaves behind, creates and produces (or helps to produce)," as Erikson wrote.

In July, the oil was continuing to flow into the sea, so as soon as the summer session of classes ended, Norma arranged to take seven Be the Change students, including her daughter Becca, who was now enrolled as a freshman at Kean, on a road trip to the Gulf Coast to help out with ongoing Hurricane Katrina relief efforts—renovating homes for the elderly—and visiting beaches to hand out water bottles and offer any other services they could to oil-spill relief workers. The group had rented a black Suburban, and the students would be sharing rooms at Holiday Inns along the way on the weeklong excursion.

"Want to come along?" Norma asked me in a last-minute email.

I showed up with a duffel bag one morning at Kean University. Norma was running late picking up the rental, and I spotted a student I knew from the death class. We sat together in the lobby of Hennings Hall, waiting for the others.

"So what's our itinerary?"

Norma had been too busy organizing to explain all the plans to me, apart from the gulf as the final destination.

"Well," the student said, "our first stop is Virginia Tech."

I gulped. I had not been back to Virginia Tech University since covering the mass shootings and the French professor's funeral in 2007.

The student explained that Norma had thought it would be a good lesson for her students from Death in Perspective at Kean University to pay their respects to Virginia Tech's dead.

Of course she did, I thought. Who would go on a road trip passing by the vicinity of the campus that had been the site of the largest school shooting in U.S. history without popping in to poke around?

The group of nine road trippers trickled in and piled their belongings into the rented van. By driving through the day and late into the night, stopping at a Waffle House to eat and a Holiday Inn in Roanoke to sleep, we arrived on the Virginia Tech campus the next morning as it was beginning to drizzle. Norma parked the van at The Inn, the stone hotel and conference center that had been overrun by media trucks and satellites that morning three years earlier, when a desperate father had turned to reporters and begged for answers before he discovered that his daughter had been killed.

From there we walked to Norris Hall.

IT SEEMED UNIMAGINABLE that Norris Hall had reopened for classes. Who would want to sit through lessons in a place once covered in bodies and blood? What could a campus do with such a building? Tear it down? Board it up?

Yet, to everyone's surprise, the wooden double doors opened. In the corridor hung a framed sign detailing the evacuation route and another that read SAFE WATCH, asking anyone who noticed suspicious behavior to call. The lights in the building were on, and a staircase leading to the second floor was unobstructed.

One by one, we reached the west wing of the second story. Its floor gleamed with boards of blond and mahogany-toned wood. The walls had been painted pale yellow and decorated with paintings in shades of turquoise, tangerine, apple, gold, rose, and aquamarine. It was bright and cheery, like the Isaiah House. To the group's left was a curved wall of cloudy blue ice-colored glass with the words: CENTER FOR PEACE STUDIES & VIOLENCE PREVENTION. Behind a glass door, we spotted two men. Norma knocked on the door to introduce herself, shuffling inside wearing her hiker's backpack, as the rest of us waited outside in the hall.

Our group had shown up unannounced. Within a few seconds, Norma motioned for everyone to join her inside. A short, white-haired man with a soft-fuzzed gray beard and a pink face approached. He wore a black dress shirt and khaki slacks and spoke with a Polish accent. I had seen him before—at his wife's funeral. She had been the French teacher, known to students as Madame Couture.

Jerzy Nowak welcomed everyone inside. The Kean students loved his name; they pronounced it "Jersey."

He explained that the older daughter of Madame Couture had first suggested the idea for a peace center, which had led to Jerzy's proposal to transform Norris Hall into the headquarters for a program to prevent violence. The university had chosen that proposal over others, and a $50,000 gift from a group called the Lacy Foundation had helped launch the center.

The very room in which we were standing had been room 211, home to the French class taught by Madame Couture. I knew the scene it had once been. My article published in the aftermath of that event had re-created that setting, from the writings in French on the overhead projector, which translated into "Britney Spears has been married more often than Christina Aguilera," to the maroon carpet and lightweight metal desks. I knew where each student had sat and what each had worn: a blue fleece, a newsboy cap, a cadet uniform. I knew where their bodies had fallen.

Jerzy's new office had been set up in the renovated space. The reality hit me: every weekday for the last year, Jerzy had been coming to work on the very spot where his wife had been killed.

What is the purpose of death education? Give examples to support your explanation.

EIGHTEEN

The Rhizome

As Jerzy remembered it, in the weeks after the shootings, plant grow-ers from across the region had loaded pickup trucks full of flowers and brought them as donations to the campus of Virginia Tech. One par-ticular perennial nearly filled an entire truck: small ruby-pink and white petals dangled from each horizontal stem, like charms on a necklace. The plant was known as a bleeding heart. The manager of the garden on campus received so many such flowers in the days after April 16, 2007, that he could not even accept them all.

You could still see the bleeding heart in the Hahn Horticulture Gar-den, where Madame Couture was memorialized and where Norma's students visited after Jerzy gave them all a tour of Norris Hall's second floor. It was the kind of flower that Jocelyne Couture-Nowak would have appreciated, given the love of horticulture she shared with her husband, who had spent most of his career researching plant stresses and plants' reactions to threats of weather, pathogens, and predators.

Madame Couture had enjoyed long days planting marigolds and poppies outside the redbrick home with the view of the Blue Ridge Mountains that they had purchased in 2007. They'd lived in the house for only five weeks before launching ambitious landscaping plans, in-cluding constructing a screen-covered deck in the backyard, a shed, and a patio; building a gazebo that overlooked the yard; and creating a rock garden. That Sunday before his wife was killed, Jerzy had spent the afternoon clearing branches from a rambling rose overgrowth in their lot. He'd suggested stopping work before dark, but Madame Couture had not been ready to quit. She'd asked him to hand over the pruners. It had taken her a half hour to trim the rest of the branches from the rosebush. She'd worn gloves, yet the thorns had pricked her anyway, and she'd left for work the next morning with scratches on her skin.

On her way to class that Monday morning, Madame Couture had stopped by the foreign language department and talked to a colleague about the spring chill. At forty-nine, the Canadian native had pebble gray and white hair that fell past her shoulders, which she often wore in a French braid. Outside, snowflakes swirled. Madame Couture had only one pressing worry on her mind, as she told her colleague: she hoped her flowers would survive the frost.

Nowadays, it was still too painful for Jerzy to go into the details of his wife's death in his public talks, so instead he had done what Norma had often suggested to her grieving students: he had written much of it down, submitting his account as a personal essay to a research journal, *Traumatology*. During the visit, he provided the Kean group with a copy of the article, which Norma read aloud to the group later in the van.

In it, he described how, on that morning, he'd had no reason to believe that his wife's class was being held in Norris Hall, where he heard the shootings had taken place. Language courses took place in various buildings, and he thought she taught in Torgersen Hall. His wife had not been answering her cell phone that morning, but that didn't surprise him either because she often turned it off when she taught. It was not until shortly after 2 P.M., when someone from his daughter's middle school called to tell him that his wife had not arrived to pick up their twelve-year-old daughter, Sylvie, that Jerzy began to sweat. He phoned her department and asked where she had been teaching that day.

The voice replied, "In Norris Hall."

Jerzy went to get Sylvie, and around 4 P.M. the two headed to The Inn at Virginia Tech, where other families had gathered, hoping for information about loved ones. But there was no information. It took hours for him to learn that she had not been admitted to any of the hospitals. He took that as a sign of good news at first.

"She could be among the dead," someone told him.

"You did not need to tell me that," Jerzy replied.

He went to join Sylvie, who had left with a family friend earlier. A hotline had been set up, and Jerzy checked in for the next several hours. Nothing. Journalists called his home, asking for updates. In those hours, Jerzy agonized about everything he had failed to tell his wife in their seventeen years of marriage. Did she know how much he cherished her? Why hadn't he taken that job offer two years earlier?

He had not yet learned the truth, but like so many other families who had not yet heard from their loved ones as night fell, he knew.

As the night ground on, Sylvie told her dad that she was going to lie down on Mom's bed; she wanted to smell her.

At 11:30 P.M., the university provost called, asking if he could come over with the vice provost of education. It took them an hour to arrive, as they went to the wrong address at first because they had not realized the family had recently moved. He let them inside.

"She did not suffer," the provost told Jerzy. "A bullet went through her head."

That detail, as horrific as it was, gave Jerzy momentary comfort. *She did not suffer.*

That morning, within twelve minutes, Seung-Hui Cho had managed to fire 174 shots, wounding twenty-five students at Norris Hall and killing twenty-five students and five faculty members. He'd killed two other students at a dorm earlier that morning. Cho's final blast at 9:51 A.M. was for himself. He died in room 211, his body falling not far from Madame Couture's.

Six others in the classroom survived, but twelve died. Only one person in the French class had not been shot. The other survivors had been hit in the shoulder, collarbone, stomach, buttocks, knee, arms, back, and head.

After the provosts left, Jerzy went to check on his daughter. He thought she might be asleep, but she was awake. Jerzy needed to be alone with Sylvie, who was still on her mother's bed. How could he break such news to a twelve-year-old?

He put his arms around her, whispering what he'd learned about her mom into his little girl's ear. They wept together. Then Sylvie gathered herself together, telling her father that a boy in her class at school had lost his mother to cancer two years before. The boy had made it through. He was okay now. Together, she told him, they would be too.

The next morning, Jerzy had so many tasks to keep his mind distracted: phone family and friends, contact the funeral home, make travel arrangements, figure out expenses and insurance issues, respond to the media requests flooding his inbox and the reporters showing up on his doorstep. It seemed as though a hundred people stopped by that day with coffee, flowers, cards, food, condolences. It was not until the beginning of day two that he really broke down.

How could he answer a teenage girl's questions about growing up— questions a mother would know the answers to far better than him? He had left so much of the day-to-day household responsibilities up to his wife, from cooking to child rearing to paying the bills. How could he learn to handle everything without his beloved wife's guidance? He had never thought about planning a funeral; now he had no idea where to begin.

The doorbell rang at 7 A.M., in the midst of Jerzy's breakdown. It was a neighbor offering coffee and help. Jerzy accepted her offer. Others from throughout the community came to his aid too. A colleague handled the media, giving interviews in front of Jerzy's home while Jerzy escaped to run errands. Family and friends began arriving the next day from around the world, as the Red Cross shuttled them from the airport.

Sylvie's teachers came to the house to set up an individualized study schedule for her and help her catch up on missed assignments. A memorial fund was established in Jerzy's wife's name. Money would go toward building a special garden for her on campus. Donations poured in from across the United States.

Six days passed. Candles flickered and burned out. The roses and carnations left on memorial stones outside Norris Hall wilted. The weather turned warm, and students returned to campus. Mourners replaced the dead flowers with fresh ones. Jerzy was not allowed to view his wife's body until Sunday evening. He asked to go in before the rest of the family, to determine whether it would be okay for the others to see her. When Jerzy entered the room, he looked at the body of the woman who for so many years had called him "darling." He searched her hands for the scratches from the rambling rose thorns. He traced the track of dried droplets of blood between the fingers of her left hand. The bullet had scratched her wedding ring and hit the left side of her forehead.

After the funeral was over, after his wife's ashes had been scattered over Cape Forchu in Nova Scotia, where the two of them had visited a lighthouse on one of their earlier dates, after the media had gone home, Jerzy began to ponder how he would live with her memory. His step-daughter, Francine Dulong, had suggested creating a peace center, and the idea had stuck with him.

Jerzy could not stand outside Norris Hall and see the memorial to the dead on the drillfield. Thirty-two slabs of limestone, each a foot wide, each bearing the name of each of Cho's shooting victims, including Jocelyne Couture-Nowak. The stones formed an arch in the grass. He took a leave from the horticulture department to launch the Center for Peace Studies and Violence Prevention, and two years after his wife's funeral, he moved into his new office in the west wing of the second floor of Norris Hall.

"PLANTS ARE NOT solitary organisms," Jerzy wrote in the *Traumatology* essay that Norma read to students en route to the Gulf Coast after they left Virginia Tech that afternoon. "Their capacity to withstand stress is heavily dependent on their interactions with other organisms in the rhizosphere, the zone that surrounds their roots."

The bleeding heart, for example, dies in midsummer and stays dormant until the following spring. But its essence lives on underground; the plant's seeds have been born in pods, where they absorbed water within the earth, flourishing into an intricate underground life system known as the rhizome. Part of this main stem bursts through the surface of earth in warm months, creating leaflets that absorb water and carbon dioxide from sunlight. Those elements transform into sugar that the bleeding heart, like most of life, needs to survive, while releasing a by-product—oxygen, which we need to survive—into the air.

As the plant matures, the heart-shaped petals blossom, ready to spread their seed to the next generation. The bloom will stay visible for a single season. Meanwhile, underground, the rhizome is storing nutrients for the winter and working for the benefit of the community, sending sugar into the soil that surrounds it, on which microbes like bacteria feast. In return, bacteria help the flower survive, absorbing nitrogen from the soil and turning it into fertilizer to create a stronger, more resilient plant.

"Life has always seemed to me like a plant that lives on its rhizome," the psychologist Carl Jung wrote in *Memories, Dreams, Reflections*. "Its true life is invisible, hidden in the rhizome. The part that appears above ground lasts only a single summer. Then it withers away—an ephemeral apparition. When we think of the unending growth and decay of life and civilizations, we cannot escape the impression of absolute nullity. Yet I have never lost a sense of something that lives and endures underneath the eternal flux. What we see is the blossom, which passes. The rhizome remains."

People, as Jerzy saw it, were not really so different from plants. In times of great stress they needed one another, needed the support of their communities, to endure. They became living proof of Erikson's generativity.

So Jerzy invited Norma and her students to return to Virginia Tech in three months to give a presentation at the Center for Peace Studies and Violence Prevention's first major event since it had been launched. They would get to meet experts from around the world who were working on nonviolence subjects.

Norma made a mental note of who would join her this time. She invited two girls from Isaiah House, and Isis was one of them. Since it was a conference on nonviolence, Norma knew there was another student she could not leave out. When she got ahold of Israel, he told the professor he would rearrange his work schedule, pitch in with driving duties, whatever she needed. He was definitely in.

ISRAEL PLOPPED HIMSELF behind the steering wheel, clipped his commercial driver's license for trucks and buses to the visor of the van, and turned up the hip-hop music on the stereo. Isis, wearing a bright pink Kean University T-shirt with an army green jacket over it, sat in the front passenger seat next to him. Leaning back in the driver's seat with his hand on the wheel, Israel proceeded to zip down the interstate with a van of ten people in tow for the 480-mile trip.

Seven hours later, Israel delivered everyone in the van to Virginia Tech in time for the keynote address. The group stayed up almost all night with Norma, practicing for the next morning's presentation in the lobby of The Inn at Virginia Tech. With the exception of Israel, most didn't have public speaking experience, and they were terrified, stuttering through their lines, forgetting the explanations of the psychological concepts they planned to bring up, such as Robert Agnew's General Strain Theory and Abraham Maslow's Hierarchy of Needs.

"What if I get up there and freeze?" one asked.

"What if I throw up?"

"You guys are going to do great," Norma assured them.

They didn't want their presentation to be all about theories and—taking a lesson out of Norma's practice—some decided to share their personal experiences with violence and discrimination. By seven the next morning, the students had already put on their fluorescent green Kean University T-shirts and gathered in a meeting room to practice more. As the first audience members trickled into the assembly hall, Norma looked at her cell phone's clock. The presentation would begin in minutes, but the room was mostly empty.

"Where is everyone?" Norma said. "Shouldn't we wait for more?"

But they couldn't. It was time to begin. The professors and other experts, the group soon learned, would not be coming. The students had been partitioned off in the basement of the Inn, while the world-renowned academics and scholars were meeting separately in the conference center upstairs.

Jerzy had not intended for the conference to be divided into two when he had begun planning it two years earlier—he'd always envisioned it as student-centered. But six months before, university officials had seized on the opportunity to build on Jerzy's vision by creating a conference for academics and researchers, inviting their own speakers, including a

Harvard Medical School specialist in children's exposure to urban violence, a speaker from the U.S. Department of Education, and a renowned researcher of antisocial and violent behavior and neuropsychology.

The Kean students didn't understand the division, and it all seemed a bit unfair to Jerzy. Why not one conference? Why couldn't students and professors present together? Wasn't it important for people with PhDs and international followings to hear about what the students had to say?

The vice president and dean of undergraduate education at Virginia Tech approached the lectern and made a few brief opening comments. When he was done, he left the stage and walked out the door.

A moderator announced, "I invite Kean University and its contingent to come forward, please." The group gathered in front of the lecture hall, the audience seats filled with about seventeen people. Norma cheered on the students from the second row.

Even with the paltry crowd, one unflaggingly supportive face in the audience made the effort seem worth it. Off to their right, in the front, sat Jerzy. He had the row all to himself.

When Israel's turn came to speak, he recounted the life of crime that had led to his reformation. He was now training to go into law enforcement. He introduced the teen homeless shelter project, explaining that in the area surrounding Isaiah House, "Just since September, there have been 87 rapes, 105 murders, and over 2,000 robberies."

When Isis took the microphone, she could not stop crying, explaining how her mother had done drugs, beaten her, and ended up in prison for eleven years. "I didn't think I was going to make it," she said. But as of the last marking period, she had received straight As and was now preparing for Kean University, along with two other girls from Isaiah House. An alumna had written her a $10,000 check to cover the tuition after hearing her story at a fund-raiser for Norma's Be the Change group. Five other college applications had been received from the shelter for Fall 2011.

When their presentation ended, Jerzy rose from his seat. He walked over to Norma and her students, his face pink as a petal. He had tears in his eyes, and a smile took over his face as he went down the line and embraced each one of them.

Of Norma's students, Jerzy said that he felt most connected to Israel. The young man reminded Jerzy of the soldiers he had been put in charge of in Poland when he had been working for the army. The men had been criminals before going under Jerzy's watch, and they were preparing to put down a rebellion in 1968. Jerzy's task was to try to humanize them. He had managed to transform some of the former criminals and considered it among the biggest successes of his life.

Later, Jerzy could not forget a particular moment at the Virginia Tech conference when the students had acted out scenes led by the drama department. Israel had been paired with a theater professor who had tried simulating holding a gun. Without uttering a word, Israel took that man's hand and redirected his finger in precisely the way it would be positioned if he were pulling a trigger.

Then Israel took his own hand and gently cupped it around the theater professor's imaginary gun, as Jerzy and everyone else watched. Israel formed a shield with his fingers to block its make-believe bullets.

UPON THE STUDENTS' return from Virginia Tech, Be the Change continued to gain traction, participating in more home makeover projects, including one for a single mom with three kids, two of whom were wheelchair-bound. Their mother ended up enrolling at Kean University. They hosted a discussion on campus with the father of a Virginia Tech shooting victim, as well as trips to the Amnesty International Northeast Regional Conference and the Omega Institute's Women & Power Conference, to which scholarships were provided to young women from Isaiah House and Kean.

Be the Change students handed out more than a thousand purple ribbons on campus to raise awareness about the issues of bullying following the suicide of eighteen-year-old Tyler Clementi, who had attended nearby Rutgers University. Clementi, who was gay, had jumped off the George Washington Bridge in September 2010 after his roommate had secretly taped him on a webcam having a romantic encounter with a man and then posted the video online.

The group launched "Operation PB&J," in which students met

weekly to make two hundred to three hundred peanut butter and jelly sandwiches and stuff each into a brown paper bag along with fruit, juice, and other snacks, handing the items out to the homeless sleeping in and around Newark's Penn Station. The cost to feed the homeless came to $100 each week, which students tried to raise; when they couldn't, Norma paid it on her own. The student group also gathered clothes and toys for victims of the tornados in Joplin, Missouri, which Norma and Norm delivered in person during the summer break.

A half-dozen girls from Isaiah House enrolled as students at Kean University. By September 2011, Isis, who had become a freshman, was going along on some of the excursions like Operation PB&J. She had relied on such handouts when she was homeless.

In 2011, Be the Change began working toward becoming an official nonprofit. Norma had hopes that students could one day work or intern for the organization to gain experience and travel around the world doing community service projects. The group inspired a Be the Change club at nearby University High School and got permission to paint a "Before I Die" wall on their campus after seeing the concept in New Orleans, where a woman named Candy Chang had turned the side of an abandoned house into a giant chalkboard on which residents wrote their fears, hopes, and dreams.

At University High, Be the Change college and high school students worked together one rainy afternoon to paint black chalkboard paint over redbrick. They took turns finishing the sentence "Before I die I want to ___" in their own words. Several dozen declarations trailed across the wall in white letters:

"Before I die I want to fall in love."
"Before I die I want to be a wife and mother."
"Before I die I want to save a life."

CLASS DISCUSSION QUESTION
How do the stories of who we are survive our death?
Erika Hayasaki
Dr. Bowe
Death in Perspective
Good-bye Letter

You should have been given a chance to graduate, Sangeeta, to fall in love with a good man, to watch your mother grow old, to lose touch with childhood friends and years later stumble across them on Facebook. I can imagine your message to me: "Hey girl, remember me? I'm a mom now. Life has been good. Hard sometimes, with this economy and all, but good."

And I would remind you of that day sophomore year when you kissed your new car and I just wouldn't let you go. How I begged you to take me for a ride instead.

How we swore to each other we would never let that night end. How we swore we would never say good-bye.

In loving memory of you.

NINETEEN

Life Cycles

For a long time, I had kept in my possession a Polaroid photo of my high school friend Sangeeta in her coffin. I don't remember exactly why I had it. Only that someone handed me the photo for safekeeping after the funeral and never asked for it back. I lost track of the person who gave it to me, so I tucked the photo away in an envelope, and then in a box, and tried to forget. Until I did forget.

Many years later, when I went digging through my boxes, I couldn't find it. The photo was gone, beyond my grasp, a memory.

I had not seen Sangeeta's mother, Parneeta, in sixteen years, but I still had one final assignment to complete. I always believed she'd packed up and gone back to Fiji. But in fact she had stayed. I discovered she lived only twenty minutes north of where Sangeeta had been killed.

One Sunday morning in 2010, after visiting my mother and grandparents in nearby Lynnwood, Washington, I arrived at a grayish blue home, walked past a colorful Big Wheel in the front yard, and knocked on her door.

Parneeta answered. She had Sangeeta's long black shiny hair, her round brown face, and her bright eyes—except there was something different about her eyes: they were surrounded by a reservoir of laugh lines.

She remembered my high school article about her daughter. Parneeta went into another room and came back with an armful of mementos and old photographs, including one of mother and daughter smiling against a billowing studio backdrop, both in floral prints, both with the front of their hair pinned back the same.

Parneeta told me that she had emigrated from Fiji to America after divorcing Sangeeta's father and that she had not known many people when she arrived. Unlike her daughter, she had not grown a crop of close friends. Sangeeta had been Parneeta's best friend. "I used to *laugh* so much with her," she said, stretching out the word "laugh" as if holding on to the note of a lullaby. "When we were together, nobody could tell we were mother and daughter."

It was a hard life. Parneeta was a single mother, raising Sangeeta and her older brother alone. At first, they lived in public housing projects, until Parneeta found work at Nintendo, and that was when they moved into the Lynnwood apartment. Then she took a second job on the weekends to cover the bills, rent, and groceries.

Parneeta had not been there for her daughter that morning when she was killed—and she had spent many years hating herself for that.

"That morning I woke up. I was having a little cold. I was thinking I should not go to work. Maybe I should call in."

She had dragged herself out of bed in the dark of the morning hour and into the shower.

Was the killer waiting for her daughter already then? She always wondered. Lurking in the shadows? Spying as he watched for her to leave the parking lot?

"She was asleep," Parneeta continued. "I checked her bedroom door. It was locked. I double-locked the front door and drove to work."

She'd been at work for several hours when the officers showed up.

After the funeral, Parneeta quit both of her jobs, believing they took her daughter away. She stared at Sangeeta's pictures for hours. She drove through red lights. Every day, she dreamed of Sangeeta. If she did not dream of her, she felt angry.

Her son, Parnesh, had been in a persistent state of trouble, which worsened. Parneeta had thrown all of his clothes into a garbage bag before Sangeeta died and told another family member to pick him up. But he ran away and got into drugs, stealing, and hanging out with gangs. Eventually he landed in prison.

Weeks disappeared into months, into years. Parneeta prayed, meditated, went to a temple every night. She went for long walks and did yoga in the mornings. She lighted incense and candles, and cried out into the air. "I could feel her around me."

Her son was locked up forty-four times—and spent about four and a half years on and off behind bars for crimes such as residential burglary and robbery.

Following the family custom, Parnesh entered into an arranged marriage in 2006. But that still did not change his ways. He felt as though he had lost his heart when his sister died. Nothing in the world could soften him again. His wife became pregnant, but when she went to the hospital in labor, Parnesh did not even go with her.

He showed up hours after the delivery. Parnesh looked at his wife holding their firstborn child in her arms. A strange feeling washed over him. He could sense something powerful in this child's presence. His mother could too.

A LITTLE GIRL shuffled into the dining room, where I had been speaking with Parneeta. She had on pink-striped socks and a pink polka-dot cotton dress and a tangerine sweater embroidered with sequined starry flowers. Her hair was swept up in a ponytail.

"Baby," Parneeta said, pulling the child into her lap. "Look who's here."

The girl looked at me. Those big eyes. Framed by long, paper fan–like eyelashes. Parneeta unfastened the girl's ponytail, and black locks went tumbling down her back.

She was three years old, Parnesh's daughter—Parneeta's granddaughter.

Her middle name was Sangeeta.

Parnesh had found a job, and his wife gave birth to a second child, also a little girl. The birth of his first daughter had compelled him to get his act together, stay out of jail, and become a devoted father and husband, and for the past three years he had done just that. The family had pitched in to buy a house with grandma. Parneeta found a new job as well. It was close to home. If they needed a babysitter she never hesitated to take off time from work.

The little girl buried her face in her grandma's chest, and Parneeta wrapped her arms around her and nuzzled back.

"That," Parneeta told me, "is how our lives changed."

TWENTY

Birthday

August 22, 2011

It was Norma's birthday, and I had been trying for months to convince her not to spend it alone, as she always preferred to do. I had moved from New York back to California, but I told the professor I would be flying back to the East Coast in the hope that she would take me to Newport News, Virginia, where she had spent her happiest years with her grandmother as a child and also where she had buried her grandmother as an adult the day after her birthday. We had been planning this trip for years, and more than once she had canceled on me.

This time around, I was not surprised when Norma didn't respond to my messages right away. I knew she did not care to dwell on the more painful parts of her past, and I knew she detested being with people on the days before, during, and after her birthday even more. Considering that she barely let her family near her those three days, I suspected the last person she would be eager to share that time with would be me. I got onto the plane anyway.

Norma had agreed to let me follow her around beginning in 2008 because she wanted to spread her class lessons to a wider audience. But she had not anticipated that I would still be tagging along and asking probing questions—particularly about *her*—three years later.

"Always the journalist," she would say in response to my questions.

"Always the nurse," I would reply.

I arrived the day before her birthday. Late the next morning, I got a response from her: she had changed her mind about our excursion. We would go to her cabin in New Hampshire. She did not think she was up for Virginia.

At that point, I was happy to take whatever I could get.

When she pulled up in her black hatchback an hour later at the shopping center parking lot where we had agreed to meet, she looked pretty in her long pale gray cotton summer dress, raisin-colored lipstick, and a necklace made of turquoise and rose-shaded buffalo charms. It turned out I had not been the only one pressuring her; she had relented and gone to a birthday breakfast with her older daughter that morning.

As soon as I sat in the front passenger seat, she looked at me and said, "I think I changed my mind."

About the trip? I asked.

No, she replied. About the destination. Her grandmother's hometown in Virginia, she felt, was pulling her.

"Let's do it," I said, and we pointed the car toward Virginia.

We stopped in Baltimore, her father's hometown, for the night and ate crab cakes for dinner. There was no birthday dessert and no singing or clapping waiters. Norma was explicit: she wanted none of that.

The next morning, she drove around Little Italy, pointing out her father's and grandfather's old neighborhood, the tenement row houses now replaced by condos, the storefronts that used to house spaghetti shops.

As she steered, she pulled out a birthday card her father had sent her. She had tucked it between the seat and gear panel. Inside the card, her father had written, "You have accomplished much, endured a tough history of memories. However you have *prevailed*. And I adore you for that."

We were almost to Virginia. I took the wheel as Norma moved to the backseat, where she pulled out some bridal shower invites. She had offered to put together the shower for a young woman she knew whose mother had committed suicide. She was also scheduled to help her pick out her wedding dress in a few days.

Norma bounced around in the back, trying to write out the invites, but she soon gave up when the bumpy road made writing impossible. She checked her Facebook messages, catching up on the hundreds of missed birthday notes from yesterday. "Oh, my God, there was an earthquake in New Jersey!"

It had rumbled the East Coast just minutes before. Students and neighbors had started posting that they had felt the jolt. "Wait," she said, clicking on more status updates. The epicenter of the quake was actually centered near Richmond, Virginia. We had just left Richmond and were about twenty minutes away when it hit. That must have been what that bumpy road was all about. Maybe, she joked, it was her mother trying to send us a message.

She pulled up a *New York Times* article on her phone. It was a 5.8 magnitude earthquake felt all the way from Washington, D.C., where it had damaged National Cathedral, to Manhattan's Wall Street, Maine, and Georgia. Geologists announced that it was the strongest quake in central Virginia's history. The only other two that had come close had struck in 1875 and 1897.

A powerful hurricane was headed for the Northeast, where it was expected to hit Virginia, New York City, and New Jersey, among other areas, over the next several days. By the time Norma returned to Highland Park the next week, her home would be flooded and her power would be out. She would end up sleeping in a motel for the next three months following Hurricane Irene, well into the new semester.

But neither of us knew any of that. We were just cruising along with Norma's Sirius XM radio station tuned to the Coffee House channel.

It was just as Norma always said: "I have no danger button," no clear sense for when to get out of harm's way. We were sixty miles from Newport News, and the skies were hydrangea blue and clear.

WE PASSED CHRISTOPHER Newport University, a statue of Leif Eriksson, and Civil War Trails and turned onto Shoe Lane, a narrow road shaded by tall pine and crab apple trees. Swings hung from tree branches in front of Savannah-style mansions. Some of the homes had pillars and rolling green lawns.

We pulled into the driveway of a white house on a high ridge with chipped green paint trimming and flowering bushes. It overlooked a dried-up creek, and two dogwood trees still stood where her grandmother had planted them. "It always felt like she was in a tree house, you know?" Norma said, walking up the driveway.

It used to be painted gray, Norma remembered. Her grandmother had sold the place when she'd gotten sick, not long before she had died. The nameplate in front now read "Beale."

"I would park at the end of the driveway and walk up," Norma said. "My grandmother would stand at the doorway waving. She was so excited. I remember she always wore a diamond necklace with a bigger diamond and two small ones."

Norma climbed the front steps, crunching pinecones on the way to a wooden deck. "They have a Jacuzzi now," she said. "Should I ring the bell? I'm sure nobody's home."

No one answered. It was a Tuesday afternoon, and the owners were probably at work. "This was her bedroom right here," Norma said, trying to peer in through a draped window. "Then the backyard . . . I was friends with the little girl that lived behind."

We got back into the car and drove down the road, to the bay overlooking the James River, where she'd used to bring her books and study while people crabbed and fished. The lion statues in the park that her grandmother had dedicated to her still stood there with puffed-out chests.

"Well, we'll just do a little cemetery field trip next," Norma said, trying to remember the name of the memorial park in which she had buried her grandmother. We headed to the nearest one listed on her GPS, the Garden of Rest, and Norma went inside the main office to get a map. The cemetery director led her to the plots himself. His family plots were near hers. "Enjoy your visit," he said.

She stared through her sunglasses at the two matching flat headstones, both with brass plates set against marbled stone.

Her great-grandmother, Celia W. Hayflich, 1887–1984.

Her grandmother's headstone had gold flower etchings: Rosalie H. Stein, 1910–1990. Norma explained that her great-grandmother and great-grandfather had come to Ellis Island from Russia by ship, after fleeing pogroms against Jews. They had made their money by going into the hatmaking business in New York.

Norma trolled the cemetery grass in search of rocks to put on their graves. She picked up two flat stones and placed them on the metal plates, sitting cross-legged before them.

In Erikson's first stage of life, mistrust threatens the life of a baby if that child has not been properly loved. In the last stage of life, despair darkens the death of a dying person if that person's life has not been properly lived. Hope, as Erikson taught, began in the first stage of life if trust was established with loving care. In his writings, Erikson quoted a *Webster's Dictionary* entry when he stated, "Trust (the first of our ego values) is here defined as 'the assured reliance on another's integrity,' the last of our values. I suspect that Webster had business in mind rather than babies, credit rather than faith. But the formulation stands. And it seems possible to further paraphrase the relation of adult integrity and infantile trust by saying that healthy children will not fear life if their elders have integrity enough to not fear death."

Each stage of life is filled with unique challenges, but the ways in which each person learns to survive, according to Erikson, create character.

Sometimes these lessons needed to be examined beyond textbooks, in the lives and life cycles of everyday people. That was what was practiced by Norma, this rare woman who respected death without trepidation. This professor who delighted in cemeteries, the overlooked classrooms beneath our feet. Her intuition led her to damaged people because she had once felt damaged too. She taught her students to understand the value of Erikson's lessons long before they reached the final stages of life. She helped create character.

The people I had encountered on this journey with Norma—Jonathan, Caitlin, Israel, Carl, Jerzy, and Isis—had learned the value of living for others. But living for others alone was not enough. Caitlin had realized that. Jonathan had realized that. And of everyone, perhaps the one person who had had to work hardest to live by it was Norma.

Norma hunched over the burial plots with her sandals off. Blades of grass tickled her feet. All around her, weeds had pushed through the earth's skin and become pretty. For a moment, she paid attention to nothing else—just her emotions and her ancestors beneath the ground. She polished the dull brass headstones with her palms, gently scraping the earth-dusted letters with her fingernails.

Norma had come into this world, fighting to live. Yet for so long she felt shame that she had survived at all.

"For the first time, really ever," she told me on the way home, "it feels like a long time ago."

Epilogue

If you look for Norma Bowe and her students today, you might find them planting gardens. They are scooping worm-filled soil into their palms, spreading seeds, waiting for tomatoes, watermelons, cantaloupes, carrots, and roses to grow. They are planting mint and lilies, clearing the way for rhizomes to flourish.

They first sowed a memory garden at Kean University, where Death in Perspective students and the campus community could honor lost loved ones, and since then Be the Change has transformed abandoned lots throughout Newark into community gardens partly inspired by the one at Virginia Tech in memory of Madame Couture.

The Newark garden project began in 2012, when Norma and a student found a vacant lot next to an elderly care facility. It was one of hundreds of such lots in the area exposed to open-air drug dealing. Norma and the student offered to bring Be the Change back to build a community garden on the weed-infested, trash-littered desert of dirt. A resident of the elder care facility contacted the councilman for the Central Ward, Darrin Sharif, who cleared the way for the project. Sharif attended the makeover and was so impressed by the students and their professor that he asked if they might be willing to take on another abandoned lot on South 14th Street, on one of the highest-crime blocks, in memory of a woman who had been known as the "mayor" of her neighborhood, Rica Jenkins. She had passed away the previous year. Norma's team planted flowers that Rica's family said she had appreciated.

Sharif noticed that Norma had been reaching into her own pocket to pay for the garden renovations. With so many vacant lots in Newark, he wanted to support Be the Change if it would be willing to continue its work. Sharif secured a spacious office with hardwood floors, a kitchen, a bathroom, desks, and sofas in downtown Newark for Be the Change to hold its meetings, fund-raisers, and other events. Be the Change would go on to transform vacant lots across the city.

Since 2011, Be the Change students have also handed out more than ten thousand peanut butter and jelly sandwiches and brown-bag meals to the homeless sleeping in and around Newark's Penn Station, and they have remained active throughout other parts of the country. The students returned to Virginia Tech three times since the first visit to meet with students, educators, and activists. Jerzy Nowak retired from the Center for Peace Studies and Violence in 2011 but remains active with the organization.

The group's spring break community service trips to the Gulf Coast became annual adventures. The students stopped in Tuscaloosa, Alabama, to deliver clothing, food, and other supplies to survivors of the 2011 tornados. Israel remained active in many of the events, including the garden projects and another one to send water, food, and six hundred pounds of toys to children and families who survived the 2011 tornado in Joplin, Missouri, which killed 158 people and destroyed around eight thousand houses and apartments. In 2013, Be the Change raised more than $2,000 in gift cards for survivors of the Moore, Oklahoma tornado.

Be the Change has continued to regularly team up with the United Saints Recovery Project in Louisiana to help rebuild homes for residents who lost them during Hurricane Katrina. While in the gulf area in 2010, the students befriended a fisherman nicknamed "Red." At six feet, six inches tall in his overalls, he had crawfish red hair, wore size 13 boots, and was built like the trunk of a live-oak tree. Before the 2010 BP oil spill, he'd worked on a shrimp boat, an oyster boat, and two charter boats. But, like so many of his neighbors, he'd lost his fishing career during the oil disaster.

Just before Christmas 2010, Red called Norma in New Jersey and explained that fishermen in the gulf area were struggling to pay their bills and buy gifts for their kids. "There was drug abuse, alcohol abuse, domestic violence had shot up," he said. "They couldn't fish. They were broke." Norma and Be the Change gathered donations of toys and raised $5,000 to cover the shipping costs. "We put toys in the hands of every fisherman, shrimper, crabber, and oysterman that needed them," said Red.

Be the Change sent toys to the fishermen's families for the holidays again the following year. Then, in late October 2012, the Tri-State Area became a victim of its own major natural disaster. Hurricane Sandy obliterated parts of New York and the New Jersey coastline. Wanting to help and remembering all that his New Jersey friends had done for his neighbors, Red got on his local news station in Mississippi and announced that he planned to travel to New Jersey with his tool set to help rebuild. His phone started ringing, and within days he had received donations and support, including a 53-foot, 18-wheel moving truck, which he packed full of food and supplies. It took two and a half days to drive the truck to New Jersey, and when he arrived he met up with Norma and her students, who had already been hard at work. Be the Change had descended upon a community called Union Beach, just twenty-six miles from Kean. Sandy had destroyed or damaged 1,600 of the town's 2,100 homes. The students visited daily, some donning hazmat suits and masks to help clean out people's flooded basements and haul away debris. Others helped cook for and feed people who'd lost their homes and power. Israel pulled nine-hour storm relief shifts. Red dropped off most of his supplies and donations in Union Beach and spent the next month washing dishes and serving meals to survivors.

Norma remains in touch with many of the other young people she has worked with over the years, those who have graduated and moved on with their lives, including Jonathan and Caitlin.

A few months after Jonathan moved out of the apartment that he had shared with Caitlin for a year, he found a new girlfriend. Caitlin wrote him an email, giving his new relationship her blessing.

"Sometimes I can't believe how different I feel inside," Caitlin said. "Something I knew would have destroyed me before hasn't this time." She is thriving in her new career as a middle school psychologist. Her personal experiences help her relate to the children she works with, and she has conquered the worst of her OCD, no longer relying on rituals to calm her. She has since crossed nine more items off her bucket list: She has visited Niagara Falls, the Grand Canyon, Uruguay, San Diego, Chicago, and gone to Disney World with Jonathan. She has parasailed, camped, and sung karaoke, and she will earn her doctorate in psychology in 2015. Jonathan continues to travel the country and share his family's story with public audiences in the hope of touching others. He has spoken before thousands.

As for Norma's Death in Perspective class, it continues to fill up quickly each semester, and the professor has added a new field trip to the list: the crematory. She also added more class projects to the syllabus, including the preservation of an abandoned cemetery near some of the gardens in Newark that Be the Change planted. Two classes of Death in Perspective students would meet at the cemetery in the warm-weather months to clear the broken tombstones of the moss and vines that obscure hundred-year-old etchings, pull the weeds, and cut the overgrown grass. In March 2013, Norma was honored with an Outstanding Human Rights Educator Award from Kean's Human Rights Institute.

To SEE SOME of Be the Change's projects in action, please check out these videos made by students:

thedeathclass.com/be-the-change/

A Note About This Book

This is a work of narrative nonfiction. The people in this book are real, their stories true. No events have been fabricated, no quotes made up. Over the course of four years, I spent thousands of hours following around the characters presented here, almost always with a tape recorder in hand. I also took handwritten notes and sometimes photographs as additional documentation. I read nearly a hundred books and articles on the subjects of death, dying, and mental health—from psychology to philosophy to science—and interviewed experts in the field, but most of that scholarly research did not make it into this book. Rather, it informed the writing of each narrative, for this is first and foremost a story about people. Israel's name was changed, along with the young gang member he mentored—to protect Israel's identity because he believed his life might have been put in jeopardy if details became public. All other names are real.

I relied heavily on three forms of reporting. The first is called "immersion journalism," also known as fly-on-the-wall reporting. In many instances, I was the journalist capturing the events going on around me, trying to blend into the background and remain as unobtrusive as possible.

The second is known as "participatory journalism," in which I participated in some events, including becoming an active member of the class, completing written assignments, and going along on field trips. As a participant, I was able to give myself permission not only to be emotionally affected by the journey, as any other human would, but also to write about my own experiences.

The third form of reporting is often referred to as "narrative reconstruction." Some events happened in the past. I could not have been present to record them, so instead I relied on an array of sources: interviews with witnesses, journal entries, class assignments, photo albums, videos, newspapers, police reports, medical records, and court documents, in some cases revisiting sites where events had occurred to capture the surroundings.

I interviewed more than fifty of Norma Bowe's students and came to know dozens of others as well. I wish I could have included all of their stories here. The main characters in this book were extremely cooperative and open when it came to my exhaustive probing and shadowing. I went back to them numerous times to make sure I had documented each of their journeys, as well as their thoughts and feelings, right. I tried my best as a narrator to capture each person's language, mannerisms, memories, and emotions, often adopting the way of talking they used in interviews. In some places, I included the exact quotes they used to describe the way they were feeling. I chose to trust their interpretations of particular moments, but I do not discount the fallibility of human memory.

In some instances in this book, where I employed narrative reconstruction, there were no additional documents or additional witnesses available to supplement the reporting of a scene. When that happened, I relied on the recollections of the main person involved and chose to include memories connected to highly emotionally charged experiences, as studies have shown that those are the memories our minds tend to preserve.

I am thankful they allowed me into their lives and minds to do this because I know that without all of our memories, stories would not be stories. The remarkableness of our lives would be lost on us. And the dead would always remain just that. So this is a book of memories and documentation, as close to the truth as I could get, appreciating that within the hard facts, we can also discover metaphor and meaning.

Acknowledgments

First I want to thank Norma Bowe for agreeing to allow me to tell the story of her life and her students' lives. When I first met her, she had no idea I would still be following her around four years later, but she hung in there because she recognized the value of bringing experiences from her class to a wider audience. Her life encapsulated the stories I love to tell, about everyday people who live through extraordinary events, as did Caitlin, Jonathan, Israel, Carl, Isis, Stephanie, Parneeta, and Jerzy. Thank you to all of the people who ended up in this book. Your resilience and courage made me work even harder to honor your truths.

To the people who have inspired and guided me the most in my career: Richard E. Meyer, who taught me how to practice narrative journalism; he holds stories to the most rigorous of standards because he believes "God is in the details," and I try to pass on his generativity to the students I teach every year. To Richard Kipling and Miriam Pawel for giving me opportunities when I was an aspiring journalist out of college, and who have remained mentors and friends ever since. To Barry Siegel, a masterful literary journalist who leads by example and believed that I could write a book. To Leslie Schwartz, who taught me how much nonfiction writers can learn from the techniques of fiction while still adhering to the journalistic foundations of truth, and who gave brutally honest yet encouraging feedback on my raw pages. To Steve Padilla, the kind of writing coach every newsroom needs, who read every page of this book and offered valuable editing and suggestions.

To Jonathan Karp of Simon & Schuster for believing in this idea, and in me, from the beginning, and for giving the time, support, and editorial guidance to make it happen. To Priscilla Painton for being a kind, patient, and rigorous editor who demands excellence. To Michael Szczerban for his thoughtful and smart suggestions, and also to Sydney Tanigawa.

To my agent, Kathy Robbins, for being on my team, and for offering instructive feedback and steady support, and to The Robbins Office, Rachelle Bergstein, Mike Gillespie, and Micah Hauser, for all of their valuable assistance.

This book arose out of a *Los Angeles Times* Column One, which was my favorite section to write for, and I want to thank my editors Millie Quan, Scott Kraft, and Roger Smith, who gave me the freedom and encouragement to stretch and push myself as a writer within that space.

From the *Los Angeles Times*, I would also like to thank Efrain Hernandez, Frank Sotomayor, Randy Hagihara, Craig Matsuda, Tracy Boucher, and Susan Denley for supporting the Minority Editorial Training Program. I always felt humbled to be working for such talented editors, especially John Carroll, Dean Baquet, Marc Duvoisin, Beth Schuster, Julie Marquis, Larry Gordon, Sue Horton, the late Don Hunt, and Shelby Grad. I learned from their leadership and guidance.

To the journalism mentors who first helped me find my voice and write about Sangeeta, among other stories, when I was in high school: Susan Best, Lynn Jacobs, and Carole Carmichael. And in college, to the professors whose literary journalism inspired me, Walt Harrington and Leon Dash.

To my mother, Bev Harris, a fearless investigator, gifted writer, nurturing soul, and the strongest woman I know. To my father, Yoshi Hayasaki, who boarded a cargo ship to America when he was eighteen not knowing English and made his dreams come true. To Lisa Hayasaki, a second mom to me, and to my siblings Casey Hayasaki, Mia Hayasaki, and Megan Melton. To my grandmother, Ruth Harris, and grandfather, the late Carl Harris, who ran his own writing group into his mid-eighties. To the other prolific writers in my family, my uncle, the late Richard Harris, and my aunt Tamalyn Dallal.

To the friends who have been my steadfast foundation: Sandra

Murillo and Steven Campos, Tanya Miller, Marjorie Hernandez, Kenyatta Anthony, Jia-Rui Chong and Bryan Cook, David and Tessa Pierson, Melissa Murillo, Portia Marcelo, Thuy Ngo, Shermaine Barlaan, Rachana Rathi, Tami Abdollah, Garrett Therolf, Kurt Streeter, and to a few other writing friends: Christopher Goffard, Miles Corwin, Amy Wilentz, Carol Burke, Cara DiMassa, Teresa Watanabe, Ching-Ching Ni, Lorenza Munoz, Lisa Richardson, Julie Price, Stephanie Hoops, Kim Gregory, Azita Fatheree, Milton Carerro, Clayton Verbinski, Lubov Dean, Tara Zucker, Victoria Aguayo, Deborah Essner, Angela Ledgerwood, Rodrigo Lazo, Lilith Mahmud, Kimi Yoshino, Arlene Keizer, and to the UC Irvine English Department faculty.

Especially to my loving husband, G. Hayward Coombs. You keep me calm and smiling, and remind me of what I appreciate most in this life each day. I love you.

Appendix: Erikson's Stage Theory

STAGE	CRISIS/CONFLICT	FAVORABLE OUTCOME
Infancy	Trust vs. mistrust	Faith in the environment and future, "an actual sense of the reality of 'good' powers, outside and within oneself."
Early childhood	Autonomy vs. shame and doubt	A sense of control, independence, adequacy and self-worth.
Play age	Initiative vs. guilt	Ability to initiate one's own activities, develop a sense of purpose.
School age	Industry vs. inferiority	Ability to learn how things work, to understand and organize.
Adolescence	Identity vs. role confusion	Seeing oneself as a unique person, with a strong sense of identity.
Early adulthood	Intimacy vs. isolation	Ability to make commitment to others, to love others by loving one's self first.
Adulthood	Generativity vs. stagnation	Concern for family and society, working to leaving something behind for the next generation, whether money, wisdom, creativity, or genes. Committing oneself to a cause, to people, or to a larger universal purpose.
Old age to death	Integrity vs. despair	A sense of fulfillment, a willingness to face death with integrity and courage, an overall acceptance of one's life cycle and the people who have become significant to it.

NFAVORABLE OUTCOME	RESOLUTION OR VIRTUE	CULMINATION OF FAVORABLE OUTCOME IN OLD AGE
uspicion, fear of the future, ouble finding a reason live in world that is full disappointment and scontent.	Hope	Appreciation of interdependence, a sense that life, humanity, and the world are not so bad.
eelings of shame and lf-doubt. *I am not good ough. Nothing I have to say important. No one will ever ve me.* A wish for invisibility.	Will	Acceptance of one's own life cycle, from birth to death.
sense of guilt or adequacy.	Purpose	Humor; compassion; resilience
sense of inferiority. A wish r invisibility.	Competence	Humility and an acceptance of life with its ups and downs, joys and disappointments.
ability to form one's own entity, confusion over who e really is, weak sense of self.	Fidelity	Integration, and understanding of life's varieties and complexities.
ability to form true lationships. Loneliness d isolation.	Love	Understanding human relationships, intimacy, and an appreciation of real love.
elf-centeredness, narcissism, allow involvement in the orld.	Care	Empathy and concern
verall dissatisfaction with e. Feelings of regret and espair. Denial of death.	Wisdom	Strength of self that is able to withstand physical disintegration.

ppendix sources are the writings of Erik Erikson and Norma Bowe's lectures.

Sources and Notes

PROLOGUE: *The Good-bye Letter*

Scene of Timothy McVeigh and Oklahoma Bombing

Clothing: Nolan Clay, "Jury Views Slogan-Bearing Shirt, McVeigh's Other Clothes," *The Daily Oklahoman*, May 16, 1997.

Traced route: Ben Fenwick, "The Road to Oklahoma City (Timothy McVeigh's alleged bombing plot)," *Playboy*, June 1, 1997.

Day care: Arnold Hamilton, "Children of the Bombing," *The Dallas Morning News*, April 17, 2005.

Murder of Sangeeta Lal

Witness accounts, timeline, crime scene: Crime records obtained from the Lynnwood Police Department in a public records request, including interviews of witnesses by police.

Aftermath and physical descriptions: Author's journals, photos, and first-person accounts.

Mother's reaction: Author's interviews with Sangeeta Lal's mother, Parneeta Lal, 2010.

School newspaper article: Erika Hayasaki, "Tragedy Strikes Lynnwood Student: Gun Violence Claims a Young Life," *The Royal Gazette*, April 1995.

No name, wrong age: "Apparent Murder, Suicide Claims 2," *The Seattle Times*, April 19, 1995.

James McCray news brief: "Murder-Suicide Figure ID'd," *The Seattle Times*, April 21, 1995.

Virginia Tech

Memorial: Maura Reynolds, Richard Fausset, and contributed to by Erika Hayasaki, "Somber Vow: 'We Will Prevail,'" *Los Angeles Times*, April 18, 2007.

"Mais oui, Madame. Mais oui": Erika Hayasaki, "A Deadly Hush in Room 211," *Los Angeles Times*, April 25, 2007.

Additional background on Erin Peterson: Molly Hennessy-Fiske, "Suddenly, a Pain They Can't Escape; Like Others, a Virginia Couple Struggles with a Child's Violent Death," *Los Angeles Times*, April 23, 2007.

"Jocelyne . . . if heaven exists": Albert Raboteau, "Students, Stories Shape French Teacher's Memorial," *Roanoke Times & World News*, April 25, 2007.

Death in Perspective

An amazing class offered at Kean: Rajul Punjabi, "Gaining a Little Life Perspective," *The Cougar's Byte*, December 11, 2006.

A three-year waiting list: Priority students received first dibs at registering for the class; open spots filled quickly, leaving Norma with a list of students requesting admission if a spot opened.

Bill Zuhoski: Interview conducted by author.

History of Death Education

Taboo subject: Kenneth J. Doka, *The Crumbling Taboo: The Rise of Death Education* (New Directions for Student Services, 1985), 85–95.

Death education as important as sex education: Dixie Dennis, *Living, Dying, Grieving*, chap. 17, "The Past, Present and Future of Death Education" (Sudbury, Mass.: Jones and Bartlett Publishers, 2009), www.jblearning .com/samples/0763743267/43267_ch17_pass1.pdf, p. 198.

Elisabeth Kübler-Ross dragging death out of the darkness: "Dying: Out of Darkness," *Time*, October 10, 1969.

First college class on death: Clifton D. Bryant, Dennis L. Peck, eds., *Encyclopedia of Death and the Human Experience* (Thousand Oaks, Calif.: Sage, 2009), 317; Daniel Leviton, "Horrendous Death," *Death and the Quest for Meaning: Essays in Honor of Herman Feifel*, ed. Stephen Strack (Northvale, N.J.: Jason Aronson, 1997), xvi.

By 1971, more than six hundred death courses were being offered

across the United States, and five years later that number had nearly doubled: Kenneth J. Doka, "The Death Awareness Movement," *Handbook of Death and Dying*, ed. Clifton D. Bryant (Thousand Oaks, Calif.: Sage, 2003), 52.

Now thousands of such classes can be found across disciplines: Darrell Crase, "Development Opportunities for Teachers of Death Education," *The Clearing House* 62, no. 9 (May 1989): 387–390.

Supplementary Reporting: From author interview with Illene Cupit, president of the National Association for Death Education and Couseling. Cupit said membership in her organization has grown by 13 percent over the last six years to more than two thousand members. "Prior to 1969 there were virtually no classes on death. Now virtually every college campus in the country has a class on death," she said.

Norma Bowe: Scenes are drawn primarily from author's interviews and observations.

ONE: *The Professor*

The Rosedale and Rosehill Cemetery scenes: Observed by author.

Ray Tse background: Mark Sceurman and Mark Moran, *Weird N.J.: Your Travel Guide to New Jersey's Local Legends and Best Kept Secrets* (New York: Sterling, 2009), 230.

Norma's description of natural death: Observed by author.

Supplementary background on final days of life: Robert E. Enck, *The Medical Care of Terminally Ill Patients (The Johns Hopkins Series in Hematology/Oncology)*, 2nd ed. (Baltimore, Md.: Johns Hopkins University Press, 2002), "The Final Moments," 173–179; A. Wutzler, P. Mavrogiorgou, C. Winter, and G. Juckel, "Elevation of Brain Serotonin During Dying," *Neuroscience Letters* 498, no. 1 (July 1, 2011): 1; Daniel B. Carr and Michael Prendergast, "Endorphins at the Approach of Death," *The Lancet* 317, no. 8216 (Feb. 14, 1981): 390.

The appearance of a newly lifeless face: Sherwin B. Nuland, *How We Die: Reflections on Life's Final Chapter* (New York: Vintage, 1995), 122.

Near-death experiences: Raymond Moody, *Life After Life* (New York: HarperOne, 2001); Sam Parnia, *What Happens When We Die?: A Groundbreaking Study into the Nature of Life and Death* (Carlsbad, Calif.: Hay House, 2007); Jeffrey Long with Paul Perry, *Evidence of the Afterlife: The Science of Near-Death Experiences* (New York: HarperOne, 2010); Erika Hayasaki, *Dead or Alive* (Amazon Digital Services, 2012).

Denial of death: Ernest Becker, *The Denial of Death* (New York: Free Press, 1973), 87.

Coroner scene: Details of coroner's office scene from Erika Hayasaki, "Finding Life's Meaning in Death," *Los Angeles Times*, Sept. 3, 2008.

Arthur Schopenhauer: Arthur Schopenhauer, *Studies in Pessimism, on Human Nature, and Religion: A Dialogue, Etc.* (www.digireads.com, 2008), 6.

Study on what kind of students take death education courses in college and why: Sarah Brabant and DeAnn Kalich, "Who Enrolls in College Death Education Courses? A Longitudinal Study," *Omega* 58, no. 1 (2008–2009): 1–18.

"I used to pray every day until one day I lost hope and it felt like it was pointless": Quoted from student letter read in class.

"After I was raped I wanted to curl up in a ball and die": Cited from student letter read in class.

"Life is made up of moments": Anna Quindlen, *A Short Guide to a Happy Life* (New York: Random House, 2000), p. 41.

Anecdote about Mary Manly: From interviews with Norma.

Then Almitra spoke: Khalil Gibran, "Death," in *The Prophet* (Eastford, Conn.: Martino Fine Books, 2011), 50.

TWO: *Life Stories of Norma Lynn*

Scenes and anecdotes from Norma's home, childhood, and life: From observations and interviews by author.

Additional background on Norma's life: From interviews with her family members, including father, daughters, and partner, Norm.

Background on Norma's mother, father, and father's Mafia history: From interviews with Norma and separate interviews with her father.

Student who gave birth in a bathroom stall: Ronald Smothers, "Guilty Plea by Mother, 20, in Prom Death," *The New York Times*, Aug. 21, 1998.

Scenes of Norma in classroom: Observed by author.

Erik Erikson

Norma's teachings on Erikson: Drawn from Norma's lectures witnessed by author.

Additional background from: Lawrence J. Friedman, *Identity's Architect: A Biography of Erik H. Erikson* (New York: Scribner, 1999); Erik Erikson, "Autobiographic Notes on the Identity Crisis," *Daedalus* 99, no. 4

(1970): 743; Paul Roazen, *Erik H. Erikson: The Power and Limits of a Vision* (Northvale, N.J.: Jason Aronson, 1997), 96; Erik H. Erikson, *The Erik Erikson Reader,* ed. Robert Coles (New York: W. W. Norton, 2001); Erik H. Erikson, *Identity and the Life Cycle* (New York: W. W. Norton, 1994); Erik H. Erikson, *Childhood and Society* (New York: W. W. Norton, 1993); Erik H. Erikson, *Identity: Youth and Crisis* (New York: W. W. Norton, 1994); Erik H. Erikson and Joan M. Erikson, *The Life Cycle Completed,* extended version (New York: W. W. Norton, 1998); Erik H. Erikson, *Insight and Responsibility* (New York: W. W. Norton, 1964); Erik H. Erikson, *Insight and Responsibility: Lectures on the Ethical Implications of Psychoanalytical Insight* (New York: W. W. Norton, 1972); Erik Erikson, "The Healthy Personality," in *Identity and the Life Cycle Notes* (original version of this paper appeared in Symposium on the Healthy Personality), Supplement II: Problems of Infancy and Childhood, Transactions of Fourth Conference, March 1950, ed. M. J. E. Senn (New York: Josiah Macy, Jr. Foundation, 1950), 59–60; Kenneth Hoover, Robert Coles, Lena Klintbjer Erickson, Lawrence Friedman, Catarina Kinnvall, and Lina Kreidie, *The Future of Identity: Centennial Reflections on the Legacy of Erik Erikson* (New York: Lexington Books, 2004), 64–65. Carol Hren Hoare, *Erikson on Development in Adulthood: New Insights from the Unpublished Papers* (New York: Oxford University Press, 2001); Edward F. Moone, "Erik Erikson: Artist of Moral-Religious Development," in *Kierkegaard's Influence on the Social Sciences,* ed. Jon Stewart (Burlington, Vt.: Ashgate, 2010); Coles, Robert, Erik H. Erikson: *The Growth of His Work* (Boston: Little, Brown, 1970).

Supplementary background on child development and attachment: Robert Karen, *Becoming Attached: First Relationships and How They Shape Our Capacity to Love* (New York: Oxford University Press, 1998); Rene A. Spitz, *The First Year of Life: A Psychoanalytic Study of Normal and Deviant Development of Object Relations* (New York: International Universities Press, 1965); Harry Bakwin, "Loneliness in Infants," *American Journal of Diseases in Children* 63, no. 1 (1942): 30–40; Harry Bakwin, "The Hospital Care of Infants and Children," *The Journal of Pediatrics* 39, no. 3 (September 1951): 383–390; *Mental Health: A Report of the Surgeon General—Executive Summary* (Rockville, Md.: U.S. Department of Health and Human Services, Substance Abuse and Mental Health Services Administration, Center for Mental Health Services, National Institutes of Health, National Institute of Mental Health, 1999); Konner, Melvin, *The Evolution of Childhood: Relationships, Emotion, Mind* (Cambridge, Mass.: The Belknap Press of Harvard University Press, 2010).

THREE: *Rewind Button*

Scenes and anecdotes from Caitlin's home, childhood, and life: From observations and interviews by author.

Scenes of Caitlin in class: From interviews with Caitlin and Norma Bowe.

Caitlin's writings: From her letters and assignments.

Norma's stories from working with the mentally ill: Observed by author during class discussions and recorded in interviews.

Scenes of Caitlin meeting Jonathan: From interviews with Jonathan and Caitlin.

"Brain on drugs" lecture by Norma: Observed by author.

Supplementary brain and love sources: Helen E. Fisher, "Reward, Addiction, and Emotion Regulation Systems Associated with Rejection in Love," *Journal of Neurophysiology* 104, no. 1 (July 2010): 51; Emory Young, "Being Human: Love: Neuroscience Reveals All," *Nature* 457, no. 148 (January 8, 2009); Bianca P. Acevedo, Arthur Aron, Helen E. Fisher, and Lucy L. Brown, "Neural Correlates of Long-Term Intense Romantic Love," *Social Cognitive Affective Neuroscience*, published online January 5, 2011.

Supplementary background on OCD: Jeremy Wolfe, "Defining Mental Illness: Are Suicide Bombers Insane?," Massachusetts Institute of Technology: MIT OpenCourseWare, Lecture 21, Introduction to Psychology, Fall 2004; Paul Bloom, "What Happens When Things Go Wrong: Mental Illness, Part II," Yale Open Courses, Psychology 110: Introduction to Psychology, Lecture 19, Oct. 12, 2009.

FOUR: *Little Boy*

Scenes and anecdotes from Jonathan's home, childhood, and life: Drawn from interviews by author.

Supplementary source material on murder of Jonathan's mother and his father's arrest: Court records of the case provided through public record request to Union County Prosecutor's Office. "Man, 37, Is Arrested in Ex-Wife's Killing," Associated Press, March 10, 1996; "Union County Man Charged with Murder of Ex-Wife," *The Record*, March 11, 1996; "Man Who Feared Alien Takeover Pleads Guilty to Killing Ex-wife," Associated Press, Sept. 3, 1998; Rick Hepp, "East Jersey Inmate Hangs Himself in Apparent Suicide," *The Star-Ledger*, Dec. 19, 2006, states, "Four other state inmates have committed suicide this year," naming "East Jersey inmate Brett Steingraber, a former Roselle Park man who said he killed his ex-wife in 1996 to save her from an alien invasion, on Feb. 15."

FIVE: *Strange Behavior*

Scene from banquet hall: Reconstructed based on interviews with Caitlin, Jonathan, Norma, and photographs capturing the graduation and party.

Scenes of Josh: Reconstructed based on interviews with Jonathan and Caitlin.

Delusions and mental illness: Background observed by author in Norma's lectures.

Supplementary information on delusions, mental disorders, and schizophrenia: Jeremy Wolfe, "Causing Mental Illness: What Can Make You Lose Your Mind?," Massachusetts Institute of Technology: MIT OpenCourseWare, Lecture 22, Introduction to Psychology, Fall 2004; Wolfe, "Defining Mental Illness"; Susan Nolen-Hoeksema, "What Happens When Things Go Wrong: Mental Illness, Part I," Yale Open Courses, Psychology 110: Introduction to Psychology, Lecture 18, Oct. 12, 2009; Bloom, "What Happens When Things Go Wrong: Mental Illness, Part II."

Argument between Caitlin and Jonathan: Reconstructed based on interviews with both of them.

Josh's attack on Jonathan: Reconstructed based on interviews with Jonathan and Caitlin, as well as police reports and medical reports.

Norma's schizophrenia lesson: Based on interviews with Norma, Jonathan, and Caitlin.

Conversations with Josh in hospital: Reconstructed based on interviews with Jonathan, as well as his personal writings.

Applebee's scene: Reconstructed based on interviews with Norma and Caitlin.

Life cycle, fifth and sixth stages: Norma's explanations observed by author during lectures and recorded in interviews.

"To a considerable extent adolescent love is an attempt to arrive at a definition of one's identity": Erikson, *Identity: Youth and Crisis*, 132.

"Unfortunately, many young people marry under such circumstances, hoping to find themselves in another": Erikson, *Identity and the Life Cycle*, 101.

SIX: *To the Rescue*

Scenes with Norma and Stephanie and in the motel with Stephanie's mother: Witnessed by author.

Norma's first death and experiences in nursing school and as a working medical professional: As told to author in interviews.

Norma teaching in women's prison: Witnessed by author.

Community service trip to Alabama: Witnessed by author.

Holiday Inn dog bereavement session: Witnessed by author.

Crashing Buddhism retreat: Witnessed by author.

Generativity: Explained by Norma in lectures and interviews observed by author.

Supplementary background on generativity found in: Erikson, *Identity and the Life Cycle*, Erikson, *Childhood and Society*, Erikson and Erikson, *The Life Cycle Completed.*

Father Hudson House makeover: Reconstructed from interviews of Norma and the students involved, as well as interviews with Sally and Jim. In addition, photos and videos used, and visits to the hospice by author.

Erikson 1969 psychobiography of Gandhi: Erik H. Erikson, *Gandhi's Truth: On the Origins of Militant Nonviolence* (New York: W. W. Norton, 1993).

Griminger funeral scene and death teacher saves life at funeral comment: Witnessed by author.

"In times of strife and crisis, she thrives on it": From author's interviews with Norma's father.

Stories of Norma's grandmother, birthdays: As told to author by Norma.

Disappearing on birthday: Observed by author.

"Shame is early expressed in an impulse to bury one's face, or to sink, right then and there, into the ground": Erikson, *Identity and the Life Cycle*, p. 154.

SEVEN: *The Trigger*

Scene of Israel in Norma's office: Reconstructed based on interviews with Norma and Israel.

Israel's story: As told to author by Israel.

Israel's participation in class: As told to author by Israel and Norma.

EIGHT: *Despair*

Men's prison trip: Scenes inside prison witnessed by author, with supplementary reporting during numerous trips inside prison. Also based on interviews with Israel, Norma, Carl, and other students.

Supplementary reporting on Northern State Prison: Meg Lundstrom, "Kean Opens Newark Prison," *The Record*, Oct. 21, 1987; "Vote Due on $198M Prison Bond November Referendum," *The Record*, April 21, 1987; "20 Inmates Moved to Unfinished State Jail," *The Record*, June

1, 1987; Alfonso A. Narvaez, "As Prison Opens in Jersey, Officials Support a Bond Issue," *The New York Times*, Oct. 21, 1987; "N.J. to Enlarge 5 Prisons; Ship Lockup on Hold," *The Record*, March 11, 1988; "Kean OKs $80.78M for 1,332 New Prison Beds," *The Record*, June 19, 1988; Todd Richissin, "Two Civilians Held Hostage for Several Hours at N.J. Prison, Freed Unharmed," Associated Press, Oct. 27, 1988; Eve Markowitz, "Prison Siege Is Over; Inmates Give Up, Free Hostages Unharmed," *The Record*, Oct. 28, 1988; Abby Goodnough, "Inmates Injure 15 Guards at Prison in Newark," *The New York Times*, May 2, 1997; Dunstan McNichol, "Tents, Double Bunks in N.J. Prisons; Crowding Blamed for Violent Episodes," *The Record*, July 31, 1997; "New Prison Unit Designed to Break Gangs," Associated Press, March 5, 1988; William Kleinknecht, "State Prisons Try to Break Inmate Gangs," *The Star-Ledger*, Feb. 8, 1999; Brian Donohue, "Harsh Unit Is Prison's Answer to Violence—Isolated Inmates Gain Release by Renouncing Gang Affiliation," *The Star-Ledger*, Jan. 23, 2000; "Passaic Man Hangs in Prison," Associated Press, April 17, 2001; Nikita Stewart, "A Fear for What Might Lie Below Shadows Jail Project—Essex Guards Worry About Toxins Under Site," *The Star-Ledger*, Sept. 7, 2003; Maya Rao, "Probers Say Street Gangs More Active in N.J. Prisons," *The Philadelphia Inquirer*, Nov. 25, 2008; "Northern State Inmate Dies in Cell Fire He Set," *The Star-Ledger*, Dec. 6, 2008.

The Northern State gang unit was closed in 2010, after author visited the prison: Kibret Markos, "Closing Gang Unit to Save State $5m," *The Record*, May 7, 2010.

Donald Paul Weber: Abbott Koloff, "Killer of 80-year-old Bernardsville Woman Set to Get Out of Prison," *Daily Record*, July 14, 2007; Abbott Koloff, "Hearing Revives Memories of Rape Attempt, Murder of Bernardsville Widow," *Daily Record*, July 15, 2007; Abbott Koloff, "Widow Killer Will Get Parole," *Daily Record*, July 25, 2007; Nyier Abdou and Ralph R. Ortega, "State Parole Board OKs Release of Murderer—Victim's Family Says Convict Still a Threat," *The Star-Ledger*, July 27, 2007.

Details of other inmates' crimes from Northern State and in Norma's class: Most details and charges based on State of New Jersey Department of Corrections inmate search. See also Bill Sanderson, "He's Hemmed In by All the Evidence; Prosecution Concludes Its Case in Teaneck Murder Trial," *The Record*, March 22, 1989; Bill Sanderson, "A Plea to Spare a Murderer's Life; Drug Use Cited in Teaneck Slaying," *The Record*, March 28, 1989; Bill Sanderson, "Killer Is Spared Death Sentence," *The Record*, March 31, 1989; Sue Epstein and Mary Ann Spoto,

"Re-accused Killer Moves to Maximum-Security Cell," *The Star-Ledger,* Sept. 1, 1999; Robin Gaby Fisher and Judith Lucas, "Death Ends Notorious Killer's Quest to Go Free—Zarinsky, Long Suspected of Slaying More than One Missing Teenager, Dies at 68," *The Star-Ledger,* Nov. 30, 2008; Giovanna Fabiano, "Man Who Raped, Killed Woman in '76 Denied Parole," *The Record,* Sept. 15, 2009.

Carl's background: From author's interviews with him in prison as well as interviews with his mother. Also used were his class essays and personal writings. The details of the crime he was serving time for came from police reports and full interviews of Carl, his accomplice, and his sister, and investigation documents obtained by author.

Finding Buddhism in prison: As recounted to author by Carl. Also interviewed about this was Dean Sluyter, a spiritual teacher in Northern State.

"Fearing death, I went to the mountains": "The Thirty-Seven Practices of Bodhisattvas," pamphlet published by Dzogchen Center, Austin Texas, June 2005, p. 6. Also found in Lama Surya Das, *Awakening the Buddhist Heart: Integrating Love, Meaning, and Connection into Every Part of Your Life* (New York: Broadway Books, 2001).

"Wisdom, then, is detached concern with life itself, in the face of death itself": Erikson, *Insight and Responsibility,* 134.

"Despair expresses the feeling that the time is too short": Erikson, *Identity and the Life Cycle,* 104–105.

Norma's memories of her mother's illness and death: Drawn from interviews with author.

The acceptance of one's one and only life cycle: Erikson, *Identity and the Life Cycle,* 104.

Israel's story of sharing his letter about Jason: Based on interviews with Israel. Young gang member's death also documented in police press releases and news stories.

NINE: *Brothers*

Jonathan and Josh's trip to Uruguay and events during subsequent return to New Jersey: Recounted in interviews with author.

Mounting medical bills and responsibilities: Documented in bank statements, bill statements, medical statements, notifications provided to author by Jonathan.

"Josh I love you so much and I don't give a fuck what I have to do to help you": Letter provided to author by Jonathan.

Psychiatrist's response: As told to author by Jonathan. Conversation was later confirmed in audiotape conversation that Jonathan recorded of the psychiatrist's response after Josh's death.

Josh's suicide: Recounted by Jonathan in interviews with author. Also used were police reports of his death, which was also documented in Richard Khavkine, "Police ID Man Killed by Train in Linden," www.mycentraljersey .com, January 14, 2009.

Josh's suicide note: Copy provided to author.

Caitlin and Norma meeting after Josh's death: Reconstructed from interviews with Norma and Caitlin.

Caitlin and Jonathan's reunion: Recounted in interviews with both of them.

Funeral services at McCracken Funeral Home: Recounted by Jonathan and Caitlin. Author also visited funeral home and attended field trips mentioned.

TEN: *Reclamations*

"We have just entered our spring semester in the midst of an economic recession": Kelly Nemeth, *The Tower,* Jan. 28–Feb. 10, 2009.

Classroom scenes: Observed by author.

"In the year of America's birth, in the coldest of months, a small band of patriots huddled by dying campfires on the shores of an icy river": President Barack Obama's Inaugural Address, www.whitehouse .gov/blog/inaugural-address.

Isaiah House makeover: Witnessed by author. Also used interviews with students and Norma, photographs, and videos.

Background on Becca: Author's interviews with Becca, and Norma.

Story of Isis: As told to author by Isis.

ELEVEN: *Jonathan*

Scene of Jonathan speaking to Norma's Death in Perspective class: Witnessed by author.

TWELVE: *Caitlin*

Caitlin's mother's suicide attempt: As recounted to author by Caitlin the day after.

Caitlin with bandages on hand next day: Witnessed by author.

Jonathan cradling Caitlin in hallway: Witnessed by author.

THIRTEEN: *To Serve*

"Man *needs* to teach": Erikson, *Insight and Responsibility*, 131.

Jonathan's visit to Northern State Prison: Witnessed by author.

Jonathan's visit to Trenton Psychiatric Hospital: Witnessed by author.

New Jersey's mental health system: Susan Livio, "A Call for Psych Workers Who Are Better Qualified," *The Star-Ledger,* March 29, 2009; Alison Evans Cuellar and Deborah Haas-Wilson, "Competition and the Mental Health System," *American Journal of Psychiatry* 166, no. 3 (March 1, 2009): 273–283; Mary Ann Spoto, "Lawmakers Seek a Mental Health System Overhaul," *The Star-Ledger,* Oct. 6, 2008; Bob Brau, "A Professor Teaches What's Wrong with Prisons," *The Star-Ledger,* June 26, 2008; "Trenton Psychiatric Hospital Celebrates 160th Anniversary," *US Fed News,* May 19, 2008; Alan Guenther, "Admission, Then Death at Psychiatric Hospital," *Asbury Park Press,* Feb. 17, 2008; "Overhaul State's Mental Health Services," *Home News Tribune,* January 27, 2008.

Greystone Park Psychiatric Hospital in Parsippany: Robert Hanley, "Troubled Center for Mentally Ill Will Be Closed in New Jersey," *The New York Times,* April 29, 2000.

Jonathan and Caitlin's presentation on mental health: Witnessed by author. The presentation slides can be seen at www.slideshare.net/jonsteingraber/brainstorming-session-at-kean.

FOURTEEN: *Roadblocks*

Norma's car accident: Recounted by Norma, Norm, and Becca.

"I was in the bathroom over my dead baby girl's body": From letter provided to author.

FIFTEEN: *Parting Ways*

Information in chapter drawn primarily from interviews with Jonathan and Caitlin.

Jonathan's message to Norma: Provided to author.

SIXTEEN: *Epiphanies*

Information in chapter drawn primarily from interviews with Caitlin.

SEVENTEEN: *Road Trip*

Native Americans in South Dakota: Chris Rodda, "Emergency

Help Desperately Needed to Heat Homes on the Pine Ridge Reservation," The Huffington Post, Jan. 27, 2010; navajo, "Emergency Help Desperately Needed to Heat Homes on the Pine Ridge Reservation," Daily Kos, Jan. 29, 2010. Keith Olbermann MSNBC clips: www.dailykos .com/story/2010/02/10/835966/-Keith-Olbermann-Links-to-Two-More -Donation-Links-for-S-D-Rezs, Feb. 8, 2010.

"The instinctual power behind various forms of selfless 'caring' potentially extends to whatever a man generates and leaves behind": Erikson, *Insight and Responsibility*, 131.

Visit to Virginia Tech and encounter with Jerzy: Witnessed by author.

EIGHTEEN: *The Rhizome*

Virginia Tech Memorial Garden: Visited by author with Norma and students.

Jerzy's story: Erika Hayasaki, contributed to by Richard Fausset, "A Deadly Hush in Room 211," *Los Angeles Times*, April 25, 2007; Jerzy Nowak and Richard E. Veilleux, "Personal Reflections on the Virginia Tech Tragedy from a Victim's Spouse with Commentary by a Close Colleague," *Traumatology* 14, no. 89 (March 2008): 89–99; also based on author interviews with him at Virginia Tech.

Road trip to Virginia Tech: Witnessed by author.

Student presentation at Virginia Tech: Witnessed by author.

Be the Change activities: Some witnessed by author; others documented in photos, videos, and interviews with participants.

NINETEEN: *Life Cycles*

Information in chapter based on author's interview with Parneeta Lal.

TWENTY: *Birthday*

Norma's birthday trip: Observed by author.

"Trust (the first of our ego values) is here defined as 'the assured reliance on another's integrity,' the last of our values": Erikson, "Eight Stages of Man," in *Childhood and Society*, 269.

Selected Bibliography and Suggested Readings

Albom, Mitch. *Tuesdays with Morrie: An Old Man, a Young Man, and Life's Greatest Lesson.* New York: Broadway, 2002.

Ariès, Philippe. *The Hour of Our Death: The Classic History of Western Attitudes Toward Death over the Last One Thousand Years.* 2nd ed. New York: Vintage Books, 1982.

———. *Western Attitudes Toward Death: From the Middle Ages to the Present.* The Johns Hopkins Symposia in Comparative History, The Johns Hopkins University Press, August 1, 1975.

Bakwin, Harry. "The Hospital Care of Infants and Children." *The Journal of Pediatrics* 39, no. 3 (September 1951): 383–390.

———. "Loneliness in Infants." *American Journal of Diseases in Children* 63, no. 1 (1942): 30–40.

Bauby, Jean-Dominique. *The Diving Bell and the Butterfly: A Memoir of Life in Death.* New York: Vintage, June 23, 1998.

Becker, Ernest. *The Birth and Death of Meaning: A Perspective in Psychiatry and Anthropology.* New York: Free Press, 1962.

———. *The Denial of Death.* New York: Free Press, 1973.

Becker, Ernest, and Daniel Liechty, ed. *The Ernest Becker Reader.* Seattle: University of Washington Press, 2005.

Blackmore, Susan. *Dying to Live: Near-Death Experiences.* Amherst, N.Y.: Prometheus, 1993.

Bryant, Clifton D., ed. *Handbook of Death and Dying.* Thousand Oaks, Calif.: Sage Publications, 2003.

Bryant, Clifton D., and Dennis L. Peck, eds. *Encyclopedia of Death and the Human Experience.* Thousand Oaks, Calif.: Sage Publications, 2009.

Butler, Robert N. "Successful Aging and the Role of the Life Review." *Journal of the American Geriatric Society* 22, no. 12 (1974): 529–535.

Byock, Ira. *Dying Well: Peace and Possibilities at the End of Life.* New York: Riverhead Books, 1997.

Coles, Robert. *Erik H. Erikson: The Growth of His Work.* Boston: Little, Brown, 1970.

Doka, K. J. "The Crumbling Taboo: The Rise of Death Education." In *Coping with Death on Campus,* ed. E. S. Zinner. San Francisco: Jossey-Bass, 1985, 85–95.

Durlak, Joseph A. "Changing Death Attitudes Through Death Education." In *Death Anxiety Handbook: Research, Instrumentation, and Application,* ed. Robert A. Neimeyer. Washington, D.C.: Taylor & Francis, 1994.

Durlak, Joseph A., and Lee Ann Riesenberg. "The Impact of Death Education." *Death Studies* 15, no. 1 (1991): 39–58.

Erikson, Erik H. *Childhood and Society.* 2nd ed. New York: W. W. Norton, 1993.

———. *Gandhi's Truth: On the Origins of Militant Nonviolence.* New York: W. W. Norton, 1993.

———. *Identity and the Life Cycle.* New York: W. W. Norton, 1994.

———. *Identity: Youth and Crisis.* New York: W. W. Norton, 1994.

———. *Insight and Responsibility.* New York: W. W. Norton, 1964.

———. *Insight and Responsibility: Lectures on the Ethical Implications of Psychoanalytical Insight.* New York: W. W. Norton, 1972.

———. *The Erik Erikson Reader.* Ed. Robert Coles. New York: W. W. Norton, 2001.

Erikson, Erik H., and Joan M. Erikson. *The Life Cycle Completed,* extended version. New York: W. W. Norton, 1998.

Feifel, Herman. *The Meaning of Death.* New York: McGraw-Hill, 1959.

Friedman, Lawrence J. *Identity's Architect: A Biography of Erik H. Erikson.* New York: Scribner, 1999.

Gibran, Khalil. "Death," in *The Prophet.* Eastford, Conn.: Martino Fine Books, 2011, 50.

Goleman, Daniel. *Emotional Intelligence.* New York: Bantam Books, 1995.

Hall, G. Stanley. "Thanatophobia and Immortality," *American Journal of Psychology* 26, no. 4 (1915): 550–613.

Hendrin, Herbert. *Suicide in America,* new and expanded ed. New York: W. W. Norton, 1996.

Hoare, Carol Hren. *Erikson on Development in Adulthood: New Insights from the Unpublished Papers.* New York: Oxford University Press, 2001.

Holden, Janice Miner, Bruce Greyson, and Debbie James. *The Handbook* of *Near-Death Experiences: Thirty Years of Investigation.* New York: Praeger, 2009.

Hoover, Kenneth. *The Future of Identity: Centennial Reflections on the Legacy of Erik Erikson.* New York: Lexington Books, 2004.

Karen, Robert. *Becoming Attached: First Relationships and How They Shape Our Capacity to Love.* New York: Oxford University Press, 1998.

Kastenbaum, Robert. "Death-Related Anxiety," In *Anxiety and Stress.* Ed. Larry Michelson and L. Michael Ascher. New York: Guilford Press, 1987.

———. *Death, Society, and Human Experience,* 10th ed. NJ: Pearson, 2009.

———. *Death, Society and Human Experience,* 11th ed. NJ: Pearson, 2011.

———. *Psychology of Death,* 3rd ed. New York: Springer, 2006.

Keen, Sam. "A Conversation with Ernest Becker," *Psychology Today* 7, no. 11 (April 1974), 70–80.

Keltner, Dacher. *The Compassionate Instinct: The Science of Human Goodness.* New York: W. W. Norton, 2010.

Kirwin, Barbara. *The Mad, the Bad, and the Innocent: The Criminal Mind on Trial—Tales of a Forensic Psychologist.* Boston: Little, Brown, 1997.

Knott, J. Eugene. "Death Education for All." In *Dying: Facing the Facts.* Ed. Hannelore Wass. Washington, DC: Hemisphere, 1979.

Konner, Melvin. *The Evolution of Childhood: Relationships, Emotion, Mind.* Cambridge, Mass.: The Belknap Press of Harvard University Press, 2010.

Kramer, Robert, ed. *A Psychology of Difference: The American Lectures of Otto Rank.* Princeton, N.J.: Princeton University Press, 1996.

Kübler-Ross, Elisabeth. *Death is of Vital Importance: On Life, Death, and Life After Death.* New York: Station Hill Press, 1995.

———. *On Death and Dying.* New York: Scribner, 1997.

———. *On Life after Death,* rev. 2nd ed. Berkeley, Calif.: Celestial Arts, 2008.

LeDoux, Joseph. *The Emotional Brain.* New York: Simon & Schuster, 1996.

Leviton, Daniel. "The Scope of Death Education." *Death Education* 1 (1977): 41–55.

Lieberman, E. James. *Acts of Will: The Life and Work of Otto Rank.* Free Press; updated ed., Amherst, Mass.: University of Massachusetts Press, 1993.

Long, Jeffrey. *Evidence of the Afterlife: The Science of Near-Death Experiences.* New York: HarperOne, 2011.

Lynch, Thomas. *The Undertaking: Life Studies from the Dismal Trade.* New York: W. W. Norton & Company, 2009.

Maslow, Abraham. *The Farther Reaches of Human Nature.* New York: Arkana, 1993.

Menaker, Esther. *Otto Rank: A Rediscovered Legacy.* New York: Columbia University Press, 1982.

Mitford, Jessica. *The American Way of Death.* New York: Fawcett, 1983.

———. *The American Way of Death Revisted.* New York: Vintage, 2000.

Moody, Raymond. *Life After Life.* New York: HarperOne, 2001.

Moone, Edward F. "Erik Erikson: Artist of Moral-Religious Development." *In Kierkegaard's Influence on the Social Sciences.* Ed. Jon Stewart. Burlington, Vt.: Ashgate, 2010.

Neimeyer, Robert, ed. *Death Anxiety Handbook: Research, Instrumentation, and Application.* Washington, D.C.: Taylor & Francis, 1994.

Neimeyer, Robert, and David Van Brunt. "Death Anxiety," In *Dying: Facing the Facts,* 3rd ed. Ed. Hannelore Wass and Robert A. Neimeyer. Philadelphia: Taylor & Francis, 1995.

Nietzsche, Friedrich. *The Case of Wagner.* Trans. Walter Kaufmann. In *The Birth of Tragedy and The Case of Wagner.* New York: Random House, 1967.

———. *The Will to Power.* Trans. Walter Kaufmann. New York: Random House, 1967.

Nuland, Sherwin B. *How We Die: Reflections on Life's Final Chapter.* New York: Vintage, 1995.

Page, Andrew C. "Fear and Phobias." In *Encyclopedia of Human Emotions.* Ed. David Levinson, James J. Ponzetti Jr., and Peter F. Jorgenson. New York: Macmillan, 1999.

Paradis, Cheryl. *The Measure of Madness: Inside the Disturbed and Disturbing Criminal Mind.* New York: Citadel, 2010.

Parnia, Sam. *What Happens When We Die?: A Groundbreaking Study into the Nature of Life and Death.* Carlsbad, CA: Hay House, 2007.

Payne, Malcolm and Reith, Margaret, *Social Work: In End-of-Life and Palliative Care.* Chicago: Lyceum Books, Inc., 2009.

Pyszczynski, Tom, Jeff Greenberg, and Sheldon Solomon. "A Dual-Process Model of Defense Against Conscious and Unconscious Death-Related Thoughts: An Extension of Terror Management Theory." *Psychological Review* 106, no. 4 (1999): 835–845.

Quindlen, Anna. *A Short Guide to a Happy Life.* New York: Random House, 2000.

Rando, Therese A., ed. *Loss and Anticipatory Grief.* New York: Lexington Books, 1986.

Rank, Otto. *Psychology and the Soul: A Study of the Origin, Conceptual Evolution, and Nature of the Soul.* Trans. Gregory C. Richter and E. James Lieberman. Baltimore, Md.: Johns Hopkins University Press, 2002.

Roazen, Paul. *Erik H. Erikson: The Power and Limits of a Vision.* Northvale, N.J.: Jason Aronson, 1997.

Schopenhauer, Arthur. *Studies in Pessimism, on Human Nature, and Religion: A Dialogue, Etc.* www.digireads.com, 2008.

———. *Will to Live: Selected Writings of Arthur Schopenhauer.* Ed. Richard Taylor. New York: Fredrick Ungar, 1967.

———. *The World as Will and Representation,* vol. 1. Trans. E. F. J. Payne. New York: Dover Publications, 1966.

Screech, M.A. ed. Michel de Montaigne, *The Essays: A Selection.* London: Penguin Books, 1993.

Shneidman, Edwin S. *The Suicidal Mind.* New York: Oxford University Press, 1996.

Spitz, René A. *The First Year of Life: A Psychoanalytic Study of Normal and Deviant Development of Object Relations.* 3rd ed. New York: International Universities Press, 1965.

Strack, Stephen, ed. *Death and the Quest for Meaning: Essays in Honor of Herman Feifel.* Northvale, N.J.: Jason Aronson, 1997.

van Lommel, P., R. van Wees, V. Meyers, and I. Elfferich. "Near-Death Experience in Survivors of Cardiac Arrest: A Prospective Study in the Netherlands." *The Lancet* 358, no. 9298 (2001): 2039–2045.

Wass, Hannelore, M. David Miller, and Gordon Thornton. "Death Education and Grief/Suicide Intervention in the Public Schools." *Death Studies* 14, no. 3 (May–June 1990): 253–268.

Webb, Marilyn. *The Good Death: The New American Search to Reshape the End of Life.* New York: Bantam, 1999.

Yalom, Irvin D. *Staring at the Sun: Overcoming the Terror of Death.* San Francisco: Jossey-Bass, 2009.

Index

About the Author

Erika Hayasaki is an award-winning reporter and assistant professor in the Literary Journalism Department at the University of California, Irvine, an undergraduate degree program dedicated to studying and practicing narrative journalism. She spent nine years covering breaking news and writing feature stories for the *Los Angeles Times*, where she was a staff metro reporter, education writer, and New York–based national correspondent.

Erika has published more than nine hundred articles for the *Los Angeles Times* and also while working as a reporter for other newspapers such as the *Tampa Tribune*, the *Seattle Post-Intelligencer*, and *The News Gazette* in Champaign, Illinois. In 2004, she won the Los Angeles Times Best Writing award for her stories about a new teacher's plight, a boy's dangerous journey to school, and a cultural divide at a Latino high school. She was a recipient of the American Society of Newspaper Editors Breaking News Award. In 2007, she won a narrative feature writing award from the American Association of Sunday Feature Editors for her *Los Angeles Times Magazine* profile, "The Daughter." She has twice been a finalist for the Livingston Award for journalists under 35, including in 2008, for her reconstruction of the Virginia Tech shootings inside a French class.

She has also served as a volunteer writing mentor and teacher for teenage girls for the Los Angeles–based WriteGirl and the New York–based Girls Write Now. Both are nonprofit organizations that pair professional women writers with teenage girls for weekly mentoring and monthly writing workshops.

She lives in Los Angeles with her husband, and their newborn daughter.

Get email updates on

ERIKA HAYASAKI,

exclusive offers,

and other great book recommendations

from Simon & Schuster.